W9-BXH-862

Additional Praise for
The Simplified Guide to
Not-for-Profit Accounting, Formation, and Reporting

"This book is fantastic! Not-for-profit accounting can be quite complex at times, but this book cuts right to the point and provides easy-to-understand answers to difficult questions. I would recommend it to anyone and everyone who works in a financial capacity at a not-for-profit organization."
—Alina Yavorovskaya,
EVP of Finance and Administration and CFO,
Seeds of Peace

"Laurence Scot has created an extremely practical, useful, and easy-to-use guide that is a must read for anyone and everyone who is interested in not-for-profits. Whether you are starting a not-for-profit or are a board member, an officer, or a current or future staff accountant, you will greatly benefit from this valuable and comprehensive book."
—Ece A.J. Yilmaz, MBA, CMA, CBM, PMP,
Executive Director,
American College Nutrition

"This is a definite read for anyone involved in the not-for-profit industry, regardless of your level of prior knowledge. The not-for-profit world has its own rules, and it is your responsibility to know them. Thankfully, Laurence Scot has managed to explain all the basic need-to-knows in very clear words."
—Filip Johansson, Director of Finance and Operations,
Swedish-American Chamber of Commerce, Inc.

"Accounting can't be made too simple for me. If you want to start a not-for-profit company or serve on a board, Laurence Scot's simplified guide will bring the mystifying world of not-for-profit accounting into focus. Clear and straightforward, this guide is the best answer to all my questions."
—Pia Lindström, TV and radio broadcasting

"As a trustee and treasurer of a private day school, this book equipped me with all of the concepts associated with not-for-profit accounting to allow me to excel at performing my responsibilities as a fiduciary."
—Susan Levitt, private school trustee and treasurer

"While there is nothing particularly simple about not-for-profit accounting, this book provides a veritable to-do list for organizations of any size. Larry Scot's book is an excellent resource."
—Eric Jorgensen, Finance Associate,
Médecins Sans Frontières/Doctors Without Borders USA

"Laurence Scot successfully integrates extensive professional, educational, and practical experience to produce a highly relevant, clearly written, and insightful book. In my opinion, *The Simplified Guide to Not-for-Profit Accounting, Formation, and Reporting* is the most concise, complete, and important resource for everyone considering and practicing not-for-profit accounting."

—Mark Carmichael, Finance Director,
World Monuments Fund

"The only not-for-profit accounting guide of its kind, this book provides a comprehensive guide to starting up a not-for-profit organization, as well the accounting requirements necessary for producing GAAP financial statements for an NFP organization. I'm recommending this book to those looking for a user-friendly desktop reference to answer all your industry-related questions."

—Kim Chadourne, Director of Management Reporting,
Columbia University

"A marvelous introduction to NFP accounting—it's like having the great teacher there in the office with me! Mr. Scot's book is a must read for anyone working in the not-for-profit sector."

—Joshua Powers, Director of Administration,
Association of Black Foundation Executives

"Scot's book is the Baedeker of not-for-profit accounting and reporting practices—guiding the reader through the organization of a NFP—responsibilities of its board of directors and critical government reports to file. It succeeds admirably in its goal to steer readers around the hazards of organizing, managing and overseeing a not-for-profit organization."

—Karen Rockey, Treasurer,
Financial Women's Association of New York

The Simplified Guide to Not-for-Profit Accounting, Formation, and Reporting

The Simplified Guide to Not-for-Profit Accounting, Formation, and Reporting

Laurence Scot

WILEY

John Wiley & Sons, Inc.

Published by John Wiley & Sons, Inc., Hoboken, New Jersey.
Published simultaneously in Canada.

For general information on our other products and services or for technical support, please contact our Customer Care Department within the United States at (800) 762-2974, outside the United States at (317) 572-3993 or fax (317) 572-4002.

Wiley also publishes its books in a variety of electronic formats. Some content that appears in print may not be available in electronic books. For more information about Wiley products, visit our web site at www.wiley.com.

Library of Congress Cataloging-in-Publication Data:
    Scot, Laurence.
        The simplified guide to not-for-profit accounting, formation & reporting/Laurence Scot.
            p. cm.
    Includes index.
    ISBN 978-0-470-57544-4 (pbk.)
    1.   Nonprofit organizations—Accounting. 2.   Nonprofit organizations—Finance. I. Title.
    HF5686.N56S36 2010
    657′.98—dc22

                                                                                    2009048436

Contents

Preface

There are very few studies showing the exact number of not-for-profit (NFP) organizations in existence in the United States. The reason for this is the enormous diversity in legal structure, type of activities performed, and level of tax exemption and reporting that NFP organizations encompass. The few studies that have been performed show the number of NFP organizations has grown almost exponentially in 30 years. In 2005 the *NonProfit Times* reported that the total number of nonprofit organizations in the United States stood at about 1.5 million. Broken down, this would be about 850,000 public charities, 100,000 private foundations, and the balance, all other types (chambers of commerce, civic leagues, etc.) In 2009, the number is probably closer to over 2 million. The Internal Revenue Service has approximately 1.5 million organizations classified as fully exempt from taxes and another 400,000 that have partial exemption, such as churches that file annual information returns (i.e., Form 990s) but never applied for tax exemption and certain pension trusts and political organizations. If all churches, including those that do not file any returns are included, as well as very small community, sports, and other groups, the number of NFP organizations could be between 2 and 2.5 million.

According to a report by the Nonprofit Employment Data Project at The Johns Hopkins Center for Civil Society Studies, employment in the U.S. NFP sector has grown faster than overall employment in 46 of the 50 states. Some states such as New York and California have an exceedingly high concentration of NFP organizations. In New York alone, there are over 100,000 registered NFPs, and some published reports state that if combined, these organizations would constitute one of the top three industries in New York. So, one would think, with so many NFP organizations requiring qualified technical staff, there would be an abundance of training material available. Surprisingly though, there isn't. As with any industry, specific knowledge is mandatory in order to function properly. In the area of accounting and finance, this is also a truism. However, despite the fact that NFPs constitute one of the largest segments of our economy, there is a dearth of books and other literature and even fewer programs geared specifically to training NFP accountants and financial employees. Hence, the reason for this book.

Accounting Is More Than Numbers

In order to account for something, one must first understand what they are accounting for. Unfortunately, many financial staff hired at NFPs do not have a good understanding of what an NFP organization is, the rules they must follow, and who they have to report to. There are also a lot of misconceptions about what an NFP can and cannot do. For example, one common misconception is that all NFP organizations can receive tax-deductible contributions. Other misconceptions include the following: all NFPs are exempt from paying all income taxes, NFPs are not allowed to have profits (i.e., have income in excess of expenses), and NFPs cannot own other entities. All falsehoods.

After servicing the NFP industry for more than 20 years, the author believes that there should be more places where recent graduates, new hires, existing employees, management, officers, and board members can go to get a basic understanding of how a typical NFP operates and the accounting and reporting rules they must follow. Whether it's accounting for government or foundation grants or assessments; unrestricted or restricted contributions; fund-raising events, trade shows or auctions; membership fees or dues; journals or programmatic services/activities; cash control or investment strategies and returns; or the numerous other unique NFP activities, accountants need to be adequately trained and knowledgeable to perform their duties at a level sufficient to support the proper functioning of the organization.

The author believes that this book will provide the reader with a fundamental understanding of how NFP organizations are formed, their structure, and the unique accounting and reporting issues they face. Although not all encompassing, the information provided here should be sufficient in assisting with maintaining the financial books of a typical NFP entity and complying with most reporting requirements. The author wishes to point out that information in this book does NOT apply to each and every organization or situation, nor will it contain every conceivable transaction, activity, or disclosure. Rather, the goal is to provide enough fundamental information to be useful in a practical way and act as a desk reference for future questions. Because the author is located in and most familiar with New York state rules, the examples used in this book will apply to that state and not necessarily be applicable to all other states or jurisdictions.

I want to thank a number of people without whom this book would not have become a reality. First and foremost Susan McDermott, senior editor at John Wiley & Sons, and her staff, who saw the need for publishing this type of book. Special thanks to Gail Rizick and my wife Mindy Scot for spending a significant amount of time providing editorial suggestions, and to Gail Donovan and numerous others for prodding me over the years to write a book on a subject near and dear to me. I also want to thank my young son, Jason Scot, for allowing me the time to write this book at the loss of many fun and enjoyable joint activities, and last, my partners William Skody and Alfred Jacob, for assisting me in providing the highest level of professional service to my NFP clients for over 20 years.

CHAPTER

Introduction

Most textbooks define not-for-profits (NFPs) as organizations exhibiting a certain set of characteristics different from a commercial enterprise. If a more descriptive definition was needed, one could say an NFP organization is *a legal entity or group formed for some purpose other than to make a profit and not owned by any one or more individuals or entity.* NFPs do not have owners, shareholders, or partners who derive a return or income from their invest- ment. Instead there are individuals entrusted with the responsibility of ensuring that the entity accomplishes its purpose for being in existence, otherwise known as their mission. These responsible individuals are known as the board of directors or the board of trustees. If you ask any large group of individuals to give a short description of an NFP organization, the most typical answers would be that it is an organization that performs a service to society, receives tax deductible contributions, and doesn't pay any income taxes. Although this is true for many NFP organizations it is much too simplistic and doesn't do justice to the myriad of different activities that NFPs engage in today, nor to the fact that not all NFPs can receive tax- deductible contributions or are exempt from paying all taxes. There is also a lot of confusion regarding terminology used to describe these non- commercial-type organizations, and many terms are used interchangeably. Terms like *NFP, nonprofit (NP or NPO), exempt organization, public charity,* and *foundation.* However, there are some technical differences and reasons why one term is preferable or appropriate over others in some instances.

Definitions

Not-for-profit vs. *nonprofit:* The term *nonprofit* is probably the oldest and most widely used term. However, it doesn't accurately describe this unique type of organization because it implies that there isn't or shouldn't be *any* profit. That is to say, either the receipts coming in equal the disbursements going out (i.e., zero net profit), which is very difficult to achieve in reality, or the expenses going out exceed the revenue coming in (i.e., net loss), which

1

would put an organization out of business if experienced on an ongoing basis. A number of years ago, the term *not-for-profit* started to be used by the accounting profession's rule-making bodies because it better described the operations of noncommercial entities. Simply put, the term means an organization that is *not* in business to make a profit but is in existence for some other purpose. That doesn't mean (and it shouldn't mean) that it can't take in more than it spends because, through simple arithmetic, if the pluses don't exceed the minuses the organization won't be able to exist on an ongoing or going-concern basis for any length of time.

Exempt Organization: Not-for-profit or nonprofit status is a state law concept and one must apply within a state to receive this status. This status makes an organization eligible (key word *eligible*) for certain benefits, such as exemptions from federal and state income tax and state sales and property taxes, but it doesn't guarantee it will receive those exemptions. Although most NFPs are exempt from paying taxes, not all are. The agency empowered with the authority to grant tax exemption is the Internal Revenue Service (IRS). After registering as a not-for-profit organization at the state level, a lengthy application must be submitted to the IRS requesting tax exempt status.

Public Charity and Foundation: A public charity is a special type of NFP that is exempt from income taxes under the Internal Revenue Code section 501 (c)(3) and signifies that the organization receives most of its support from the *public* instead of from a small group of individuals. A public charity differs from a *private foundation* in that a foundation receives most of its funds from a small number of individuals or entities such as from one family or corporation. Its primary activity is the making of grants to other charitable organizations and individuals, rather than operating charitable programs. When an organization applies for exempt public-charity status but doesn't meet the public test, it is classified as a foundation. The application process to be an exempt organization (public charity, foundation, or other) will be explained in more detail later in the Chapter 2.

Unique Characteristics and Types of NFPs

In addition to the general characteristic of NOT being in business to make a profit, not-for-profit organizations have a number of other characteristics that distinguish them from a typical commercial entity. The most widely known is their exemption from paying taxes. The allowance can include exemption from paying federal, state, and local income tax, sales tax, property tax, utility tax, and many other types of taxes and fees. However, as will be explained later in this book, not all NFPs are exempt from paying all taxes.

Another widely known characteristic of NFPs is their ability to receive tax deductible contributions from an individual or entity that isn't getting something in return of equal or greater value. Can all NFPs receive tax-deductible contributions? No. Only those recognized and classified as a certain type of exempt organization by the IRS qualify, such as public charities and private foundations. The justification for the deduction is to provide an incentive for supporting the activities of private organizations that provide a valuable and needed service to society. Other types of NFPs such as membership organizations and civic leagues generally can't receive tax-deductible contributions.

There are even differences in the maximum amount of contributions that an individual or corporation can deduct from their taxes based on the type of NFP organization they give to. For example, the tax code currently allows an individual to deduct up to 50 percent of their adjusted gross income (AGI) for contributions made to a public charity but typically only up to 30 percent of their AGI if their donations are made to a private foundation.

Other typical characteristics that distinguish NFPs from commercial enterprises include the following:

Administrative/Employment-Related

- Not concerned with serving the interests of owners, partners, or share-holders but rather serving the competing interests of many external parties such as donors (individual, corporate, and foundations), government granting agencies, other NFP organizations (contributors, affiliates), regulatory agencies (IRS, state, local) and the general public.
- Role of the board of directors—NFP boards play a much more active role in the day-to-day activities of the organization and many times assist management with various programs and events.
- Board compensation—Board members don't usually get paid for their duties and conversely are often expected to make contributions or assist in raising funds through events or other fund-raising activities.
- Budget development and utilization—Most successful organizations use budgets to control costs. With NFPs, budgets are used not just to control costs but also to obtain government and foundation grants, to meet restrictions imposed by donors, and, by way of transparency, to show their board and external parties that they are prudent with their funds and other assets.
- NFPs receive many free services from volunteers who help with administrative duties, programs, events, activities, and so forth. Imagine a bank asking people to work as bank tellers for free!

Accounting and Reporting Related

- Tracking contributions by restrictions (unrestricted, temporarily restricted, and permanently restricted).

- Tracking and reporting contributed services and facilities.
- Tracking and reporting expenses by function (e.g., program, management).
- Accounting for investments on a fair market value basis instead of cost basis.
- Allocating and accounting for joint costs and direct costs related to fund-raising activities
- Most nonpublic small to medium-size commercial enterprises don't have their financial statement audited by a CPA. NFPs on the other hand are required by many states to have an independent audit performed if they exceed a certain level of support (e.g., New York requires a financial audit if *revenues* exceed $250,000).
- NFPs receiving federal grants are required to have a specialized audit (in compliance with Office of Management and Budget A-133) performed if their *grant expenditures* exceed $500,000.
- Many NFPs are audited by government agencies, foundations, and other NFPs who provide them with donations and grants.
- Providing increased transparency and disclosures in financial reporting.

Types of Not-for-Profit Organizations

When most people think of a typical NFP organization, they envision a public charity that performs some public service like the Salvation Army, Goodwill, United Way, Boy Scouts, and so on. It is not generally known that there are many different types of NFPs and, depending on the type, they have different reporting requirements and are eligible for different tax and other exemptions. There are many different ways to group NFP organizations such as by activities, revenue source, asset size or number of employees, local, national, or international operations, and so forth. The most prominent and accepted classification basis is the one used by the IRS to determine an organization's tax-exempt status as categorized by an Internal Revenue Code section. The IRS has a publication (Publication 557—*Tax-Exempt Status for Your Organization*) that lists 27 major categories (501(c)(1) to 501(c)(27)) and numerous additional categories and subcategories.

The most widely known Internal Revenue Code section is the *501(c)(3)*. This is the code section for *public charities* and there are many different types, performing many different functions such as:

- Charitable (food, clothing, shelter, financial support)
- Religious (church, synagogues, mosques)
- Educational (elementary through high school, colleges and universities)
- Scientific, research, and literary

- Museums and performing arts (opera, ballet)
- Health and welfare (hospitals, drug treatment, counseling)
- Prevention of cruelty to children or animals
- Amateur sports

Other common categories of NFPs listed by code section are: 501(c)(4)—civic leagues, local associations of employees; 501(c)(6)—membership organizations, business leagues, chambers of commerce, real estate boards, and economic development; and 501(c)(7)—social and recreation clubs. There are many other categories including political groups, cemetery companies, mutual insurance companies, and so on (see Appendix A for a complete list).

NFP Organization Formation

Many NFP organizations are started by one or more people who have an idea that they believe will enrich people's lives in some beneficial or productive way, either individually or in groups, and can benefit communities, towns, cities, states, society domestically or internationally, or affect the whole planet (e.g., global warming). Because the idea consists of something that will be ongoing, as opposed to a one-shot activity, they need to create an entity to convert this idea into a reality. The entity that would be created is an NFP whose business goal is to create products or services that have some benevolent purpose and not exist simply to generate income and maximize profits.

There are numerous ways of creating and building a successful NFP organization, and there is no one absolute or perfect method. That being said, the author believes there are certain fundamental steps that should be taken to increase the chance that the outcome will be successful.

How Does One Start an NFP?

The first step after envisioning your idea is to create a name for your organization. Like any commercial business, the name should be descriptive of the entity's mission but not so long that it becomes cumbersome. For example, The Society for the Advancement of People Who Believe in Peace on Earth and Brotherhood of All Mankind is a tad too long. A much better name would be EarthPeacePeople (maybe not perfect, but you get the idea). For purposes of this book, the author has created a fictitious organization called Job Training Now, Inc., or JTN for short.

After creating the organization's name, the next step is to develop a plan of how the organization will achieve its goals. The plan will be the result of answering the 4W-H questions: *What, How, Who, When,* and *Where.* This plan is similar to what is known in the business world as a business plan. It doesn't have to be a formal, 40-page, bound document with color financial projections, but it should be documented in writing to provide the creators with direction and clarity. It doesn't have to cover every conceivable and possible situation but should cover the basic goals of the new organization to provide a guide to move forward.

The first question to be answered is the *What* question. What programs or major activities will the organization perform? In the case of our fictitious organization, JTN, the two major programs will be simulated on-the-job training and corporate on-site training. Next, *how* will the programs or activities be performed and *how* will support and revenue be obtained? If prioritization was required, the *How* question should be the first to be addressed before moving on. Too many times NFPs with great missions are created without first determining how support will be obtained only to end up closing up within a short period because of a lack of funds. In JTN's case, the creators believe they can obtain funding from government grants and program fees earned from corporate customers.

The next question to be answered: *Who* will perform the programs and manage the organization. In many startup situations the creator of the organization will be the person who performs most of the organization's functions, and in JTN's case, it will be the creator whose title will be president. In many cases the creator will be assisted by several individuals who will serve as members of the initial board of directors or trustees. For purposes of this book, the term *board of directors* will be inclusive of the term *board of trustees.*

The final two questions to be answered: *When* will activities begin? and *Where* will the organization be located and activities take place? The president of JTN plans on running the organization out of her apartment initially, and performing the training in a rented school room. The activities are planned to begin at the end of the summer.

After writing the plan and answering the 4W-H questions, the creator needs to form an initial board of directors and decide who will act as initial officers. Usually this is accomplished by getting together a few like-minded individuals who are interested in the NFP's mission. Many states require several names in order to incorporate.

After a draft operating plan is written and the initial board of directors and officers are determined, what is the next step? Answer: creating the actual NFP entity.

Registration

A not-for-profit organization is created by registering the NFP name as a legal entity or unincorporated association. The registration process takes place at the state level because not-for-profit status is a state law concept. An NFP can form as any legal structure such as a partnership, limited liability company (LLC), or corporation. The most common legal entity is the corporation, and in most cases, a special type of corporate classification. Because the author is most familiar with New York State (NYS) laws, rules, and regulations, those will be the ones referred to throughout this book. Other state rules will be mentioned if appropriate.

To apply to be an NFP corporation in NYS you must file Articles of Incorporation, which define the activities of the entity. The Articles of Incorporation are filed with the Secretary of State, Division of Corporations. To become an NFP corporation in the state of New Jersey you must file a Certificate of Incorporation, which must be filed with the New Jersey Division of Revenue, Corporate Filing Unit. In both cases, a copy of the organization's bylaws must be included with the incorporation papers. The bylaws is a document that specifies in broad terms *how the organization will operate and be governed.* That is to say, it states the rules and regulations that the entity must follow. Typically, bylaws will include: the purpose of the organization, the number of board members, how board members are elected, how board members are removed, the voting rights of board members, number of board members required for a quorum (number required to pass any resolution), number of minimum board meetings per year, titles and responsibilities of officers, the name and number of any required board committees, and any other guiding operating rules that the organization must follow. Once submitted, bylaws should be adhered to but can be revised in the future. Revisions are sometimes necessary as an organization grows but special care should be taken before making any revision and the number of revisions should be kept to an absolute minimum.

Although anyone can prepare the Articles or Certificate of Incorporation and bylaws, it is preferable to have these documents prepared by a qualified attorney. Qualified in this context means being knowledgeable about not-for-profit organization structure and terminology. This is very important because the lack of inclusion of certain provisions in your organizing document might prevent the organization from getting tax-exemption approval in the future. Attorneys, like other professionals, typically charge fees for their services. Fortunately, the American Bar Association suggests that attorneys perform a certain percentage of their annual services free of charge or on a pro bono basis, and many attorneys comply. The search for a pro bono attorney then becomes the first of a never-ending process of trying to obtain free services or products for the NFP organization. It is in the context of soliciting something for free that the author has coined the phrase "beg for profits" to describe the type of activities that so many NFPs engage in on a daily basis, in order to accomplish their mission.

Other Initial Steps

After registering your entity (incorporating, etc.), the next step is to obtain an Employer Identification Number (EIN), also know as a Taxpayer Identification Number (TIN). Years ago this took several days. Today an EIN can be obtained online simply by going to the IRS web site www.irs.gov and completing the SS-4 application form. Upon completion of the form you receive a number immediately.

Once you have your legal name and EIN, the next step is to open a bank account. Prior to going to the bank it should be decided who will have signatory rights, that is, rights to handle all bank-related transactions (e.g., sign checks). Usually this will be at least two of the following: the president, chairperson, executive director, treasurer, or secretary.

Other decisions or actions that should be made prior to providing any products or services include deciding who will handle the bookkeeping or accounting duties, getting solid commitments from several people to be members of the first board of directors, and obtaining initial funding.

Exemption Applications and Other Registrations

One of the most important things that a new NFP organization should do is apply for tax exemption, that is, exemption from paying income and other taxes. A general misconception is that an NFP corporation or association is automatically tax exempt after it becomes a corporation. NFP corporate status only makes an organization *eligible* for certain benefits, such as exemption from state sales tax, property tax, and federal and state income tax. To actually receive exemption, the organization must apply and be approved for exemption.

Federal Income Tax Exemption (IRS)—General

To qualify as being exempt from federal income taxes, an NFP organization must meet the requirements set forth in the Internal Revenue Code. The IRS has issued a publication, Pub. 557, to assist organizations seeking recognition of exemption from federal income taxes. To qualify for exemption under the Internal Revenue Code (code section 501(a)), an organization must be organized for one or more purposes specifically designated in the code. Most organizations seeking recognition of exemption from federal income taxes must use one of two specific application forms prescribed by the IRS. The two forms are Form 1023, *Application for Recognition of Exemption Under Section 501(c)(3) of the Internal Revenue Code*, and Form 1024, *Application for Recognition of Exemption Under Section 501(a)*. Both forms are lengthy but Form 1023 is more comprehensive because it allows the organization to receive tax-deductible contributions from individuals, corporations, and other entities. Great care should be taken in preparing these applications because of the importance of receiving numerous tax exemptions. The next section will discuss the preparation of Form 1023 and will highlight certain important sections (Form 1024 will not be discussed in this book).

It should be noted that there is one major exception to applying for tax exemption and this applies to religious organizations classified as churches. IRS *Publication 1828* defines churches as organizations with specific characteristics developed by the IRS and court decisions over time and includes: distinct legal existence, recognized creed and form of worship, definite and distinct ecclesiastical government, formal code of doctrine and discipline, distinct religious history, membership not associated with any other church or denomination, organization of ordained ministers, literature of its own, regular religious services, and so forth. They are exempt from filing the application because of the First Amendment of the U.S. Constitution, which is part of the U.S. Bill of Rights. The First Amendment prohibits the federal legislature from making laws respecting an establishment of religion (establishment clause) or that prohibit the free exercise of religion (free exercise clause). In addition to not being required to file for tax exemption, churches are also not required to file an annual information return (Form 990). They can, however, voluntarily file the form if they desire to show that they are being compliant with all required rules and regulations.

Other Registrations and Filings

Most states also require some type of NFP registration if an organization plans on operating or soliciting funds through fund-raising or gambling (e.g., raffle) activities within their state. In New York, the regulatory agency responsible for monitoring the NFP sector is the New York State Charities Bureau, which is part of the office of the Attorney General. In New Jersey it is the Department of Consumers Affairs. Under two New York state statutes (Article 7-A & EPTL), an NFP organization wishing to operate or receive charitable contributions in the state must file Form 410, *Registration Statement for Charitable Organizations* and Schedule E, *Request for Registration Exemption for Charitable Organizations.* Article 7-A of the Executive Law (Article 7-A) requires registration of charitable and other not-for-profit organizations that solicit contributions from New York state entities (residents, foundations, corporations, government agencies, and other entities). Section 8-1.4 of the Estates, Powers and Trusts Law (EPTL) requires registration of charitable organizations that are incorporated or formed or otherwise will conduct activity in New York state. When both elements apply, an NFP must apply as a dual registrant.

Exemption from federal and state income taxes is one benefit that most NFPs enjoy. However, there are a number of other tax exemptions available to NFPs depending on their federal exemption status and the state in which they operate. To receive a particular exemption, an NFP organization must file the appropriate application. For example, New York state law allows public charities an exemption from paying state and local sales and use tax on purchases. Qualifying NFPs should file Form ST119.2, *Application for an Exempt Organization Certificate* with New York State Department of Taxation and Finance. For a similar exemption in New Jersey, the application must be made with the New Jersey Department of Taxation.

Another available exemption to New York public charities is the exemption from New York state real estate taxes for property the organization owns and uses for exempt purposes. To obtain exemption, the organization must file an *Exemption from Real Estate Taxation for Property Owned by Nonprofit Organizations* form with the New York City Department of Finance. Other exemptions might also be available depending on state and local laws. Professional advice should be sought to determine all available exemptions.

Application for Recognition of Exemption—IRS Forms 1023 and 1024

As mentioned previously, to qualify as being exempt from federal income taxes, an NFP must meet certain requirements set forth in the Internal Revenue Code. In order to determine whether they are eligible for an exemption they must submit either Form 1023, *Application for Recognition of Exemption Under Section 501(c)(3) of the Internal Revenue Code*, or Form 1024, *Application for Recognition of Exemption Under Section 501(a)*. Form 1024 would be used by various NFP organizations such as civic leagues, membership organizations, chambers of commerce, economic development corporations, labor, fraternities, and others.

Form 1023   Form 1023 is used by any organization organized and operated exclusively for religious, charitable, scientific, testing for public safety, literary, educational, fostering national or international amateur sports competition, or for the prevention of cruelty to children or animals (i.e., any organization wishing to be treated as a public charity or private foundation). This form is very important and a great deal of care should be taken when completing it because of the importance and ramification of receiving tax exemption in order to fulfill the stated mission of the organization. Although the IRS does not release statistics on the number of incomplete applications filed and the number returned requesting elaboration or additional information, it is the author's experience that the number is more than insignificant and could reach as high as 25–40 percent of all applications. Unlike other filings with the IRS (e.g., individual income tax returns), every application for recognition for exemption is reviewed by an agent of the IRS. Since the IRS takes their role of approving exemptions very seriously, and approval is based more on a facts and elements basis rather than a quantitative basis, computer algorithms cannot be used for acceptance or rejection. This means more scrutiny by a real person and, consequently, more questions. Fortunately, at the end of the process, most applications are approved.

Form 1023 is quite lengthy and consists of 26 pages (12 core and 14 pages of schedules), so a complete review of the form is beyond the scope of this book. Certain significant sections, however, will be covered to assist the reader in avoiding errors or omissions or to highlight various elements that the IRS will scrutinize to validate providing the organization with a tax exemption. Many questions require a yes or no answer, and many others require a written explanation. In accordance with Form 1023 instructions, if there is insufficient space to legibly and accurately respond to a question, answers should be put on an 8½ × 11-inch paper and attached to the application.

IRS regulations require that Form 1023 be filed within 27 months after legal formation. The reason for allowing such a long period of time is to give the organization sufficient time to develop its programs and seek support. Although a number of organizations will opt to apply immediately upon formation, many decide to wait a while. In a number of situations, waiting until the completion of 12–15 months of activities is preferable because it better supports the organization's proposition that its mission is not to make a profit but to provide some acceptable benefit to society.

Figures 2.1–2.9 have been extracted from the most current Form 1023. Below each figure you will find information related to questions on the form. Some suggestions for appropriate answers are provided.

Part I, Line 1 asks for the organization's legal name. Many organizations have long legal names and sometimes use an abbreviation when referring to themselves (e.g., AICPA for the American Institute of Certified Public Accountants or NYSSCPA for New York State Society of Certified Public Accountants). The exact legal name as stated in the organizing documents (e.g., Articles of Incorporation, bylaws, etc.) must be used on this form. A slight variation will cause a follow-up communication from the IRS.

Part I, Line 7 asks if you are represented by someone other than an empowered officer of the organization. If the individual preparing the application is not an officer, a power of attorney (POA) form (*Power of Attorney and Declaration of Representative*) must be completed and submitted with the 1023 application. A POA allows a representative to act on behalf of an authorized person.

Part II, Line 5 asks if the organization has adopted *bylaws*. Many states such as New York require that bylaws be included with the organizing documents submitted to the state. If bylaws are not required, this question wants an explanation of how officers and board members are selected. The more democratic and less dictatorial the process, the better it is.

Part III, Lines 1 through 2c are very important. As stated on the form, these questions ensure that the organizing documents contain the required

Form **1023** (Rev. June 2006) Department of the Treasury Internal Revenue Service	**Application for Recognition of Exemption Under Section 501(c)(3) of the Internal Revenue Code**	OMB No. 1545-0056 Note: *If exempt status is approved, this application will be open for public inspection.*

Use the instructions to complete this application and for a definition of all **bold** items. For additional help, call IRS Exempt Organizations Customer Account Services toll-free at 1-877-829-5500. Visit our website at www.irs.gov for forms and publications. If the required information and documents are not submitted with payment of the appropriate user fee, the application may be returned to you.

Attach additional sheets to this application if you need more space to answer fully. Put your name and EIN on each sheet and identify each answer by Part and line number. Complete Parts I - XI of Form 1023 and submit only those Schedules (A through H) that apply to you.

Part I   Identification of Applicant

1 Full name of organization (exactly as it appears in your organizing document)	2 c/o Name (if applicable)

3 Mailing address (Number and street) (see instructions)	Room/Suite	4 Employer Identification Number (EIN)

City or town, state or country, and ZIP + 4	5 Month the annual accounting period ends (01-12)

6   Primary contact (officer, director, trustee, or **authorized representative**)
   a   Name:
   b   Phone:
   c   Fax: (optional)

7   Are you represented by an authorized representative, such as an attorney or accountant? If "Yes," provide the authorized representative's name, and the name and address of the authorized representative's firm. Include a completed Form 2848, *Power of Attorney and Declaration of Representative,* with your application if you would like us to communicate with your representative.   ☐ Yes   ☐ No

8   Was a person who is not one of your officers, directors, trustees, employees, or an authorized representative listed in line 7, paid, or promised payment, to help plan, manage, or advise you about the structure or activities of your organization, or about your financial or tax matters? If "Yes," provide the person's name, the name and address of the person's firm, the amounts paid or promised to be paid, and describe that person's role.   ☐ Yes   ☐ No

9 a   Organization's website:
   b   Organization's email: (optional)

10   Certain organizations are not required to file an information return (Form 990 or Form 990-EZ). If you are granted tax-exemption, are you claiming to be excused from filing Form 990 or Form 990-EZ? If "Yes," explain. See the instructions for a description of organizations not required to file Form 990 or Form 990-EZ.   ☐ Yes   ☐ No

11   Date incorporated if a corporation, or formed, if other than a corporation. (MM/DD/YYYY)   /   /

12   Were you formed under the laws of a foreign country?   ☐ Yes   ☐ No
   If "Yes," state the country.

For Paperwork Reduction Act Notice, see page 24 of the instructions.   Form **1023** (Rev. 6-2006)

Figure 2.1   Form 1023, Part I

provisions (i.e., language) to meet the requirements set forth under Internal Revenue Code section 501(c)(3). To ensure that they do, copies of the organizing documents (Incorporation, bylaws) and any amendments must be submitted with Form 1023. Many applications are rejected because the Articles or Certificate of Incorporation don't contain required wording. This is the reason it is so important that an experienced professional assist with the preparation and submission of the application.

Part III, Lines 1 requires that organizing documents state that the purpose of the organization is charitable, religious, educational, or scientific (i.e., purpose clause). The applicant must disclose the page, article, and paragraph (or line) number where this information exists in the document. A sample of an appropriate answer to this question is as follows:

Form 1023 (Rev. 6-2006)	Name:	EIN:	Page 2

Part II Organizational Structure

You must be a corporation (including a limited liability company), an unincorporated association, or a trust to be tax exempt. (See instructions.) DO NOT file this form unless you can check "Yes" on lines 1, 2, 3, or 4.

1 Are you a **corporation**? If "Yes," attach a copy of your articles of incorporation showing **certification of filing** with the appropriate state agency. Include copies of any amendments to your articles and be sure they also show state filing certification. ☐ Yes ☐ No

2 Are you a **limited liability company (LLC)**? If "Yes," attach a copy of your articles of organization showing certification of filing with the appropriate state agency. Also, if you adopted an operating agreement, attach a copy. Include copies of any amendments to your articles and be sure they show state filing certification. Refer to the instructions for circumstances when an LLC should not file its own exemption application. ☐ Yes ☐ No

3 Are you an **unincorporated association**? If "Yes," attach a copy of your articles of association, constitution, or other similar organizing document that is dated and includes at least two signatures. Include signed and dated copies of any amendments. ☐ Yes ☐ No

4 a Are you a **trust**? If "Yes," attach a signed and dated copy of your trust agreement. Include signed and dated copies of any amendments. ☐ Yes ☐ No

 b Have you been funded? If "No," explain how you are formed without anything of value placed in trust. ☐ Yes ☐ No

5 Have you adopted bylaws? If "Yes," attach a current copy showing date of adoption. If "No," explain how your officers, directors, or trustees are selected. ☐ Yes ☐ No

Part III Required Provisions in Your Organizing Document

The following questions are designed to ensure that when you file this application, your organizing document contains the required provisions to meet the organizational test under section 501(c)(3). Unless you can check the boxes in both lines 1 and 2, your organizing document does not meet the organizational test. DO NOT file this application until you have amended your organizing document. Submit your original and amended organizing documents (showing state filing certification if you are a corporation or an LLC) with your application.

1 Section 501(c)(3) requires that your organizing document state your exempt purpose(s), such as charitable, religious, educational, and/or scientific purposes. Check the box to confirm that your organizing document meets this requirement. Describe specifically where your organizing document meets this requirement, such as a reference to a particular article or section in your organizing document. Refer to the instructions for exempt purpose language. Location of Purpose Clause (Page, Article, and Paragraph): _____ ☐

2a Section 501(c)(3) requires that upon dissolution of your organization, your remaining assets must be used exclusively for exempt purposes, such as charitable, religious, educational, and/or scientific purposes. Check the box on line 2a to confirm that your organizing document meets this requirement by express provision for the distribution of assets upon dissolution. If you rely on state law for your dissolution provision, do not check the box on line 2a and go to line 2c. ☐

2b If you checked the box on line 2a, specify the location of your dissolution clause (Page, Article, and Paragraph). Do not complete line 2c if you checked box 2a. _____

2c See the instructions for information about the operation of state law in your particular state. Check this box if you rely on operation of state law for your dissolution provision and indicate the state: _____ ☐

Part IV Narrative Description of Your Activities

Using an attachment, describe your *past, present, and planned* activities in a narrative. If you believe that you have already provided some of this information in response to other parts of this application, you may summarize that information here and refer to the specific parts of the application for supporting details. You may also attach representative copies of newsletters, brochures, or similar documents for supporting details to this narrative. Remember that if this application is approved, it will be open for public inspection. Therefore, your narrative description of activities should be thorough and accurate. Refer to the instructions for information that must be included in your description.

Part V Compensation and Other Financial Arrangements With Your Officers, Directors, Trustees, Employees, and Independent Contractors

1a List the names, titles, and mailing addresses of all of your officers, directors, and trustees. For each person listed, state their total annual **compensation**, or proposed compensation, for all services to the organization, whether as an officer, employee, or other position. Use actual figures, if available. Enter "none" if no compensation is or will be paid. If additional space is needed, attach a separate sheet. Refer to the instructions for information on what to include as compensation.

Name	Title	Mailing address	Compensation amount (annual actual or estimated)

Figure 2.2 Form 1023, Parts II, III, and IV

The ORGANIZATION shall be a not-for-profit corporation organized for charitable, educational, and scientific purposes, within the meaning of section 501(c)(3) of the Internal Revenue Code, as amended, including, for such purposes, the making of distributions to organizations that qualify as exempt organizations under 501(c)(3) of the Internal Revenue Code, as amended. Its additional purposes are . . . (describe).

Part III, Lines 2a–2c require that organizing documents state that upon dissolution of the organization, your remaining assets will be used exclusively for exempt purposes (e.g., charitable, religious, educational, or scientific). Like any other organization, there will be times when there is no longer a need for an organization's activities or services or the organization is unable to function due to a lack of funds or a myriad of other reasons. The IRS wants to ensure that an organization accepts responsibility that all remaining assets are used in a manner similar to its operating exempt purpose. Line 2b requires that you disclose the page, article, and paragraph (or line) number where this information exists in the organizing document. A sample statement might read as follows:

> Upon dissolution of the corporation, the board of directors shall, after paying all liabilities, distribute all of the assets of the corporation to one or more organizations operated exclusively for charitable, educational, or scientific purposes . . .

Part IV is also very important. This question requests a narrative description of your activities (past, present, or planned). It covers past, present, or planned activities to allow flexibility because of the varying stages of development an organization might be in at the time of application. For example, if applying immediately after incorporation, activities described would be planned, and if applying after a year, activities might be past, present, and planned. The directions state that you can attach to the form all promotional material describing your NFP activities. Because promotional materials (web site, brochures, etc.) are not always created and available when an organization first begins operations, the organization might be in a better position to support its statements of benevolent activities if it waits a year or so until they are available. Also, many times the narrative description is too long. It might seem to the applicant that more is better. But sometimes when the description becomes too elaborate and tries to cover every conceivable activity, it ends up causing confusion. Many applications have been rejected because of inconsistencies in the narrative. The narrative should be descriptive enough to clearly convey all past, present, or planned major activities and should reinforce the fact that activities are being conducted for a purpose other than based on a profit motive.

Part V (partial presentation illustrated in Figure 2.3) also asks a number of very important questions. This section asks questions related to compensation and financial arrangements paid to an organization's officers, directors, trustees, key employees, highest compensated employees, and highest compensated independent contractors. More specifically, these questions seek to disclose the method the organization uses to determine compensation payments to influential individuals or individuals who have an economic relationship with influential individuals. Line 2 asks relationship (related-party) questions. Lines 6a and 6b are looking for answers related to compensation arrangements based on profit (e.g., salary is based on a percentage of contributions raised) rather than a fixed fee based on the

Part V	Compensation and Other Financial Arrangements With Your Officers, Directors, Trustees, Employees, and Independent Contractors

1a List the names, titles, and mailing addresses of all of your officers, directors, and trustees. For each person listed, state their total annual **compensation**, or proposed compensation, for all services to the organization, whether as an officer, employee, or other position. Use actual figures, if available. Enter "none" if no compensation is or will be paid. If additional space is needed, attach a separate sheet. Refer to the instructions for information on what to include as compensation.

Name	Title	Mailing address	Compensation amount (annual actual or estimated)

————————— Lines Skipped —————————

2a Are any of your officers, directors, or trustees **related** to each other through **family** or **business relationships**? If "Yes," identify the individuals and explain the relationship. ☐ Yes ☐ No

b Do you have a business relationship with any of your officers, directors, or trustees other than through their position as an officer, director, or trustee? If "Yes," identify the individuals and describe the business relationship with each of your officers, directors, or trustees. ☐ Yes ☐ No

c Are any of your officers, directors, or trustees related to your highest compensated employees or highest compensated independent contractors listed on lines 1b or 1c through family or business relationships? If "Yes," identify the individuals and explain the relationship. ☐ Yes ☐ No

————————— Lines Skipped —————————

6a Do you or will you compensate any of your officers, directors, trustees, highest compensated employees, and highest compensated independent contractors listed in lines 1a, 1b, or 1c through **non-fixed payments**, such as discretionary bonuses or revenue-based payments? If "Yes," describe all non-fixed compensation arrangements, including how the amounts are determined, who is eligible for such arrangements, whether you place a limitation on total compensation, and how you determine or will determine that you pay no more than reasonable compensation for services. Refer to the instructions for Part V, lines 1a, 1b, and 1c, for information on what to include as compensation. ☐ Yes ☐ No

b Do you or will you compensate any of your employees, other than your officers, directors, trustees, or your five highest compensated employees who receive or will receive compensation of more than $50,000 per year, through non-fixed payments, such as discretionary bonuses or revenue-based payments? If "Yes," describe all non-fixed compensation arrangements, including how the amounts are or will be determined, who is or will be eligible for such arrangements, whether you place or will place a limitation on total compensation, and how you determine or will determine that you pay no more than reasonable compensation for services. Refer to the instructions for Part V, lines 1a, 1b, and 1c, for information on what to include as compensation. ☐ Yes ☐ No

Figure 2.3   Form 1023, Part V

fair value of the services provided (i.e., typical salary for fund-raising employee). For abbreviation purposes, throughout this book the acronym DOTKEY will be used to refer to directors, officers, trustees, and key employees. The IRS defines a key employee as someone who earns a significant salary (e.g., >$150,000) and has authority to make major organizational decisions or has significant control over the organization's activities.

Part VI (partial presentation illustrated in Figure 2.4) relates to goods and services your organization provides to outside parties and members of your organization. Both Part V and Part VI are seeking to make sure that someone is not unjustly benefiting from a financial or economic arrangement that, in essence, is misusing contributions, grants, and other support. A fundamental requirement for tax-exempt organizations under IRS Code is that they must be organized and operated in a way that NO part of their net earnings *inure* (accrue) to the benefit of any private individual. They are trying to determine whether any Inurnment exists.

Part VI   Your Members and Other Individuals and Organizations That Receive Benefits From You
The following "Yes" or "No" questions relate to goods, services, and funds you provide to individuals and organizations as part of your activities. Your answers should pertain to *past, present,* and *planned* activities. (See instructions.)

1a In carrying out your exempt purposes, do you provide goods, services, or funds to individuals? If "Yes," describe each program that provides goods, services, or funds to individuals.	☐ Yes	☐ No
b In carrying out your exempt purposes, do you provide goods, services, or funds to organizations? If "Yes," describe each program that provides goods, services, or funds to organizations.	☐ Yes	☐ No
2 Do any of your programs limit the provision of goods, services, or funds to a specific individual or group of specific individuals? For example, answer "Yes," if goods, services, or funds are provided only for a particular individual, your members, individuals who work for a particular employer, or graduates of a particular school. If "Yes," explain the limitation and how recipients are selected for each program.	☐ Yes	☐ No
3 Do any individuals who receive goods, services, or funds through your programs have a family or business relationship with any officer, director, trustee, or with any of your highest compensated employees or highest compensated independent contractors listed in Part V, lines 1a, 1b, and 1c? If "Yes," explain how these related individuals are eligible for goods, services, or funds.	☐ Yes	☐ No

Figure 2.4   Form 1023, Part VI

In order to determine whether an organization should be granted a tax exemption, the IRS wants to know about certain activities the organization will be conducting. Questions related to organizational activities are covered in Part VIII (partial presentation illustrated in Figure 2.5). Some questions in this part seek to determine whether an applicant has or will be engaging in prohibited activities, whereas other questions, if answered in the affirmative, will require the applicant to file other forms or schedules. Lines 1–2a ask if the organization is or will be involved in political campaigns of candidates for public office and whether the organization will try to influence legislation (i.e., lobbying activities). Public charities and private foundations (i.e., 501(c)(3) organizations) are prohibited from supporting or opposing

Part VIII Your Specific Activities
The following "Yes" or "No" questions relate to specific activities that you may conduct. Check the appropriate box. Your answers should pertain to *past, present,* and *planned* activities. (See instructions.)

1 Do you support or oppose candidates in **political campaigns** in any way? If "Yes," explain.	☐ Yes	☐ No
2a Do you attempt to **influence legislation**? If "Yes," explain how you attempt to influence legislation and complete line 2b. If "No," go to line 3a.	☐ Yes	☐ No
b Have you made or are you making an **election** to have your legislative activities measured by expenditures by filing Form 5768? If "Yes," attach a copy of the Form 5768 that was already filed or attach a completed Form 5768 that you are filing with this application. If "No," describe whether your attempts to influence legislation are a substantial part of your activities. Include the time and money spent on your attempts to influence legislation as compared to your total activities.	☐ Yes	☐ No
3a Do you or will you operate bingo or **gaming** activities? If "Yes," describe who conducts them, and list all revenue received or expected to be received and expenses paid or expected to be paid in operating these activities. **Revenue and expenses** should be provided for the time periods specified in Part IX, Financial Data.	☐ Yes	☐ No
b Do you or will you enter into contracts or other agreements with individuals or organizations to conduct bingo or gaming for you? If "Yes," describe any written or oral arrangements that you made or intend to make, identify with whom you have or will have such arrangements, explain how the terms are or will be negotiated at arm's length, and explain how you determine or will determine you pay no more than fair market value or you will be paid at least fair market value. Attach copies or any written contracts or other agreements relating to such arrangements.	☐ Yes	☐ No
c List the states and local jurisdictions, including Indian Reservations, in which you conduct or will conduct gaming or bingo.		

Form **1023** (Rev. 6-2006)

Figure 2.5   Form 1023, Part VIII

candidates for public office in any political campaign and will be denied an exemption if they engage in this activity. The instructions state:

> Organizations described in section 501(c)(3) are prohibited from supporting or opposing candidates for public office in any political campaign. If you answer "Yes," you are not qualified for tax exemption under section 501(c)(3) and should reconsider whether the filing of application Form 1023 is appropriate.

On the other hand, a 501(c)(3) public charity will be allowed to engage in limited lobbying activities. The instructions state that "Organizations described in section 501(c)(3) are prohibited from engaging in a substantial amount of legislative activities." Whether you are engaged in substantial legislative activities depends on all of the facts and circumstances. By filing Form 5768 (Election/Revocation of Election by an Eligible Section 501(c)(3) Organization to Make Expenditures to Influence Legislation), the organization can have their legislative activities measured solely by an expenditure test to support the contention that this activity is not substantial.

Part VIII has a total of 22 questions. In addition to questions about whether the organization will engage in political campaigns or lobbying activities, Part VIII asks whether the organization will engage in various activities including the following (partial list):

- Gaming (e.g., bingo).
- Method of raising funds (e.g., mail or telephone solicitation or from government grants).
- Engaging in economic development.
- Providing child care, operating a school, or providing low-income housing.
- Publishing, owning, or having rights to music, literature, or other intellectual property.
- Operating in a foreign country.
- Making grants or loans to other organizations or providing scholarships to individuals.

It is evident from these questions that the IRS wants specific information about how the organization performs fund-raising and what type of activities it currently engages or plans to engage in before it grants the organization a tax exemption.

Parts A and B in Part IX (partial presentation illustrated in Figure 2.6) request financial information. Part A (*Statement of Revenue and Expenses*) deals with income and expenses and Part B (*Balance Sheet*), assets and liabilities. Up until 2009, Part A required four years of revenue and expenses (current year plus three prior years) unless an organization was in existence

Form 1023 (Rev. 6-2006)   Name: EIN: Page **9**

| Part IX | **Financial Data** |

For purposes of this schedule, years in existence refer to completed tax years. If in existence 4 or more years, complete the schedule for the most recent 4 tax years. If in existence more than 1 year but less than 4 years, complete the statements for each year in existence and provide projections of your likely revenues and expenses based on a reasonable and good faith estimate of your future finances for a total of 3 years of financial information. If in existence less than 1 year, provide projections of your likely revenues and expenses for the current year and the 2 following years, based on a reasonable and good faith estimate of your future finances for a total of 3 years of financial information. (See instructions.)

A. Statement of Revenues and Expenses

| | Type of revenue or expense | Current tax year | 3 prior tax years or 2 succeeding tax years | | | |
			(a) From _ _ _ _ To _ _ _ _ _ _	(b) From _ _ _ _ _ To _ _ _ _ _ _	(c) From _ _ _ _ _ To _ _ _ _ _ _	(d) From _ _ _ _ To _ _ _ _ _ _	(e) Provide Total for (a) through (d)
Revenues	1 Gifts, grants, and contributions received (do not include unusual grants)						
	2 Membership fees received						
	3 Gross investment income						
	4 Net unrelated business income						
	5 Taxes levied for your benefit						
	6 Value of services or facilities furnished by a governmental unit without charge (not including the value of services generally furnished to the public without charge)						
	7 Any revenue not otherwise listed above or in lines 9-12 below (attach an itemized list)						

Form 1023 (Rev. 6-2006)   Name: EIN: Page **10**

| Part IX | **Financial Data** *(Continued)* |

B. Balance Sheet (for your most recently completed tax year)   Year End:

Assets		(Whole dollars)
1 Cash...	1	
2 Accounts receivable, net...	2	
3 Inventories	3	
4 Bonds and notes receivable (attach an itemized list)	4	
5 Corporate stocks (attach an itemized list)	5	

Figure 2.6   Form 1023, Part IX

less than four years. In those cases, it would be the current year, any completed prior years, and a projection of up to two future years. In 2009, the rules were changed to provide five years of activity. Consistent with prior rules, if the organization was in existence less than five years, it should complete the statement for each year in existence and provide projections of likely revenues and expenses for all remaining years. Future revised forms will have columns for five years but if using an older 1023 form, an attachment should be used to include the fifth year.

As with all sections of the 1023 application, the applicant should try to answer all questions as honestly and accurately as possible. But when an organization is first created and just beginning its operations, it is very difficult to project with any degree of certainty how much money will be received and how much will be spent on various expenses. Therefore, an exorbitant amount of time should not be spent trying to project exact figures. The IRS will not compare the projected amount on Form 1023 to future actual amounts and penalize the organization if they are not the same. Only an honest and best guess estimate is required.

One of the requirements for being classified as a public charity is that a significant portion of an organization's support and revenue must come from the public. That makes Line 1 of Part A (*Statement of Revenue and*

Expenses) very important. Line 1 discloses how much has or will be received in the form of cash and noncash gifts, contributions, and grants from foundations and government agencies. The larger of this amount is compared to all other support and revenue, the more publicly supported it is and, in turn, the more the classification of public charity is substantiated.

Part X (*Public Charity Status*) (Figure 2.7) is a very important section. In this section you request whether the organization wishes to be treated as a

Figure 2.7   Form 1023, Part X

Line 5
a) 509(a)(1) & 170(b)(1)(A)(i) - Church/convention/association of churches
b) 509(a)(1) & 170(b)(1)(A)(ii) - School
c) 509(a)(1) & 170(b)(1)(A)(iii) - Hospital/Coop. hospital service org., or medical research organization operated in conjunction with a hospital
d) 509(a)(3) – Organization supporting other publically supported NFPs
e) 509(a)(4) – Organization organized & operated for testing for public safety
f) 509(a)(1) & 170(b)(1)(A)(iv) – Organization benefiting college/university owned/ operated by government unit
g) 509(a)(1) & 170(b)(1)(A)(vi) – Org. that receives a substantial part of its financial support in the form of contributions from publicly supported organization from a government unit or from general public
h) 509(a)(2) – Organization that normally receives <1/3 of its financial support from gross investment income & receives >1/3 of its financial support from contributions, membership fees, & gross receipts from activities related to its exempt functions (subject to certain exceptions)

i) A publicly supported organization, but unsure if it is described in 5g or 5h. The organization would like the IRS to decide the correct status.

Figure 2.8   Form 1023, Line 5

private foundation or as a public charity. Public-charity status is a more favorable tax status than a private foundation. For example, private foundations typically pay an excise tax of 1 to 2 percent of their net investment earnings or pay excise tax on certain activities such as lobbying. Lines 1–4 deal with private foundation status.

Private foundation status is the default status. All NFP organizations that complete and submit Form 1023 are classified as a private foundation unless they qualify for a special exclusion. If the applicant checks No to Line 1a and believes that the organization qualifies for this special, public-charities exemption, the applicant must check off one of the boxes in 5(a)–5(i) that best describes the type of organization in terms of its activities or sources of obtaining support. The nine choices for qualifying as a public charity, and not a private foundation, are as shown in Figure 2.8.

As previously mentioned, the more publically supported the organization is, the more its attributes are that of a public charity. Hence, by checking the box on Line 5g, the applicant is stating that the organization will be receiving most of its funds from the general public. However, simply stating that the organization will be substantially supported by the general public is not enough. The organization will be required to substantiate this fact through the information provided on their information returns (Form 990) filed each year. This will be covered later in this book.

For years up through 2008, if Line 5, box g, h, or i were checked, the applicant was required to request either an advance or definitive ruling from the IRS by selecting either Line 6a (advance) or b (definitive) ruling. When the applicant requested an advance ruling, the IRS provisionally allowed the NFP organization to operate as an exempt organization for a period of five

6 If you checked box g, h, or i in question 5 above, you must request either an **advance** or a **definitive ruling** by selecting one of the boxes below. Refer to the instructions to determine which type of ruling you are eligible to receive.

a Request for Advance Ruling: By checking this box and signing the consent, pursuant to section 6501(c)(4) of the Code you request an advance ruling and agree to extend the statute of limitations on the assessment of excise tax under section 4940 of the Code. The tax will apply only if you do not establish public support status at the end of the 5-year advance ruling period. The assessment period will be extended for the 5 advance ruling years to 8 years, 4 months, and 15 days beyond the end of the first year. You have the right to refuse or limit the extension to a mutually agreed-upon period of time or issue(s). Publication 1035, *Extending the Tax Assessment Period,* provides a more detailed explanation of your rights and the consequences of the choices you make. You may obtain Publication 1035 free of charge from the IRS web site at *www.irs.gov* or by calling toll-free 1-800-829-3676. Signing this consent will not deprive you of any appeal rights to which you would otherwise be entitled. If you decide not to extend the statute of limitations, you are not eligible for an advance ruling.

☐

Consent Fixing Period of Limitations Upon Assessment of Tax Under Section 4940 of the Internal Revenue Code

For Organization

(Signature of Officer, Director, Trustee, or other authorized official)

(Type or print name of signer)   (Date)

(Type or print title or authority of signer)

For IRS Use Only

IRS Director, Exempt Organizations   (Date)

b Request for Definitive Ruling: Check this box if you have completed one tax year of at least 8 full months and you are requesting a definitive ruling. To confirm your public support status, answer line 6b(i) if you checked box g in line 5 above. Answer line 6b(ii) if you checked box h in line 5 above. If you checked box i in line 5 above, answer both lines 6b(i) and (ii).

☐

(i) (a) Enter 2% of line 8, column (e) on Part IX-A. Statement of Revenues and Expenses. _____

(b) Attach a list showing the name and amount contributed by each person, company, or organization whose gifts totaled more than the 2% amount. If the answer is "None," check this box.

☐

(ii) (a) For each year amounts are included on lines 1, 2, and 9 of Part IX-A. Statement of Revenues and Expenses, attach a list showing the name of and amount received from each **disqualified person.** If the answer is "None," check this box.

☐

(b) For each year amounts are included on line 9 of Part IX-A. Statement of Revenues and Expenses, attach a list showing the name of and amount received from each payer, other than a disqualified person, whose payments were more than the larger of (1) 1% of line 10, Part IX-A. Statement of Revenues and Expenses, or (2) $5,000. If the answer is "None," check this box.

☐

7 Did you receive any unusual grants during any of the years shown on Part IX-A. Statement of Revenues and Expenses? If "Yes," attach a list including the name of the contributor, the date and amount of the grant, a brief description of the grant, and explain why it is unusual.   ☐ Yes   ☐ No

Form **1023** (Rev. 6-2006)

Figure 2.9   Form 1023, Line 6

years. Then, after five years, it had to file Form 8734, *Support Schedule for Advance Ruling Period,* showing the IRS that it actually met the public support test. In essence, the IRS is giving the organization the benefit of the doubt that it will operate in the manner stated in the 1023 application. If not, the IRS wants the ability to go back and assess the organization an excise tax for not meeting the required support test. Normally, the statue of limitations restricts and prevents the IRS from going back past a certain point to assess any penalties (usually three years). By signing the consent section of the advance ruling, the applicant is allowing the IRS to go back 8 years, 4 months, and 15 days to assess those penalties.

Effective 2009, there are new rules. An organization is no longer required to file Form 8734 after completing its first five tax years. Moreover, the organization retains its public charity status for its first five years regardless of the public support actually received during that time. Instead, beginning with the organization's sixth taxable year, it must establish that it meets the public support test by showing that it is publicly supported on Form 990 (*Return of Organization Exempt from Income Tax*), Schedule A (*Public Charity Status and Public Support*).

Up until 2009, if the organization had operations for at least eight months, the applicant could check the box on Line 6b for a *definitive ruling* from the IRS. By checking this box the applicant is asking the IRS to make an immediate determination about the exempt status of the organization. Under the new rules, this box is only checked if the organization is in existence five or more years.

Form 1023 Checklist

To assist the applicant in completing Form 1023 and to ensure that they include all required attachments, the IRS created the Form 1023 Checklist (in Figure 2.10). A completed checklist must be included with the application sent to the IRS.

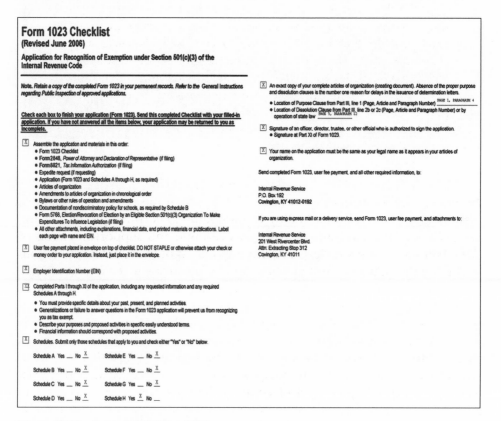

Figure 2.10 Form 1023 Checklist

Application for Recognition for Tax Exemption—Conclusion

Since approval for tax exemption from the IRS and, subsequently, state and local taxing authorities is so vital to the achievement of a NFPs mission, great care should be taken to complete Forms 1023 or 1024. Assistance completing these forms should be sought from an experienced professional.

Who Regulates Not-for-Profits?

NFP organizations are afforded a special privilege in our society (e.g., exemption from paying income taxes or the ability to receive tax deductible contributions). As such, various federal and state agencies have a responsibility to ensure that these types of organizations are acting in accordance with their stated purpose or mission. Since NFPs are created and organized on the state level, it is the state that has ultimate responsibility for protecting the public. The following is an excerpt from the New York attorney general's office web site, which clearly states their responsibility.

> New Yorkers donate billions to charity every year. The Attorney General's Charities Bureau is responsible for supervising charitable organizations to insure that donors and beneficiaries of those charities are protected from unscrupulous practices in the solicitation and management of charitable assets. The Bureau also supervises the activity of foundations and other charities to ensure that their funds and other property devoted to charitable purposes are properly used, and protects the public interest in charitable gifts and bequests contained in wills and trust agreements. The Bureau also maintains a registry of charities and fundraising professionals.

One of the ways New York's attorney general performs its regulatory function is by requiring that certain NFP organizations have their financial statements reviewed or audited by an independent certified public accountant (CPA). All organizations with gross revenue and support in excess of $100,000 must have a review, and those in excess of $250,000 must have an audit. In the simplest terms, when a CPA performs a review, he or she performs analytical and numeric tests to determine that an organization's financial statements are materially correct and free of misstatement. When an audit is performed, the auditor seeks to corroborate amounts and other information disclosed on the financial statements by examining documents (e.g., vendor invoices, bank statements) and performing other tests that provide assurance that the financial statements are materially correct. An audit provides a higher level of comfort than a review (but not absolute assurance) that the financial statements are accurate. Financial audits will be discussed in more detail later in this book.

State governments are not alone in regulating NFP-related activity. Many other regulatory bodies are involved, some with larger roles than others. Probably the next most important regulatory body is the IRS. The IRS plays such a large role because of the authority given to them by federal legislation, and in turn embodied in Internal Revenue Code [e.g., Section 501(a), to grant tax exemption to qualifying organizations]. As previously mentioned the IRS is responsible for granting exemption from paying federal income taxes and allowing an entity to receive tax-deductible contributions. They are also responsible for protecting the public by ensuring that NFP activities are consistent with the NFP's mission. They ensure compliance by:

- Requiring that NFPs file annual information returns describing their activities (i.e., Form 990).
- Requiring public availability of certain documents (e.g., Form 990, auditors reports, etc.).
- Requesting additional information from NFPs for clarification through notices.
- Performing desk or field audits to substantiate the veracity of reported information.

The federal government (aside from the IRS) also plays a regulatory role. In addition to giving billions of dollars of federal money to states and local governments, the federal government gives billions of dollars each year to NFP organizations. Money is provided in the form of grants or payments for contractual services and distributed directly from federal agencies (e.g., department of state, department of defense) or through block grants that first go to state and local government agencies and then, in turn, to NFP organizations. The department responsible for monitoring federal expenditures and other disbursements is the Office of Management and Budget (OMB). To assist in their regulatory role, OMB requires that certain NFPs that receive federal funds and expend over $500,000 of those funds in an operating year must have a special audit performed by an independent CPA. This special audit is called a *compliance audit* and must comply with OMB Circular A-133 rules. These types of audits will be discussed in more detail later in this book.

In addition to state attorney generals, the IRS, state taxing authorities, and, if applicable, the federal government through the OMB, there might be other agencies or entities that perform some level of oversight over part or all the activities of NFPs. This includes state and local government granting agencies that provide grants and other support and require periodic financial or other reports, and sometimes perform their own field audits. Lastly, sometimes foundations and other NFP organizations will monitor or regulate the activities of NFPs they provide support or services to.

It can be definitely said that the NFP world is highly regulated. Yet, despite so many competing requirements to be transparent, there is a never-ending push for NFPs to be *even more* forthcoming with their disclosures. A perfect example of the public's desire for more transparency is the totally revised federal annual information return, Form 990. From a totally objective viewpoint this is understandable, because of the incredible amount of money that flows to NFPs from individuals, foundations, corporations, and the government, and the fact that many NFPs are exempt from paying any income taxes on their net earnings.

NFP Organizational Structure

NFPs share many of the same organizational attributes that commercial entities have. These include having a physical location (office), compensating service providers (e.g., employees), hierarchal reporting structure (i.e., chain of command), marketing or promoting the organization (brochures, web site), accounting and reporting, collecting receivables, paying expenses (e.g., bills), and the list goes on. Aside from the similar attributes, most NFPs have structural and operational attributes that are distinct and different from a typical, commercial entity. The following section describes some of the similar and dissimilar attributes.

Typical Reporting and Responsibility Structure

What is an organizational reporting and responsibility structure? It is a hierarchical structure that delineates both levels of responsibility and levels of decision-making authority and supervision within an organization. All properly functioning organizations have some type of responsibility and reporting structure. Although similar on some levels, a typical NFP organizational structure is different in a number of ways from a commercial enterprise. For example, typically the highest management position in a commercial corporation is the president, who is a legal officer. By contrast, the highest management position in many NFP organizations is the executive director (ED). And, although EDs hold the top management position in these organizations, they are not legal officers and in most states cannot legally bind the organization or have authorization to sign contracts or agreements. Also, since they are not corporate officers, most EDs are not voting members of the board of directors, although they usually attend all board meetings.

How does an organization create its reporting structure? To begin with, an NFP's bylaws define the organization's responsibility and reporting structure. More specifically, the bylaws might specify:

- Minimum number of officers by title such as President, Secretary, and Treasurer
- Responsibilities and duties of each officer
- How board members are elected (e.g., nomination process, annually)
- Number of board members required for a quorum and to approve major decisions
- How board members and officers are removed from office
- Minimum number of board meetings required each year (e.g., monthly or quarterly)
- Board Committees, powers and duties
- Who's authorized to hire staff (e.g., President or ED alone or in consultation with the board)

A more expansive organizational structure for an NFP (see Figure 3.1) classified as a public charity might include the following levels:

- Board of directors
- Officers
- Advisory boards
- Board committees
- President/CEO/ED
- Management (VPs, program directors)
- Staff (full-time and part-time)
- Interns
- Volunteers

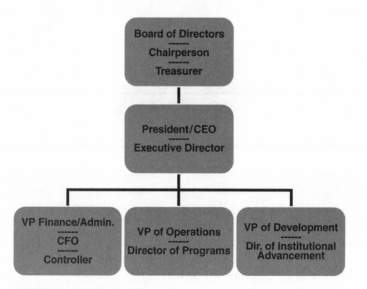

Figure 3.1 NFP Organizational Structure

It should be noted that there is no perfect structure, and each organization should design a structure that is appropriate to its particular operation and circumstances. The ultimate goal is to provide a structure that allows the organization to perform its mission in the most efficient manner possible and to provide a proper level of supervision that protects the organization's assets and ensures the organization is complying with all required laws and regulations.

Role of the Board of Directors and Committees

If one were to sum up the role of an NFP board of directors (board) it would be that they are responsible for the governance of the organization and to ensure that their organization performs all necessary activities to accomplish its mission in an ethical and legal manner. Many individuals who join NFP boards are unaware that they have legal, fiduciary, and ethical obligations and responsibilities, and under many state laws can be held accountable and prosecuted for violating these duties. Although never verbalized, a common belief held among current or prospective board members is, if things ever get too hot, they will just drop off the board and poof, they will be alleviated from any responsibility, and the remaining board members will be stuck dealing with the existing problems or issues. The fact is, even former board members can be held accountable for improper acts committed during their tenure. The reality is though, former board members are rarely ever held accountable, so this belief is not without merit. What's more, many board members feel protected from any personal liability as long as the organization has directors and officers (D&O) liability insurance. D&O insurance does afford some level of protection but will not protect a board member who willfully and knowingly authorizes or permits an organization to engage in any unlawful behavior.

In New York, as in many other jurisdictions, the primary legal duties of an NFP board member include the duties of care, loyalty, and obedience or in short, CLOBER: C(are) L(oyalty) OBE(edience) o(R) else. The following describes these duties.

What is *care*? Care requires directors to act in good faith using the degree of diligence, care, and skill, which prudent people would use in similar positions and under similar circumstances. Simply put, it means that members must take their board position seriously. They can't just show up once a year or rubber-stamp every management proposal. At a minimum, they need to review board minutes and periodic financial statements (budgets), review and approve auditors' reports and 990 information returns, monitor and evaluate ED/president activities, and question suspicious activities and expenditures.

What is *loyalty*? Loyalty requires that directors act in the best interest of the organization. That means there must be no conflict of interest or self-serving acts, not even perceived conflict-of-interest acts that might falsely allude to misdeeds. An example of this would be the organization paying a board member for some product or service and the board member donating the proceeds back to the organization. Better not to charge the organization in the first place. Activities that would violate this duty of loyalty include disclosing privy (confidential) information to unauthorized individuals such as a staff member or another organization or having the organization engage in a transaction or activity that directly or indirectly benefits the board member financially or otherwise. To reduce the possibility of becoming involved in a conflict-of-interest situation, each board member should be required to sign a *conflict-of-interest policy statement* that states that no conflict of interest activities exist. Conflict-of-interest policy statements should be a required part of an organization's policies and procedures.

What is *obedience*? Obedience requires that the board ensure that the organization complies with all applicable laws, rules, and regulations, and its internal governance documents and policies. This means not promoting, knowingly allowing, or accepting unethical or illegal behavior. Activities that would infringe on the obedience duties could include paying employees off the books (i.e., not reporting wages on Form W-2), not filing all necessary information or tax returns Forms 990 or 990-T), treating service providers as outside contractors instead of employees, engaging in discriminatory personnel practices or engaging in any activity that is in violation of the law or might negatively impact the NFP's operations.

Board Size

What is the optimum board size for a typical organization? There isn't one. The size of an NFP's board of directors varies and depends on many factors such as the type of organization (e.g., hospital, museum, chamber of commerce), size of organization in terms of revenue and expenditures, source of funds (e.g., government agencies, foundations), and the types of programs and services that the organization offers. Even when most attributes are similar, there are variations in the membership size of board of directors. Some organizations have very active board members, which allows the board to accomplish a lot with only a few members. Other organizations aren't as fortunate and require more members to assist the organization in accomplishing its mission.

Board size can range from three to one hundred. Many states have rules dictating a minimum number of required board members (e.g., New Jersey requires three). New Jersey also requires a specific number (three) of required corporate officers (president, treasurer, and secretary). There is no general rule or consensus whether a smaller board is better than a larger one. It all depends on facts and circumstances. There are, however, general characteristics that distinguish a small board from a larger one. Generally speaking, smaller boards are more intimate, usually more congenial (but not always), and can effectuate decisions more quickly than a larger board. However, there are benefits to having a larger board where there are more people to provide technical expertise and assistance with events or programs and more potential for fund-raising (i.e., more members making personal contributions or soliciting contributions from friends, etc). The negative side of larger boards is the potential for more disagreements and discord.

Board Functions and Reasons for Joining an NFP Board

Board functions can range from basic oversight to board members performing many functions pro bono (for free), such as legal advice and promotion services (commercial businesses must pay for these and other services).

Typical responsibilities include:

- Hiring upper management (e.g., ED/president/CEO).
- Approving major programs.
- Fund-raising or assisting with fund-raising events.
- Approving annual budget and periodically reviewing financial activity.
- Hiring or approving independent auditors and reviewing and approving their reports.
- Providing technical advice in a board member's field of expertise.
- Volunteering their time to assist with activities and organization programs.

There are numerous reasons an individual would want to join an NFP board of directors and equally numerous reasons why an NFP organization would want a specific individual or type of individual to join their board. Here is a sampling of reasons on both sides of the aisle.

Why would an individual want to join an NFP board?

- The individual is a founder or creator of the NFP or one of the organization's initiators.
- The individual is a donor or grantor wishing to ensure that their contributions are being properly used.
- The individual is a bank representative wishing to ensure that NFP is operating properly and able to repay all outstanding debt.

- The individual has a personal interest in NFP programs or mission (e.g., has a family member with a disease).
- The individual is successful and wishes to give something back to his or her community or to society because it feels good or they want to get into heaven.
- The individual wants to take advantage of networking opportunities for personal business by meeting other board members (although not inherently wrong, this should never be the primary reason for joining a board).
- The individual wants to offset something negative in their life (e.g., guilty about a life of greed).

Why would an organization want someone to join their board?

- The individual has the ability to raise funds.
- The individual is a provider of expertise or beneficial contacts.
- The individual is famous and can provide media exposure (famous actor, Michael J. Fox; musician, Bono; business-person-Trump).
- The individual is required to be a board member by granting agency (e.g., requires hospital to have three doctors on board).
- Conversely, NFPs do not want anyone on their board who is infamous, embroiled in some controversy, or can taint the organization in some negative way through association.

With so many competing needs and desires, and the fact that performing board duties in an effective and productive manner can take up a significant amount of a person's time, it is understandable that there exists an unfulfilled demand for qualified board members. Despite this fact, the majority of NFPs have board members who perform their basic duties, if not more.

Committees

Sometimes it is difficult to convene numerous board meetings during the year to properly handle all board functions and make important and timely decisions. To alleviate this problem and reduce the board's workload, many NFPs form one or more board committees. A board committee is a board subgroup that is empowered by the full board to perform certain limited functions. An agreed-upon number of board members either volunteer or are elected to these committees based on a particular interest or expertise (e.g., an accountant joining the budget and finance committee). By allocating and dispersing various duties, the board as a whole becomes more viable and productive.

Typical committees and responsibilities include the following:

- Executive committee, consisting of officers and other members (make all major decisions)
- Budget/finance/audit committee (approving budgets, monitoring financial activity, and selecting and reviewing auditors' report)
- Board development/nominating committee (soliciting, interviewing, and recommending all new board members)
- Fund-raising or events committees (assisting to raise support and coordinating fund-raising events)
- Programs committee (assisting with program development)
- Strategic planning committee (developing long-term programs or formulate plan for organizational restructure)
- Personnel/benefits committee (assist with developing and monitoring personnel policies and procedures; usually more prevalent with larger NFPs)
- Facilities committee (assisting with ensuring buildings and other facilities are maintained properly; usually more common with hospitals, museums, libraries or NFPs with buildings)
- Communication and marketing committee (assisting in communicating the NFP's message and promoting the NFP's mission)

Advisory Boards

What is an *advisory board?* An advisory board is a group of people who provide some level of advice to the board or management. Members of this group are not usually board members and do not have the same legal and fiduciary responsibilities of board members. The expertise they provide is very useful to the NFP in accomplishing one or more functions of the organization. The benefit to the advisory board member is one of prestige. Basically the advisory board member gets the fame without the pain. They get to tout their role and association with a worthwhile organization without any of the fiduciary or other legal responsibilities that board members have. Examples of NFP advisory boards include *research* for a hospital, educational, or medical facility; *collections* for a museum; *program acceptability* or *suitability* for an educational facility or a foundation giving scholarships.

Role of Management and Staff

Management

The role of NFP management is very similar to the role that managers play in a commercial enterprise. Generally speaking, their job is to run the day-to-day operations of the entity and perform all duties necessary to fulfill the organization's mandate or mission and perform those duties in a legal and ethical manner to the best of their ability. If one were to look for differences, it would be in management titles and who management reports to. A president or CEO of a commercial corporation tactically reports to its corporate board of directors but ultimately to the corporation's shareholders. An NFP's president/CEO is also subservient (and reports) to their board of directors. But NFPs do not have shareholders or owners to report to. Rather, they are beholden to the public and external funding sources. Therefore, management has to be concerned with the needs, mandates, and reporting requirements of such parties such as donors, government granting agencies, and government regulatory agencies (e.g., IRS, attorney general, and OMB).

NFP management titles tend to be a little different than commercial management titles. Although many NFPs have presidents (or CEOs) running their organization, many others have executive directors in the top spot. EDs perform all the same functions of a president such as hiring staff, managing resources, and overseeing daily operations. But, as mentioned previously, in most states an ED is not a legal officer of the corporation and cannot legally bind the organization or have a vote on its board of directors. Other title differences may be deputy director, program director, associate director, or assistant director instead of vice presidents or department managers.

Staff, Volunteers, and Donated Services

Many NFP staff responsibilities are similar to those in commercial enterprises. They handle various functions such as administration, accounting, and performing services or providing products. Salaries traditionally are lower at NFP organizations because of their exempt purpose and because a significant portion of their income is not earned but donated or granted. As such, NFPs can't justify asking (or begging) for support if they in turn pay out exorbitant salaries. Many people who donate money to public charities might think differently about their contributions if they believe their hard-earned salary was going to enrich someone else's lifestyle rather than going to support some charitable or beneficial activity.

Due to budgetary constraints, many NFPs operate with smaller staffs and function by employing part-time employees and using the services of interns or unpaid volunteers (board members and outside volunteers). The availability and use of unpaid volunteers is unique to NFP organizations. Imagine a supermarket asking for volunteers to work their cash register and stock their food aisles! Without unpaid volunteers many NFPs couldn't function. Volunteers are an integral part of their operations. Unpaid volunteers perform every conceivable function including the following:

- Board-members' duties (note, many large commercial entities pay their board members)
- Fire, emergency, evacuation, and security duties
- Telethons and telephone answering
- Event development and operation

- Collection and distribution of donated goods (cars, clothes, food)
- Clerical
- Transportation (delivery)
- Care giving (daycare, schools, hospitals, nursing homes, help centers)
- Legal, accounting, and tax

Role of Accounting Department

Accountants or other individuals working in some financial capacity at NFP organizations perform many of the same duties that staff accountants in commercial enterprises perform. Typical duties performed by accounting-department staff include the following:

- Tracking and paying vendor bills (i.e., accounts payable and cash disbursements)
- Receiving and tracking revenue (i.e., invoicing, accounts receivable, and cash receipts)
- Processing payroll and payroll tax (internal or through outside service providers such as ADP)
- Monitoring employee benefits (e.g., health, retirement, flex benefits)
- Monitoring bank activity (bank transfers, bank charges, bank reconciliations)
- Monitoring and accounting for investments (securities, other entities)
- Preparing budgets and explaining variances
- Maintaining the general ledger and recording journal entries and other adjustments
- Tracking capital purchases and related depreciation
- Tracking loans payable and recording related interest
- Preparing financial reports and financial statements
- Preparing for internal and external financial (e.g., CPA) and other audits (e.g., IRS)
- Preparing and filing annual tax statements such as forms W-2 and 1099

The NFP accounting department also performs duties unique or specific to NFP organizations. Depending on the type of NFP, the following duties could include:

- Tracking contributions/pledges and notifying donors of their tax deductible amounts.
- Classifying, recording, and tracking contributions by restriction (e.g., temporary, permanent).
- Tracking investments and related income by restrictions (e.g., permanently restricted endowment) and allocating pooled investment income.

- Tracking membership or chapter dues.
- Accounting for events, auctions, telethons, and other fund-raising activities.
- Tracking sales from retail-type operations such as store sales (museums and other cultural institutions), sales of publications (membership organizations), and other program activities such as health (hospitals), educational services (schools, universities), etc.
- Preparation of financial information for grant proposals.
- Preparation of financial reports to contributors, foundations, and government agencies (e.g., expense reimbursement requests).
- Preparing for audits related to:
  - State or local grants or contracts (government granting agencies or subdivisions).
  - Federal grants (OMB A-133 compliance audits).
  - Foundations or other NFPs providing funds.
- Preparing periodic financial reports to board or board committees and explanation of budget variances. Many times budget preparation and explaining budget variances are more important to NFPs than to a commercial enterprise because NFP finances are more transparent and public, and the world needs to be assured that no one individual or entity is benefiting unjustly from the NFP's special tax exemptions.
- Responding to financial questions raised by the general public.

Accounting Department Staff Structure

As with any organization, the size of the accounting staff at an NFP varies and depends on many factors including the size and complexity of the organization. In order to keep administration costs to a minimum, it is common for NFP organizations to have the absolute minimum number of accounting or financial personnel necessary to accomplish most required tasks. Consequently, there is sometimes a lot of pressure on the accounting department to complete multiple tasks simultaneously (e.g., prepare grant expense reimbursement reports, prepare for independent audit, prepare financial reports on fund-raising events, and perform all other normal duties required, such as paying bills). Furthermore, due to a lack of available training in NFP accounting and the desire to keep salaries as low as possible, NFPs are frequently forced to hire individuals who are less technically qualified than needed. For this reason, you will find more part-time staff or interns, outside contractors, or volunteers performing higher level accounting functions at many NFP organizations. Unfortunately, when qualified staff is lacking, the accounting department's ability to complete all necessary tasks on a timely and accurate basis is hampered. In these situations, the organization has to rely to a much larger extent on the technical skills of the treasurer or other board members with financial expertise or the organization's outside CPA firm.

Another difference between the accounting departments of NFPs and commercial entities is in the hierarchical reporting structure. With commercial entities, the reporting structure is much more linear. Staff accountants report to an accounting supervisor who reports to an accounting manager who reports to a controller who reports to a chief financial officer (CFO), and on up to the board of directors. With NFPs, the reporting structure is not so linear. CFOs, controllers, or vice presidents of finance and administration many times answer to the president (or ED), board treasurer, board chairperson, members of the board budget/audit/finance committee, and even other board members. Even lower positions such as staff accountant or accounting interns are sometimes given directives directly from board officers or other board members. Problems can arise in situations in which there are competing and conflicting demands and dictates (e.g., grantors, reports are overdue but the treasurer demands special reports immediately).

Accounting staff titles also vary significantly from organization to organization and are not always representative of the level of responsibility that an individual has. For example, smaller NFPs tend to have either one full-time or one part-time employee handling all internal accounting duties. Depending on the organization, the financial employee's title can be bookkeeper, accounting manager, staff accountant, and sometimes even controller. Many other titles are given to accounting department staff and can include comptroller, fiscal director, accounting director, fiscal manager, and director of finance. It is safe to say, regardless of their title, there is no shortage of tasks that NFP financial staff needs to perform on any given day.

CHAPTER

Introduction to NFP Accounting and Reporting

In order for any entity to function effectively and efficiently there must be rules and controls in place to ensure that it operates properly, that assets are protected from misuse, that employees are performing all duties, and that required responsibilities are met, and that those in authority are protecting the reputation and continuation of the entity.

Basic Tenets/Principals of Internal Controls Systems

What is the *control environment* and what are *Internal Controls?* The control environment encompasses the organization's general philosophy, the organizational structure and methods of authority, personnel procedures, external influences, and the ability to monitor its activities. Internal controls are defined as the system of policies and procedures that an organization uses to: ensure the reliability of financial reporting, comply with all required laws and regulations, protect its assets, and ensure that its resources are used properly to achieve its organizational mission efficiently and effectively. Internal controls as they relate to NFP organizations include procedures and processes for:

- Managing cash, investment, and all funds received and disbursed.
- Protecting organization assets from improper use or theft.
- Maintaining appropriate and accurate accounting records.
- Process information in such a manner that allows for the timely preparation of financial reports to management, the board of directors, and external parties.
- Maintaining appropriate records of all assets, liabilities, and financial activity to allow an independent financial or compliance audit to be conducted and completed.

- Implementing controls on the dissemination of privileged information that relates to personnel and other private matters.
- Reducing conflict of interest or other situations where someone is unjustifiably benefiting from an organization's exempt status.

As with everything else in life there is a cost/benefit to having controls and required procedures. The question is not whether there should be accounting and other internal controls but how many and what kind of controls an organization should have. Most people would agree that some level of control is needed in most situations. For example, who wouldn't lock the front door of the office or leave cash lying around in open envelopes. So deciding which controls are beneficial and needed and which are unnecessary becomes the real issue. Since there is a cost to implementing internal controls and enforcing their compliance, an organization should try to balance this against the real benefits derived. There is no one-size-fits-all structure, and policies and procedures should be instituted based on an NFP's specific set of circumstances.

The following is a sampling of five internal control-related questions and preferable answers based on cost-versus-benefit considerations:

Questions:

1. Do you require time sheets that track every minute of every day?
2. Do you install a $40K, high-end accounting software system for a small NFP with an annual operating budget of $100K?
3. Do you bother the executive director ED/president to sign every check, or do you allow the bookkeeper or accountant who prepares the checks to sign them?
4. Do you have the board treasurer also sign every check or only those over a set limit?
5. Should the board spend time reviewing and approving an organization's budget and monitoring the variances between actual expenditures and budget?

Answers:

1. **No.** The cost in time would outweigh the benefit of such detail. Tracking activity by increments of an hour or half hour would be sufficient for most organizations.
2. **No.** In most cases a popular low-cost accounting program such as QuickBooks or Peachtree would suffice.
3. **Yes.** In most cases the president, ED, or CFO will be the primary signer of every check, and **No** the bookkeeper or accountant who prepares the checks should NOT be allowed to sign them even if this saves time.

4. **No.** Having the board treasurer sign every check as a second signatory in most situations is overkill. Rather, they should be required to sign all checks over a certain limit (e.g., >\$2,000 or >\$5,000) based on the size of the organization and the volume of checks generated on a regular basis.

5. **Yes.** In almost all circumstances, the board of directors should take the time to review and approve the NFP's budget and monitor its expenditures throughout the year.

Internal controls should be fluid (not inflexible) and allow for changes in operations or situations (e.g., NFP opens a second location or creates a subsidiary). As previously mentioned, there is no perfect internal control structure and the number and extent of necessary controls should be based on each organization's specific operating environment. That being said, there are some basic tenets of internal controls that would apply to almost all organizations. One of the most basic principles of internal controls is *separation of duties.* Separation of duties means that certain functional duties, tasks, or responsibilities should be given to different individuals to handle. The reason for the separation is to remove the degree of control a single individual has over a particular process, thereby reducing the opportunity of someone doing something improper or illegal, such as misappropriating assets. The more people involved in an activity, the less likely they will collude or join together to do something wrong. Having different people handle different functions in a large NFP with a large accounting department is easy to implement. By definition, separation of duties isn't possible when the accounting department only has one or two employees. And, an NFP with an annual budget of \$300,000 cannot afford to hire four staff accountants. So what can be done to provide some degree of assurance when separation of duties is not possible? A few basic things can be done.

Cash Controls

Cash is the most susceptible of all assets because it is the most liquid and, therefore, needs the most controls. Even with limited staff, a few procedures will provide some level of control and protection. First, the number of individuals who are authorized to sign checks should be limited to only a few. A signatory (empowered to sign checks) who is no longer associated with the organization should be removed as a signatory as soon as possible. Signatory stamps should be avoided unless only used by the person whose signature is on the stamp and the stamp should be kept in a secure location (e.g., safe) to protect misuse. *Bank reconciliations* should be performed on a timely basis (as close to the receipt of the bank statement as possible). A bank reconciliation is a comparison of transactions listed on a bank statement with the transactions listed on an organization's books (i.e., cash account in the general ledger). By performing monthly bank reconciliations on a timely basis, errors or irregularities can be discovered, investigated, and resolved quickly, thereby preventing a small problem from possibly becoming a big problem. The author is aware of a number of times that bank reconciliations were either not performed or not performed in a timely manner, and it was discovered much too late that someone had stolen money or had misused the organization's funds in some improper way. To add a level of control when there is only one person handling all accounting functions, the board treasurer should periodically examine and approve, on a random basis, the prepared bank reconciliations. The staff member should be told this is only a control procedure and is not being done because of any suspicion of fraud to alleviate any ill or negative feelings.

Other Controls

Since smaller NFPs have limited staff, officers and other board members are asked to assume more oversight duties and responsibilities than those associated with larger NFPs. Typical control duties related to accounting functions include reviewing and authorizing purchases over an appropriate dollar limit; co-signing as a second signatory for checks over a certain dollar amount (e.g., >$3,000); and reviewing and approving all salary increases, employee benefits, and travel-expense reimbursements.

As important as it is to have board involvement and oversight of various accounting functions, it is equally important that board officers or other members do not over control or micromanage all or most accounting functions. An example of this is requiring dual signatures on every check generated regardless of the check amount (e.g., a telephone bill for $49.75) or questioning every expense on the cash-disbursement list. Oversight should be reasonable and appropriate to the current situation. Board members shouldn't second-guess everything that the president or ED does or wants to do. On the other hand, they also shouldn't rubber stamp everything the president or ED does.

Internal Controls of Larger NFPs

In most cases, larger organizations have more staff and more staff accountants. With more staff, accounting duties, functions, and responsibilities can be separated in such a way as to provide the highest level of control possible. An example of allocated duties in an accounting department with a controller, an accounting supervisor, and two bookkeepers/staff accountants is as follows:

- Accounting staff 1—Prepares all organization invoices, performs monthly bank reconciliations, maintains all event schedules, tracks contributions, and sends required notices to contributors.

- Accounting staff 2—Records all vendor bills (accounts payable), generates all checks, assists with preparation of grant budgets and grant reports.
- Accounting supervisor—Handles payroll and employee benefits, approves all check requests, reviews monthly bank reconciliations, prepares all grant reimbursement requests, assists with all government agency and annual financial audits, reviews all notices sent to third parties (contributors, event sponsors, etc.), maintains petty cash and safe with important documents.
- Controller—Approves all check requests over a specific limit, signs all checks, reviews and approves all budgets, works closely with ED, treasurer, and other board members, and presents financial information at board meetings.

Typical internal control procedures for purchasing and paying for goods and services include the following: requiring that a Purchase Request Form be prepared by an employee wishing to make a purchase and having it signed by the employee's supervisor; requiring Check Request Forms for all payments to be signed by a supervisor or department head and reviewed and co-signed by the accounting supervisor; and having checks over a specific limit co-signed by the board treasurer or board chairperson. Another control procedure is having an Accounting Policy and Procedure Manual, which spells out the rules and procedures that must be followed.

NFP Accounting Rules and GAAP

It is generally understood that society needs rules to function properly. The same applies to organizations and their ability to truthfully report their financial operations, and for readers of financial reports to be able to rely on the validity of those financial reports in order for them to make informed decisions regarding those organizations. For financial information to have validity and comparability there also must be rules, and the rules that accountants follow are called Generally Accepted Accounting Principles or GAAP. GAAP is not an absolute set of rules that dictate the precise method of handling every conceivable financial transaction. Rather it is a composite of various standards, conventions, and rules for recording, categorizing, and summarizing transactions and preparing financial statements or reports that accurately reflect an organization's operations at a particular point in time, and with the *least amount* of subjectivity or variability. Least amount doesn't mean that there is *no* subjectivity, just that the subjectivity is minimized as much as possible.

GAAP was developed over time and common usage and encapsulated in written documents prepared by various U.S. accounting rule making bodies. Some practices go back hundreds of years, and some rules are more current and reflect new methods of conducting business. Some standards, conventions, and rules have more prominence than others and take precedent, depending on various factors, including the particular set of circumstances and which body is pronouncing the rule (e.g., AICPA, OMB).

NFPs follow GAAP just like every other entity. However, because of their unique not-for-profit characteristics, NFPs must adhere to general GAAP accounting rules as well as GAAP that are specific to the operations of NFP organizations. The following is a brief history of the rule-making bodies and related pronouncements and documents that relate specifically to NFP organizations.

Up until 1973 the accounting rule-making body in the United States was the American Institute of CPAs (AICPA), its predecessor, the American Institute of Accountants (AIA), and various other committees or subgroups that included the following:

- The Committee on Accounting Procedure (AIA): Published 51 Accounting Research Bulletins (ARBs) between 1938 to 1959.
- Accounting Principals board (AICPA): Published 31 Accounting Principal Board Opinions (APBs) between 1959 and 1973.
- Audit and other committees: Publishes various industry audit and accounting guides, statement of position (SOP), practice bulletins, accounting interpretations, and so on.

At the end of the 1960s and beginning in the 1970s, there were a number of corporate scandals (e.g., Penn Central) that shook the public's confidence on the accuracy of financial statements and ability of auditors to uncover corporate malfeasance. There was a lot of pressure on Congress to pass laws to regulate the accounting and auditing profession (sound familiar?). To avoid the loss of the ability to regulate its own industry, the AICPA assisted in the creation of an independent rule-making body called the Financial Accounting Foundation (FAF) and its rule-making subdivision, the Financial Accounting Standards Board (FASB). It then became the FASB's job to issue all accounting pronouncements going forward. Between 1973 and 2009 the FASB has issued 168 statements known as Statements of Financial Accounting Standards (SFAS). Several of those statements were directed specifically toward NFPs and significantly altered the accounting principles that NFPs must follow.

Before the 1990s, there was little specific guidance to assist NFPs in accounting for financial transactions unique to their type of operations. The AICPA had an audit and accounting guide titled *Not-for-Profit Entities*, and a statement of position (SOP 98-2) titled, *Accounting for Costs of Activities of Not-for-Profit Organizations and State and Local Governmental Entities That Include Fund Raising*. Other than these few reference sources, NFP accountants were left to apply, as best they could, existing for-profit accounting rules to their not-for-profit activities.

In June, 1993, the FASB issued two statements that fundamentally changed the accounting rules that NFP entities would have to follow in order to be in compliance with GAAP. The two statements were SFAS 116, *Accounting for Contributions Received and Contributions Made*, and SFAS 117, *Financial Statements of Not-For-Profit Organizations*. SFAS 116 deals with contributions and how they should be valued (i.e., fair value), reported, and disclosed. Some of the major accounting changes this statement required were the immediate recognition of restricted contributions and the nonrecognition of conditional pledges or promises to give a contribution. SFAS 117 established which general-purpose financial statements would be required by NFPs and the standards for preparing and presenting those statements. One of the main premises behind SFAS 117 was that users and other readers of NFP financial statements were more interested in the restrictions placed on assets and the disclosure of expenditures by activities or programs than anything else. Prior to the issuance of this statement, a large percent of NFPs followed an accounting methodology called *fund accounting*.

Simply put, fund accounting required an organization to separate its major activities into separate categories or funds (e.g., operating fund, special-use fund). Each fund would maintain its own assets and liabilities, sources of revenue, and support and expenses. Each fund would also be self-balancing and have its own general ledger accounts. The premise behind fund accounting was that it report its operations by funds rather than by how profit was generated (i.e., revenue less expenses). The usefulness of fund accounting and its ability to properly depict an NFP's financial activities have been debated by the accounting profession for many years, and the debate wasn't resolved until the release of SFAS 117. With that release, fund accounting was no longer deemed an acceptable method for reporting NFP financial activity.

FASB SFAS 117—Financial Statements of Not-For-Profit Organizations

SFAS 117 requires all NFP organizations to provide three financial statements: a statement of financial position (balance sheet), a statement of activities (income statement), and a statement of cash flows. It also required the issuing of a fourth statement, a statement of functional expenses, for any NFP characterized as a voluntary health and welfare organization (VHWO). VHWOs are defined as organizations formed for the purpose of performing voluntary services for various segments of society. They are tax exempt, supported by the public, and operated on a not-for-profit basis. Their major source of revenue is voluntary contributions from the general public that is used for general or specific purposes connected with health, welfare, or community services.

SFAS 117 also requires classification of an organization's net assets and its revenues, expenses, gains, and losses based on the existence or absence of donor-imposed restrictions. It requires that the amounts for each of three classes of net assets—permanently restricted, temporarily restricted, and unrestricted—be displayed in a statement of financial position and that the amounts of change in each of these classes be displayed in a statement of activities. Although SFAS 117 doesn't require a statement of functional expenses unless an organization qualifies as a VHWO, the author believes that all NFPs should present this statement to provide a more complete picture of the organization's results of operations.

FASB SFAS 116—Accounting for Contributions Received and Contributions Made

SFAS 116 establishes accounting standards for contributions and applies to all entities that receive or make contributions. Generally, contributions received are recognized as revenue in the period they are received, and they are recorded at fair value. Contributions made by the organization are recognized as expenses in the period made and also recorded at fair value. This statement makes it clear that conditional promises to give (whether made or actually received), are only recognized when they become unconditional. For example, if a donor promises to give an organization $100,000 if it raises $200,000 on its own from other sources, the organization would not record that pledge as contribution income until the condition (raising $200,000) was met. SFAS 116 requires NFPs to distinguish and categorize contributions received by type of restriction (if any) placed on them (i.e., temporary, permanent, or unrestricted). It also requires that NFPs record the release of the restriction in the period the donor-imposed restriction expires (i.e., when the terms of the restriction have been met).

Other Important FASB Pronouncements

In November 1995 FASB issued SFAS 124, *Accounting for Certain Investments Held by Not-for-Profit Organizations*. This statement established standards for accounting for certain investments held by NFP organizations. It required that stocks (equity securities), bonds (debt securities), and other investments (where objective fair values are obtainable) be reported at fair value. That means that all unrealized gains and losses caused by fluctuation in value would get recorded in the year that the value changed. Before this rule, no gains or losses in value were recorded until a security was sold. This statement also required that certain disclosures about investments held by NFPs be disclosed such as the composition of investments (e.g., stock, bonds, etc.) and investment return (e.g., interest, dividends, gains, and losses).

In June 1999 FASB issued SFAS 136, *Transfers of Assets to a Not-for-Profit Organization or Charitable Trust That Raises or Holds Contributions for Others*. This statement established rules that an NFP must follow when it receives assets from a donor to be used on behalf of another entity (i.e., a beneficiary). An example of a transaction that would fall under the rules in SFAS 136 is a donor who gives an NFP $1,000,000 to invest and tells the NFP that they can retain half the income earned on that investment but must give the other half to another specified NFP.

In June 2009 the FASB issued its last SFAS, SFAS 168, *The FASB Accounting Standards Codification and the Hierarchy of Generally Accepted Accounting Principles.* This statement took all previous accounting rules, bulletins, opinions, and statements that constituted GAAP and put them (codified) into one document. It didn't change any of the accounting rules that constituted GAAP, it just consolidated and reorganized GAAP pronouncements into 90 accounting topics within a consistent structure and removed any reference to ARBs, APBs, SFAS, and so on. Throughout this book, we will at times refer to GAAP rules by their original pronouncement number (e.g., SFAS). It should be noted in the future that these will be referred to as sections of the accounting codification.

Other Accounting and Reporting Considerations

As mentioned, financial activity is recorded in an organization's financial records (i.e., general ledger) in accordance with rules promulgated by GAAP. However, NFPs must also be aware of the need to track and report certain financial information for purposes other than preparing financial statements. Examples include the following:

- Tracking variances (differences) between actual receipts and expenditures and budgeted amounts for internal (management) and external (grantors) purposes.
- Tracking data needed for disclosure on Form 990 (*Annual Information Return*) or Form 990-T (*Exempt Organization Business Tax Return*) such as number of members or chapters, identifying contributors making donations over $5,000, transactions between related parties, amounts of goods or services provided in exchange for donations received, amounts of support and revenue subject to unrelated business taxes, and fair value of qualifying donated services or facilities.
- Tracking expenditures by donor or grantor and sometimes by grant and grant year.

It is important to note that although GAAP provides specific and general guidance for handling most financial transactions, it is not all encompassing, and there are times when elements of a transaction are convoluted or unclear and personal judgment is necessary. In those cases, professional advice should be sought. And, it is important to mention, even experienced accountants disagree on which accounting rules apply to a given situation. However, when the rules are clear, accounting treatment is not optional and needs to be followed.

It is also important to mention that even though NFP organizations are not profit motivated, they are not immune from pressures to misrepresent their financial activities in the form of inaccurate or misleading financial statements. As with commercial entities, CFOs, controllers, accounting staff, and even auditors sometimes face pressure from management, officers, and board members to present financial activities in a biased way for a predetermined reason. Pressure is sometimes exerted to bury (i.e., hide) transactions or to classify transactions incorrectly. Commercial enterprises might want to show their creditors (e.g., banks or vendors) how well they are doing or want to show how bad they are doing for income tax purposes. With NFPs, the reason for the misrepresentation might be more altruistic (e.g., raise more money to provide more programs) but just as biased. For example, NFP management or boards might want to misrepresent financial activity because:

- Their organization didn't meet projected support and revenue goals.
- Actual financial results varied significantly from budgeted amounts.
- Government grant expenditures were too low or too high.
- Need restricted contributions for operations, so they misclassified contributions as unrestricted.
- Support expenses (management, fund-raising) were too high, so they wanted to reclassify expenses to programs to appear to be more efficient or to show funds were being used in a more acceptable manner.

Regardless of the reason, financial statements and other financial reports must be materially accurate and free of errors or misstatements to be useful and reliable. Just because someone in authority in an organization wants to present something in a certain way doesn't make it okay. Board members and officers are *not* rule-making bodies. Many times they don't understand accounting rules and demand that financial information be presented in a certain way that they understand. However, it is not in their purview to decide what is correct, and attention should be given to educating them in order for them to understand the reasons for the required treatment and presentation.

Basic Tenets/Principles Underlying Accounting

Basic tenets, principles, or theory of accounting are foundation concepts. They dictate in the most general terms how financial activity should be treated and form the underpinnings of GAAP. Although not all-inclusive, the following cover the major core accounting principles or concepts:

- Double-entry system
- Bookkeeping

- Debits and credits
- Basic accounting model
- Measurement
- Materiality
- Conservatism
- Consistency
- Recognition and realization
- Matching principle
- Accounting basis (cash vs. accrual)
- Cost versus fair value
- Operating period

Double-Entry System

It is commonly believed that the *double-entry bookkeeping system* was developed by an Italian mathematician and Franciscan friar name Fra Luca Pacioli in 1494 because of his description of the method for accurately recording and maintaining financial transactions. For this discovery, he was bestowed the title the father of accounting. However, he actually didn't create the double-entry bookkeeping (accounting) system but was the first one to publish a book about the bookkeeping method that Venetian merchants used during the Italian Renaissance. He described the use of various journals and ledgers that they used to track financial activity. He also described the system of double-entry bookkeeping that promulgates the idea that every entry made to a business's financial records (also known as books) has two sides and is balanced. More specifically, every entry made to the financial records should have a debit and a credit. Although Fra Luca Pacioli wasn't the inventor of this system, he did develop a mathematical formula (as a good mathematician would) to depict the way financial records (books) were balanced.

Bookkeeping

The term *bookkeeping* (or maintaining one's books) and the methodology and process used to track and report financial transactions goes back hundreds of years. Bookkeeping consists of tracking financial transactions in various written documents (i.e., books) called journals or ledgers. So, bookkeeping is not the maintenance of one book but rather the maintenance of several different types of books. One type of book is called a *journal*. Journals track (i.e., record) similar type of transactions such as sales, purchases, cash receipts, cash disbursements, payroll, and so on. After a certain period of time (day, week, month), all entries in each journal for that period of time are added together (totaled) and entered in the appropriate account in a book called the general ledger. A general ledger is made up of a number of accounts, each with a unique characteristic. A typical general ledger will include a separate account for every asset and liability category a business has, such as cash, accounts receivable, inventory, investments, equipment, accounts payable, and loans payable. It will also have a separate account for all equity accounts (unrestricted, temporarily restricted, and permanently restricted net assets), revenue accounts (contributions, grant income, etc.), and expense accounts (salaries, supplies, rent, etc.). To summarize what was just said, the process of bookkeeping requires the recording of all transactions in journals, the totaling of all transactions in each journal within a specific time period, and the recording (posting) of all journal totals to an appropriate account in the entity's general ledger.

The next step in the bookkeeping process is to total up all entries in each general ledger account and write the total in another document called the *trial balance.* The trial balance is simply a list of the totals of each general ledger account at a particular point in time. Because bookkeeping is a double-entry system, all the positive and negative numbers on the trial balance total up to zero. The last step in the bookkeeping process is to take the totals from the trial balance and place them on an appropriate financial statement. Which financial statements they go to depends on what type of account the totals represent (e.g., assets and liabilities go on the statement of financial position, revenue and expenses go on the statement of activities).

A very basic illustration of the transactional process of bookkeeping is as follows: ABC organization sells three publications during the month on credit for $100, $250, and $300. By the end of the month the organization received payment for the first two sales ($100 and $200) and the third is still outstanding (unpaid). The bookkeeping entries would be entered on the Journals and General Ledger during the month as follows:

Journals

Sales Journal	
01/05/10	$ 100
01/05/10	250
01/05/10	300
Total	$ 650

Cash Receipts Journal	
01/18/10	$ 100
01/25/10	250
	—
Total	$ 350

General Ledger

Cash	
01/31/10	$ 350
	—
Total	$ 350

Accounts Receivable	
01/31/10	$ 650
01/31/10	(350)
Total	$ 300

Sales	
01/31/10	$ 650
	—
Total	$ 650

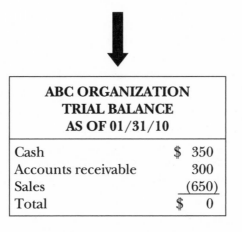

ABC ORGANIZATION TRIAL BALANCE AS OF 01/31/10	
Cash	$ 350
Accounts receivable	300
Sales	(650)
Total	$ 0

As you can see, the total on the trial balance is zero. That is because the double-entry bookkeeping system ensures that all transactions (entries) have two sides and all positive amounts (debits) and negative amounts (credits) cancel each other out. Whether a transaction is a debit or a credit depends on the type of transaction and the type of account it affects.

It should be mentioned here that the term *bookkeeping* has become an antiquated term because it implies by definition that a physical set of books are being maintained. And since (with little exception) financial transactions are no longer written in physical books, there aren't any true bookkeepers anymore. Today, computers and numerous bookkeeping/ accounting software programs have replaced physical books and the necessity of writing transactions by hand into journals, copying (posting) totals to a general ledger, copying totals to a trial balance, and finally copying balances to the appropriate financial statements. Despite the anachronistic terminology, the term *bookkeeper* is still being used to describe individuals who track and record an organization's financial transactions and the term *bookkeeping* to describe the activity they perform.

Debits and Credits

Debit comes from the Latin word *debitum* and credit from the Latin word *credere*. Debits and credits are one of the most confusing terms to most beginning accounting students, and to almost everyone else for that matter. In the simplest terms, a debit means the left side and a credit means the right side. The confusion comes into play when one is trying to determine whether a transaction should be debited or credited to a particular account on the books and whether that debit or credit is an increase or a decrease to that account. Pacioli used the concept of debits and credits to explain how every transaction is entered on an organization's books and how every entry is balanced. An example of a balanced bookkeeping transaction is the receipt of a $1,000 cash donation. The cash asset account is debited $1,000 and the contribution revenue account is credited $1,000. In order to create a balanced equation, it was postulated that certain types of ledger accounts would be positive-type accounts and amounts entered into these accounts would typically be positive numbers, and other accounts would be negative-type accounts and amounts entered into these accounts would typically be negative numbers. An abbreviation for *debit* is Dr. and *credit* Cr.

Basic Accounting Model

One of the first things taught in an introductory accounting class is the basic accounting model (or formula) devised by Fra Luca Pacioli to describe a complete and balanced set of financial books. The formula is deceptively simple and states that a business's assets less its liabilities equal its equity. The formula is:

(A)ssets	−	(L)iabilities	=	(E)quity
Own or have		Owe or are		Left over
rights to		Obligations		(cumulative)

OR (rearranging the formula)

$$A \quad = \quad L \quad + \quad (E)quity \text{ (or Net Assets)}$$

In the simplest terms, *assets* are defined as something tangible or intangible that an entity owns or has rights to; *liabilities* as something an entity owes or an obligation, and *equity* (referred to as net assets or NA for NFPs) as what is left over. Examples of assets are cash and accounts receivable (own), contributions and grants receivable (have rights to), and property and equipment (own). Examples of liabilities are accounts payable (owes) and deferred revenue (obligation). Examples of net assets (equity) are unrestricted, temporarily restricted, or permanently restricted net assets. The trick is to know whether an increase or decrease to an asset, liability, or equity (net assets) account is a debit (left side) or credit (right side) bookkeeping entry.

As previously mentioned, in order the make the accounting model work (and balance) certain types of accounts are typically classified as positive (debit type or left-side accounts) and others typically classified as negative (credit type or right-side accounts). This is illustrated as follows:

(A)ssets	=	(L)iabilities	+	(N)et (A)ssets
A	=	L	+	NA
Positive		*Negative*		*Negative*
Debit type		Credit type		Credit type

Once it is understood how certain types of accounts are handled, additions and subtractions to those accounts simply become a mechanical process. To elaborate, all additions to assets, which are positive type (left-side) accounts, are positive numbers, and all additions to liabilities and net assets, which are negative type (right-side) accounts, are negative numbers. For example, if an organization receives $500 in cash (an asset), which is a debit (left-side) account, it would appear in the general ledger cash account as follows:

Cash Account	
Debit	Credit
500.00	

Another example: If the organization owes a telephone company $250 (a liability), which is a credit (right-side) account, it would appear in the general ledger account as follows:

Accounts Payable Account	
Debit	Credit
	250.00

To recap, *increases* or additions to *asset* accounts are *debits. Increases* or additions to *liability* and *net asset* accounts are *credits.* When there are subtractions or reductions to these accounts the opposite is true. When there is a *reduction* or subtraction from an *asset* account, it is a *credit,* and when there is a *reduction* or subtraction from a *liability* or *net asset* account it is a *debit.* Let's say the organization pays the telephone company the $250 it owes it. The entry would appear in the appropriate general ledger accounts as follows:

Cash Account			Accounts Payable Account	
Debit	Credit		Debit	Credit
	250.00		250.00	

Knowing whether to debit or credit a transaction takes a little getting used to. The best way to start out is to first determine what type of accounts a transaction applies to (e.g., contributions receivable, accounts payable), then recall from memory whether an increase or decrease to this account is a debit or a credit, then make the entry.

To review, so far we covered account types that are classified as assets (something the organization owns or has rights to), *liabilities* (something the organization owes or is an obligation), and *net assets* (what is left over). There are two other major categories or types of accounts, namely, revenue/support and expenses. In the most basic terms, *revenue* can be defined as a benefit received (typically cash at some point) as a result of the sale of goods or service. NFPs also receive *support*, which is a benefit received that is not an exchange transaction and is not the result of any sale of goods or services. Support is unique to NFP organizations, because commercial enterprises are in business to make a profit and don't generally receive income without giving something in return. Examples of support are contributions and government grants.

Most people understand the term *expenses* because our society is based on a marketplace principle where goods and services are exchanged for some value, and individuals incur expenses as a normal part of life. The terms *expenses* and *expenditures* are used interchangeably but technically are slightly different. *Expenses* are defined as the using-up of an asset or incurring some type of liability (or obligation) to create or generate revenue. Whereas, *expenditures* are simply outflows of cash or other resources. Since the meanings are so similar, either term can be used to mean the using-up of assets or using resources to generate revenue.

Many people also understand the terms *profit* or *net income*, which is the excess of revenue/support earned or received over the expenses incurred or spent. Since NFPs are not in business to earn a profit, the excess of revenue/support over expenses are called increase in net assets. What is not very clear is how revenue/support and expense transactions are treated in the accounting records (i.e., are they debit- or credit-type accounts). As a matter of fact, their treatment seems to be backward. To explain this, let's review the basic accounting model (formula) of assets minus liabilities equal net assets. Assets are typically debit (positive) accounts, whereas liabilities and net assets are typically credit (negative) accounts.

$$A(\text{ssets}) \quad - \quad L(\text{iabilities}) \quad = \quad N(\text{et}) \, A(\text{ssets})$$

Because revenue/support increases net assets, revenue and support accounts are typically credit-type (negative) accounts, and because expenses decrease net assets, expense-type accounts are typically debit (positive) accounts.

As mentioned, most people new to accounting and most everyone else find the classification of accounts as debit-type or credit-type bewildering at best and beyond comprehension at worse. One reason for this is the general perception that something positive is good and something negative is bad. For example, why record revenue as a credit or negative? Revenue is good, so it should be positive or recorded as a debit, right? The answer is that different accounts are recorded as debits or credits to simply comply with the basic accounting model (or formula) devised by Fra Luca Pacioli, not because positive or negatives are good or bad.

To recap, the following shows the typical debit or credit treatment of accounts by all five major account classifications:

(A)ssets	−	(L)iabilities	=	(N)et (A)ssets	
Positive		*Negative*		*Negative*	
Debit type		Credit type		Credit type	
				Revenue	Expenses
				Negative	Positive
				Credit type	Debit type

Measurement

Another core accounting principle is the concept of measurement. In order to account for something you have to be able to measure it. Our accounting system is based on measuring activity and transactions in currency (i.e., dollars). If something can't be measured with a degree of accuracy, it shouldn't be recorded. This doesn't mean absolute certainty, just that the measurement can't be arbitrary. Examples of activities where measurement can't be made: a number of attendees say they plan on making a large contribution but never say how much they plan on giving, or a museum had a fire but it is unable to estimate the amount of the loss or how much they will receive in insurance reimbursement.

Materiality

Materiality is a concept of recording or tracking something significant in terms of overall financial effect. There is a cost to everything in life, and there is a cost to tracking activity and performing accounting functions. Consequently, many times decisions are made about how to record a particular transaction based on the cost/benefit of recording it perfectly according to GAAP. For example, the purchase of equipment is classified as an asset because it will not be used up in one year but rather be used for operations to generate revenue over several years. However, if an organization purchases six staplers totaling $66, the cost of recording it as equipment and depreciating a piece of it (e.g., $11 per year) would outweigh the benefit of recording it perfectly. As such, the purchase would typically be recorded as office-supplies expense instead of as equipment. On the other hand, you shouldn't always say everything is immaterial because you want to record something as an expense instead of as an asset or because it is easier. The question of whether something is material or not is based on facts and circumstances, such as the size of overall expenditures or the combined value of numerous small-value purchases (e.g., grouping expenditures together can make them material). Consideration of materiality is a concept that pervades all aspects of accounting.

Conservatism

Conservatism as it relates to accounting principles is not the same as the definition used to describe a person's political or religious philosophy. It means that if there are two likely outcomes, pick the one that will result in the least impact on inflating the end result, that is, the least favorable immediate effect on net income or net assets.

Consistency

Consistency means that you should apply the same set of assumptions or rules from one similar situation to the next or from one period to the next. It means an organization should apply all accounting principles, standards, and so forth on a consistent basis in order for financial data to be comparable from year to year. It doesn't mean that amounts can't vary significantly from one period to the next, but rather that the rules or basis followed shouldn't change every year. For example, NFPs should estimate and record the amount of telephone pledges made each year that will not be collected. If experience shows that 15 percent is never collected, then that is the percent that should be used to calculate uncollectible pledges each year. The organization shouldn't just change the percent in order to make their bottom line (i.e., increase in net assets) look good. However, changes can be made if it is based on something verifiable or there is a substantive reason for the change.

Recognition and Realization

Recognition and realization terms are commonly confused and used interchangeably. Recognition is including a transaction in the organization's general ledger (e.g., recognizing or recording a promise to make a contribution or pledge receivable). Realization is converting an asset or right to an asset into cash (i.e., actually receiving a donation that was pledged).

Matching Principle

The matching principle is a concept that says in order to understand how productive an organization is in any given year it is important to match or relate the revenue generated with the expense incurred to generate that revenue. Salaries are paid to employees to perform services that generate revenue and support. Hence, an organization needs to record the amount of salary expense it incurred in a year related to the revenue and support it received (or earned) in that same year. As is the case with the relationships of many accounting principles, the matching principle is related to the recognition principle. For example, say an organization wants to prepay its rent for 10 years (crazy, but theoretically possible). Under the matching principle, rent relates to generating revenue over a period of time (i.e., the need to have an office to run programs) and under the recognition principle, rent should be recognized in the period it relates to or 1/10 each year. If the organization gives the landlord $120,000 for 10 years worth of rent, it would only record $12,000 as an expense in the year paid and the rest would be recorded as an asset (i.e., prepaid rent).

There is one big exception to the matching principle with regard to NFPs. This has to do with recognizing all unconditional contributions (cash and pledges or promises to be received) in the year received even if the donor imposes a restriction on the use of the donation until some future period or occurrence. To elaborate, if a commercial enterprise receives income prior to the period it has earned it, the revenue would be recorded as a liability and classified as *deferred income* on the balance sheet. Then, when the entity provides the product or service, the entity would reclassify the deferred income and recognize it as income. The reason for this is the entity hasn't earned the income when it was received and if for some reason the product or service was not provided, the organization would have to refund the money to the payer. This complies with the matching principle of accounting. The FASB allowed an exception to the matching principle with regard to contributions and NFP organizations. Over the years there was a lot of disagreement over the proper treatment of restricted contributions, with some NFPs handling the transaction one way (e.g., picking it up in the year contributed) and others handling it a different way (recording it as deferred income). Because of this, and the fact that many restrictions are not documented in writing and easily verifiable, the FASB decided that it would require all contributions to be recognized in the year received or pledged. However, to better identify these different types of contributions, FASB 116 required that contribution income be separated into unrestricted, temporarily restricted, and permanently restricted. The treatment of contributions is explained in more detail later on.

Accounting Basis (Cash versus Accrual)

GAAP requires the accrual basis of accounting. The Statement of Financial Accounting Concepts 6 states that "accrual accounting attempts to record the financial effects on an entity, transactions and other events and circumstances that have *cash consequences* for the entity in the periods in which those transactions, events and circumstances occur, rather than only in the periods in which cash is received or paid by the entity." This means that revenue is recorded when *earned* (not when received) and expenses are recorded when *incurred* (not when paid). However, no entry should be made if the chance of realization (i.e., collection or payment) is unlikely.

Although not sanctioned under GAAP, the cash basis of accounting is much easier to understand than the accrual basis of accounting, and for this reason many organizations maintain their accounting records on the cash basis. Many board members, EDs, and even accounting staff who are not financially literate, intuitively understand cash-basis accounting. It's just like their checkbook. Revenue is recorded when cash is received and expenses are recorded when cash is paid. Many organizations maintain their books on the cash basis during the year but switch to the accrual basis at year's end.

Some organizations use a hybrid method of accounting called modified cash basis. When used, only some types of transactions are recorded on the accrual basis like accounts payable and others on the cash basis such as revenue earned. But accrual accounting is more accurate and better reflects an organization's operations in any given period. NFPs following the preferred accrual method would have a number of accrual-related accounts, such as accounts, contributions and grants receivable, accounts payable, and prepaid expenses. When the organization sends out invoices for services performed and when someone promises to make a donation, revenue is recorded. Conversely, when the organization purchases goods or services and receives a bill from a vendor or service provided, an expense is recorded.

Cost versus Fair Value

GAAP requires that the valuation method used for recording transactions should be cost (historic cost). The definition of cost is the money paid or other resource given up or foregone to acquire, produce, consume, or exchange another asset. Fair value on the other hand, is a more subjective basis. SFAS 157 defines fair value as follows: *the price that would be received to sell an asset or paid to transfer a liability in an orderly transaction between market participants at the measurement date.* Therefore, under the historic cost method, the value maintained in the organization's financial records is the cost of an asset when it is first acquired or when a liability is first incurred, not its current value. Accountants have discussed switching to the fair-value method for many years to better reflect the true value of what an organization owns and owes. However, because of the subjective nature of valuing many types of assets and some liabilities, the cost method of accounting has remained the method acceptable under GAAP. Fortunately (or unfortunately) valuation isn't a major problem with many NFPs because, with the exception of very large organizations or those with buildings, many do not have highly valued assets.

There is one exception to the historical cost method of valuing assets, namely, publicly traded investments with readily determinable values. Their values are objective and easily verifiable because the values are listed on public exchanges.

Operating Period

An organization's operating period is typically a discrete 12-month period that captures one full cycle of operations. Although most commercial entities and many NFP organizations use a calendar year as their operating period (since it is easy to follow), there is no absolute rule that the operating year must be on a calendar-year basis. Many NFPs use a period that coincides with their major revenue source, such as a government agency's operating year or the period covered by a government agency grant (e.g., July 1–June 30). At the end of an organization's operating year, all revenue and expense-account balances are combined and the resulting total representing either net income or net loss (or excess of revenue over expenses) is transferred to net assets. After the accounting entry is made, all revenue and expense accounts are zeroed out in order to start fresh for the next operating year.

NFP Accounting System and Financial Statements

As mentioned in the Chapter 4, the term *bookkeeping* is an antiquated term because accounting transactions, generally speaking, are no longer written in books, such as journals and ledgers. The following is an illustration of standard pages and a binder used to record bookkeeping transactions.

Automated Bookkeeping

Instead of writing financial transactions on paper by hand, almost all transactions are now entered and maintained on computers using accounting and other software. As with so many other functions in today's society, computers have reduced significantly—even exponentially—many manual and tedious tasks that bookkeepers used to perform. What used to take one or more bookkeepers days or even weeks to do, now takes only hours. For example, data only has to be input once from some source document (e.g., invoice, bill) and it automatically flows to the appropriate journals (e.g., accounts receivable or accounts payable), general ledger accounts (e.g., accounts payable and appropriate expense accounts), trial balance, and ultimately to the appropriate financial statement (e.g., statement of financial position and statement of activities). What's more, once data is entered into an accounting software program, the data can be used in many different ways to generate different types of reports. So the use of computers didn't just reduce manual labor; it also increased the functionality and application of the data.

However, with every advancement comes some loss or obsolescence (anyone remember the typewriter?). In the case of automated bookkeeping there was also a loss, although a small one relative to the benefits gained. The loss was the ability to follow transactions and seeing how they move through the accounting system. In the past, a bookkeeper had to understand double-entry bookkeeping and how all entries in the financial records had to balance. They understood how to move (post) data from journals to ledgers, and so forth. Today, this knowledge is lost because, with the exception of some general journal entries, most entries are made in a singular fashion, with the software automatically making the balancing entry. Entering vendor bills is an example. An individual would enter the pertinent data from each bill received from a vendor. Once entered, the software program would automatically post each amount (along with date, description, etc.) to a unique vendor card and also post the amount to the appropriate general ledger account (e.g., telephone expense, office expense, repairs expense, etc.) and also post an automatic balancing entry to the accounts-payable account.

Accounting Software

Computer technology has been advancing exponentially since the second half of the 20th century. What once took a whole room full of computers to process can now be performed on a device no larger than a person's hand. In the simplest chronological terms, technological changes have taken us from large mainframe computers, which cost millions of dollars and used punch cards and wire boards, to mini computers, which cost much less but had limited storage and processing capacity, to micro or personal computers (or *PC* for short), which have almost unlimited processing and storage capacity at a nominal cost, to networked desktop computers, which can be accessed from almost anywhere in the world. Over the last 15 years, PC prices have dropped significantly. During the early years, a typical personal computer system cost between $2,500 and $4,000 depending on its speed, memory, and so forth. Today, a typical PC costs under $1,000. Even better, due to improvements in technology, PCs now boast speeds and storage capacity thousands of times greater than in the past.

Along with computer hardware advances, came software advancements. With the advent of personal computers in the 1980s came more and more powerful software programs. Smaller companies were now able to afford accounting software programs to perform many if not all their bookkeeping functions. Years ago, accounting software could be separated into two major categories: low end and high end. Low-end programs were much less expensive but had limited functionality. For example, a program costing $500 might have a limit on the total number of vendors that could be entered (e.g., 99), might lack a payroll function to process salary information, or might be limited in the type of reports it could produce. High-end accounting software could perform many more functions and process significantly more data but was much more expensive. It also typically came with encyclopedia-size manuals that took a great deal of time to understand and learn.

Today, there are a large number of general-purpose, off-the-shelf commercial accounting programs as well as industry-specific software available. Accounting software for small- to medium-sized organizations can be grouped loosely into two major categories: low-cost and high-cost with multiple modules. Low-cost software can range from $50 to under $1,000, based on the number of users. High-cost software can range from several thousands to tens of thousands of dollars based on the number of modules purchased. Modules typically include general ledger, accounts payable, accounts receivable, payroll, inventory, and others depending on the software. Although there are no hard statistics, it is safe to say the type of accounting software that NFPs use varies from low cost to high cost, with some using commercial accounting programs and others using software geared specifically toward NFP organizations. The following lists some of the more popular accounting software by category as of 2009:

Low Cost (under $1,000)

- Quicken and QuickBooks Pro (Intuit, Inc.).
- Peachtree (Sage North America).

- MYOB (MYOB, Ltd.).
- Office Accounting (Microsoft Corp.).

Commercial High Cost

- Sage MAS 90 and Sage AccPac (Sage North America).
- Microsoft Dynamics (formerly Great Plains, Microsoft Corp.).

NFP Industry-Specific Software

- Fund E-Z (Fund E-Z Development Corp.).
- Sage MIP Fund Accounting (Sage North America).
- CYMA Fund Accounting (CYMA Systems, Inc.).
- The Financial Edge (Blackbaud, Inc.).

In addition to accounting software, NFPs use a number of other types of software to manage certain NFP activities such as fund-raising (e.g., Blackbaud, Inc.), auctions and events, membership, and grant writing and reporting.

In the author's experience, a significant number of NFP organizations do not spend adequately on accounting software, software design, and training. The reasons vary but they usually boil down to cost, lack of time, or lack of understanding of the importance of purchasing the right accounting software and configuring it in a way that best suits the organization's needs. These reasons are elaborated in the section that follows. It is not an understatement to say that an organization's accounting software system is the foundation from which all financial information flows. Inadequate software or a poorly configured system will invariably prevent an organization from capturing financial data at the level needed to provide timely and useful financial reports.

Cost

Because many NFPs are on such a tight budget and the overriding goal is to keep expenditures as low as possible, especially with overhead expenses, spending on accounting software or training is not a high priority. Too many times the cheapest program is purchased, even if a more powerful one is needed. Or, people install copies of programs they own personally or have borrowed from someone else (bootleg). Installing a personal or borrowed copy is known to be illegal, but the law is ignored because it is believed to be too insignificant for anyone to care about and the chance of getting caught and punished is slim. In an effort to save money, especially when money is tight, the misguided belief is to use cheaper software now, and then upgrade to better software when more money is available. The problem with this thinking is the misunderstanding about the true cost of switching software at a later date. It isn't just the cost of new software but also the cost in time to transfer data from the old system to the new one. Another flaw in using the cheapest software (or illegal copy) is the potential for software problems to arise due to improper installation (incomplete software files), missing software documentation, and no software customer support due to lack of ownership (license) or discontinued software version. To save money, the organization is often reluctant to pay an independent consultant to install and configure the new software properly, which ends up costing more money in lost productivity.

Lack of Time

Even when management decides it's willing to spend money to upgrade its accounting software, there can be resistance to do this from the very department that needs it the most, the accounting department. The reason is time, or lack thereof. The person in charge of the accounting department knows that it will take a great deal of time to input all necessary setup information such as vendors and customers and even longer if changing programs in the middle of the year and having to migrate (copy or move) data to the new program. Because there never seems to be enough time to complete everyday tasks, the thought of adding something else to the workload is enough to dissuade even the most ambitious individuals from upgrading.

Lack of Understanding of Importance

Sometimes the reason for not purchasing the most appropriate accounting software is simply ignorance. Ignorance about what an accounting software program does (*Can't you just use Microsoft Excel?*) or the difference in accounting software capabilities (*I use QuickBooks for my own business, why do we need a special Not-for-Profit accounting software program?*). In all cases, lack of understanding can prevent an organization from spending the necessary time to evaluate the costs versus the benefits of purchasing the right accounting software, and from understanding how important accounting software really is.

General Ledger and Chart of Accounts

Let's be positive and say appropriate accounting software is purchased. After purchasing it, the next important task is to properly setup and configure the chart of accounts, which is the framework for the core accounting structure known as the general ledger. The general ledger can be defined as a file (or book, when bookkeeping was maintained in a written format) that stores all detail or summary financial transactions of an entity. Transactions are either directly entered into the general ledger or summary information is posted (i.e., copied) from the information entered in various journals such as accounts payable, accounts receivable, or cash receipts journals. The general ledger is composed of numerous accounts that are classified by account type such as assets, liabilities, net assets, revenue/support, and expense. If you print out a list of every general ledger account created, you would have something called a chart of accounts. So, a chart of accounts is defined as a list of all account names and numbers in an organization's general ledger.

In order to capture and maintain financial information in such a way that useful and meaningful reports can be generated, the chart of accounts *structure* must be configured properly. A chart of accounts structure is the format the organization assigns to one or more letters or numbers (alphanumeric) or the order in which they are placed together. For example, an organization could create a simple six-place account structure XX-XXXX, where the first two places signify a department and the other four places signify the type of revenue, expenses, asset, and so forth. So telephone expenses (account 6500) for department one and two would be 01-6500 and 02-6500.

The design of the chart of accounts is extremely important and shouldn't be done in haste. Unfortunately, in the author's opinion, it is done too quickly all too often. As with the purchase of accounting software, lack of understanding of its importance, or lack of time or expertise is the main cause of a poorly constructed account structure. One of the biggest misconceptions is that the structure is not that important or can be easily modified at a later date. This is false. It is either not modifiable or very difficult to modify. The more data that is entered into the accounting system, the harder it is to rearrange the chart of accounts structure at a later date without convoluting financial reports.

The second factor, time, or lack thereof, is also a major cause of a less appropriate design. All too often, there is a great deal of pressure to get the accounting software implemented and functioning quickly, so a proper evaluation of the current and future reporting needs of the organization is not done.

Lastly, the lack of expertise is probably the major contributor to a poorly designed chart of accounts structure. Although the mechanics of setting up a chart of accounts structure is relatively easy, the decision of how many alphanumeric characters to use and what those characters should represent requires a certain level of experience and a broad-based knowledge of current organizational operations and possible future needs. Typically NFP staff members do not have the requisite skills and the organization is not willing, or is financially unable, to hire an outside consultant to perform this function.

In summary, the result of an inadequate account structure is that it will prevent the organization from separating and maintaining its financial transactions in such a way that it can generate, in a timely manner, all the necessary reports requested and required by management, the board of directors, and external parties such as donors and various auditors. This will cause the accounting department staff to work harder at mining the general ledger for necessary information and force them to use Microsoft Excel or another spreadsheet program to generate all required reports (e.g., by program, project, grant, event, restriction, location, department, etc.).

Chart-of-Accounts Structure

There is no standard NFP chart-of-accounts structure. The appropriate structure varies depending on the size and complexity of the organization. Typically, the more programs or activities an organization has, the larger and more complex the chart of accounts is. For ultimate functionality, the chart of accounts should be set up (configured) with both internal and external tracking and reporting requirements in mind. For example internal requirements might include the following:

- Tracking all revenue and expenses by department and location.
- Tracking expenditures by program, grant, and grant period.
- Monitoring cash position.
- Generating variance reports comparing actual to budgeted activity.
- Generating reports to program directors or division heads.
- Generating financial reports to board of directors or board committees.

External reporting requirements might include the following:

- Generating cash receipts reports to chapters and affiliated organizations.
- Generating reports to grantors, contributors, and government agencies.
- Generating detail reports needed by independent auditors and government agency auditors.

As previously stated, chart-of-accounts code structures can vary and can be as short as four characters and as long as 15. An example of one possible code structure follows, using a 12-character structure where # means number of characters; natural (core) means account name, restriction means whether something is unrestricted, temporarily restricted, or permanently restricted; program is a specific program; project or grant is a specific project or grant; and year is the specific year a project or grant relates to.

Illustration

Natural (core)	Restriction	Program Function	Project or Grant	Year
####	#	##	###	##
8050	1	90	020	09
	Unrestricted			
Travel	Management		Dept of Edu.	2009

A complete example of a chart of accounts for a small NFP organization is provided in Appendix B. That chart uses a simplified seven-character structure (e.g., 1106000) where the first character is used for restriction (unrestricted, temporarily restricted, and permanently restricted); the next two characters are used to identity a function (e.g., program, management, and general), and the last four characters are used for the core account, illustrated as follows:

#	##	—	####
1	10	—	6150
Unrestricted	Educ. Program 1		Printing Expense

Introduction to NFP Financial Statements

As discussed in Chapter 4, GAAP, as promulgated in SFAS 117, requires all NFP organizations to provide three financial statements: statement of financial position (balance sheet), statement of activities (income statement), and statement of cash flows. It also required the providing of a fourth statement, statement of functional expenses, for any NFP characterized as a voluntary health and welfare organization (VHWO), along with notes to financial statements. Financial statements are very important because this is what external parties see and many times rely on to make informed decisions regarding the organization. These statements summarize in only a few pages the major components of what an organization owns, owes, income it earned, and the related expenses it has incurred during the year.

Some statements are easier for nonfinancial individuals to understand. For example more people seem to understand the statement of activities rather than the statement of financial position. And, practically no one, even some accountants, seems to understand the statement of cash flows. The statement of functional expenses, when presented, is generally understood, whereas the notes to financial statements are avoided by many.

The following discussion is an overview of each financial statement using a fictitious NFP organization called Job Training Now, Inc. and should provide the reader with a basic understanding of each financial statement. Subsequent chapters will elaborate on how financial transactions move through the accounting system and how they are ultimately presented on the appropriate financial statements, which should increase the readers understanding of financial statements even more.

Job Training Now, Inc. (JTN) is a composite organization developed from a number of existing and functioning NFP organizations in New York City. The specifics of JTN are as follows: The mission of the organization is job training for inner-city youths, and is accomplished by performing two programs: simulated on-the-job training (on the NFP's premises) and corporate on-site training (training low-skilled employees at their employers' premises). The organization's budget is approximately $5,000,000, it has 20 employees (program coordinators and directors, instructors, and management), and an accounting department staff of three employees (vice president of finance and two staff accountants). Revenue is received from unrestricted contributions from corporations, foundations, and individuals; restricted contributions from corporations for program expenses (attendees, business attire and transportation to/from NFP training site or transportation to/from job site); program service income (training revenue and sales of training manuals); two major fund-raising events, one with an auction; two government grants from New York City government agencies; professional services received as in-kind contributions (grant writer and web master/computer consultant); and investment income earned mostly from a permanently restricted endowment created by a donation from the organization's founder, a retired high school teacher. Expenses consist of rent at two locations, some auction inventory, classroom training supplies, stipends and attendee expenses, salaries and related expenses, and all the other typical operating expenses.

Statement of Financial Position

The statement of financial position (called the balance sheet for commercial entities) shows the totals of major categories of assets, liabilities, and net assets at a particular point in time (e.g., December 31, 2010). These categories are explained in Table 5.1, along with how increases or decreases to accounts in these categories are treated in the general ledger (i.e., debited or credited). Table 5.1 is an illustrated statement of financial position.

Assets—FASB statement of accounting concepts 6 ("Elements of Financial Statements") defines assets as probable future economic benefits obtained or controlled by a particular entity as a result of past transactions or events. Assets are basically something owned or owed to you that will be converted to cash or some other asset in the future. Assets can be further classified into current and noncurrent, and, if displayed this way, the statement would be called a classified statement of financial position (not illustrated). Current assets are assets that will be sold or converted to cash within a year (e.g., accounts or contributions receivable, prepaid expenses,

Table 5.1   Statement of Financial Position

<table>
<tr><th colspan="3">Job Training Now, Inc.
Statements of Financial Position
December 31, 2010 and 2009</th></tr>
<tr><th></th><th>2010</th><th>2009</th></tr>
<tr><td>ASSETS</td><td></td><td></td></tr>
<tr><td>Cash and cash equivalents</td><td>$ 249,609</td><td>$ 671,697</td></tr>
<tr><td>Accounts receivable</td><td>60,755</td><td>113,390</td></tr>
<tr><td>Government grants receivable</td><td>66,254</td><td>337,488</td></tr>
<tr><td>Contributions receivable</td><td>75,500</td><td>216,730</td></tr>
<tr><td>Prepaid expenses</td><td>36,836</td><td>31,151</td></tr>
<tr><td>Inventory</td><td>18,000</td><td>25,000</td></tr>
<tr><td>Investments</td><td>205,000</td><td>225,000</td></tr>
<tr><td>Property and equipment - net</td><td>116,000</td><td>109,000</td></tr>
<tr><td>Security deposits and other assets</td><td>39,303</td><td>2,740</td></tr>
<tr><td>Total assets</td><td>$ 867,257</td><td>$ 1,732,196</td></tr>
<tr><td colspan="3"></td></tr>
<tr><td>LIABILITIES AND NET ASSETS</td><td></td><td></td></tr>
<tr><td>Liabilities:</td><td></td><td></td></tr>
<tr><td>Accounts payable & accrued expenses</td><td>$ 233,288</td><td>$ 354,746</td></tr>
<tr><td>Loans & notes payable</td><td>168,147</td><td>215,000</td></tr>
<tr><td>Refundable advances</td><td>10,000</td><td>0</td></tr>
<tr><td>Deferred income</td><td>23,738</td><td>364,222</td></tr>
<tr><td>Total liabilities</td><td>435,173</td><td>933,968</td></tr>
<tr><td>Commitments and contingencies (see notes)</td><td></td><td></td></tr>
<tr><td>Net assets</td><td></td><td></td></tr>
<tr><td>Unrestricted</td><td>146,321</td><td>586,588</td></tr>
<tr><td>Temporarily restricted</td><td>185,763</td><td>211,640</td></tr>
<tr><td>Permanently restricted</td><td>100,000</td><td>0</td></tr>
<tr><td>Total net assets</td><td>432,084</td><td>798,228</td></tr>
<tr><td>Total liabilities and net assets</td><td>$ 867,257</td><td>$ 1,732,196</td></tr>
</table>

See accompanying notes to financial statements.

inventory). Noncurrent assets (longer than a year) include such assets as property and equipment and security deposits. Even when not separated into current and noncurrent categories, assets are listed in the order of liquidity or ability to be converted to cash (e.g., first cash—the most liquid, then accounts receivable, and so on). When assets are increased they are debited and conversely when they are decreased they are credited.

Liabilities—FASB statement of accounting concepts 6 ("Elements of Financial Statements") defines liabilities as probable future sacrifices of economic benefits arising from present obligations of a particular entity to transfer assets or provide services to other entities in the future as a result of past transactions or events. Liabilities are basically obligations (something you owe) to another entity. They are listed on the statement of financial position according to their nearness to maturity or needing to be satisfied with cash. If a classified statement of financial position were presented, liabilities would be further separated into two groups called short term (e.g., accounts payable, deferred income) and long term (e.g., mortgage payable). When liabilities are increased, they are credited (increase what is owed), and conversely, when they are decreased they are debited.

Net Assets —Net assets are the difference between what you own and what you owe. With commercial enterprises, what is left over is called equity or capital and is due to the owners, shareholders, or partners. With NFPs, what is left over is not due to anyone. It remains in the NFP as a residual value of the organization. When net assets are increased, they are credited (increase what is left over). When net assets accounts are decreased, they are debited. The complication with net assets is that what is left over is broken up into three categories: unrestricted net assets, temporarily restricted net assets, and permanently restricted net assets. Unrestricted net assets are very similar to the capital account of a commercial company. It is the excess of NFP's assets over their liabilities, and it can be used for any legitimate purpose. Temporarily and permanently restricted net assets are different. Temporarily restricted net assets are accumulated assets (cash, receivables, etc.) received over one or more years that are restricted by the donor until some future time or purpose. Permanently restricted assets are endowments, and are restricted from use by one or more donors. Typically the stipulations made are that the donations received must be invested and only part or all the earnings received from the investments can be used by the organization for operations. The principal amount (i.e., the amount of the original gift) must be held in perpetuity (i.e., forever) by the organization and never used.

Presentation Issues

The heading at the top of the statement of financial position should show the legal name of the NFP, the statement name, and the date of the statement as follows:

Job Training Now, Inc.

Statements of Financial Position

December 31, 2010 and 2009

It is preferable to show two years together because it is more informative when the reader has something to compare to and can see if the organization is in a better or worse position than the year before. However, it might not be beneficial to show two years together when there are significant changes in accounting methods used that make comparability difficult (e.g., the organization switched from cash-basis method of accounting to the accrual basis). Also, the financial statement should include a footnote (usually at the bottom of the page) that instructs the reader to look at the notes to financial statements for additional information.

Statement of Activities

Statement of Activities (called income statement or statement of profit and loss for commercial entities) shows the major categories of income and support and total expenses by major program and supporting services (management and general and fund-raising) and covers a specified period of time (usually one year). Table 5.2 is an example of a statement of activities.

Table 5.2   Statement of Activities (vertical presentation)

	2010	2009
Job Training Now, Inc.		
Statements of Activities		
Years Ended December 31, 2010 and 2009		
Support and Revenues:		
Unrestricted:		
Government grants	$ 2,441,632	$ 2,855,000
Contributions	1,265,854	1,575,260
Program service revenue	358,875	415,920
Total before special events	4,066,361	4,846,180
Special events:		
Auction sales	15,200	18,800
Less: cost or fair value of auction items	−5,300	−6,700
Event-related income and support	565,000	595,000
Less: event-related direct costs	(249,111)	(231,460)
Net special events income and support	325,789	375,640
Contributions in-kind	91,000	92,000
Investment and other income	21,487	18,442
Release of restricted assets	211,640	—
Temporarily restricted:		
Corporate contributions	185,763	211,640
Release of restricted assets	(211,640)	—
Permanently restricted:		
Corporate contributions	100,000	—
Total support and revenues	4,790,400	5,543,902
Expenses:		
Program expenses:		
Simulated on-the-job training	3,756,128	3,790,268

(Continued)

Table 5.2   (Continued)

Corporate on-site training	272,458	265,363
Total program expenses	4,028,586	4,055,631
Supporting services:		
Management and general	1,042,475	1,052,908
Fund-raising	85,483	81,763
Total expenses	5,156,544	5,190,302
Increase/(decrease) in net assets:		
Unrestricted	(440,267)	141,960
Temporarily restricted	(25,877)	211,640
Permanently restricted	100,000	—
Increase/(decrease) in net assets	(366,144)	353,600
Net assets, beginning of year	798,228	444,628
Net assets, end of year	$ 432,084	$ 798,228

See accompanying notes to financial statements.

In addition to being titled differently, this statement is different from a typical commercial enterprise income statement in several ways. A commercial entity's income statement typically shows sales less cost of goods sold (if inventory is involved), net sales, and then expenses listed by natural classification (e.g., salaries, telephone). NFPs differ by reporting more categories of revenue and support, such as government grants, contributions, program service income, and event income. Because NFP GAAP rules changed in 1994, NFP expenses are required to be categorized and reported by functional category (e.g., program and supporting services). Expenses listed by natural classification are reported on the statement of functional expenses, if presented. Also, instead of showing net income as one line, NFPs are required to show their net income (described as changes in net assets) as three distinct lines broken down by increase (or decrease) in unrestricted net assets, temporarily restricted net assets, and permanently restricted net assets. At the bottom of the statement, the net increase or decrease from all three categories are added to net assets at the beginning of the year to arrive at net assets at the end of the year. The end of year net assets amount is the same number that appears as total net assets on the bottom of the statement of financial position.

As mentioned in the Chapter 4, when earnings exceed expenses, there is an increase in net assets, and conversely, when expenses exceed revenue and support, there is a decrease in net assets.

Presentation Issues

The same titling rules apply to the statement of activities as the statement of financial position. The heading at the top of the statement of activities should show the legal name of the NFP organization, the statement name, and the period the statement covers as shown here:

Job Training Now, Inc.

Statements of Activities

Years Ended December 31, 2010 and 2009

Note: The term *years ended* is not a typo and is correct and should not *read years ending.*

As with the other statement, it is preferable to show two years together because it provides the reader with a better perspective of how well or poorly the organization is doing. However, here too, there are exceptions to the two-year presentation, such as when significant programs are added or discontinued or when the NFP changes it operating year and the two periods being compared are not the same (e.g., 12 months vs. 6 months). This statement should also include a footnote that the reader should see the notes to financial statements for additional information.

Presentation Formatting Options

The presentation method illustrated earlier (1 column vertical) is the format preferred by the author. It is believed to be the cleanest and most concise way to present the statement of activities. However, there are many other acceptable presentation formats for this statement. Variability is acceptable as long as the basic tenets of accounting as they apply to NFPs and this statement are followed. Some presentation formats are more prevalent than others. The most widely used presentation method is the multiple-column presentation method. In this method, separate columns are used to present unrestricted (UR), temporarily-restricted (TR), and permanently restricted (PR) operations. The reason this method is so popular is because it clearly separates revenue by restriction in each column. The reason this method is not favored by the author is because for many organizations it uses a great deal of presentation space in order to display only a few numbers, hence the reason the first presentation method is preferred. A third commonly used presentation method is what can be called the by-restriction method. This method shows the unrestricted activity first and then displays the temporarily restricted activity followed by the permanently restricted revenue and support. The multiple column method and restriction methods are illustrated in Tables 5.3 and 5.4.

Statement of Cash Flows

GAAP requires that a statement of cash flows be included with all external financial statements. In the simplest terms this statement shows the cash

Table 5.3   Statement of Activities (Multiple Column Method)

	2010				2009
	UR	TR	PR	Total	Total
Support and Revenues:					
Unrestricted:					
Government grants	$ 2,441,632	$ —	$ —	$ 2,441,632	$ 2,855,000
Contributions	1,265,854	185,763	100,000	1,551,617	1,786,900
Program service revenue	358,875	—	—	358,875	415,920
Total before special events	4,066,361	185,763	100,000	4,352,124	5,057,820
Special events:					
Auction sales	15,200	—	—	15,200	18,800
Less: cost or fair value of auction items	(5,300)	—	—	(5,300)	(6,700)
Event-related income and support	565,000	—	—	565,000	595,000
Less: event-related direct costs	(249,111)	—	—	(249,111)	(231,460)
Net special events income & support	325,789	—	—	325,789	375,640
Contributions in-kind	91,000	—	—	91,000	92,000
Investment and other income	21,487	—	—	21,487	18,442
Release of restricted assets	211,640	(211,640)	—	—	—
Total support and revenues	4,716,277	(25,877)	100,000	4,790,400	5,543,902
Expenses:					
Program expenses:					
Simulated on-the-job training	3,756,128	—	—	3,756,128	3,790,268
Corporate on-site training	272,458	—	—	272,458	265,363
Total program expenses	4,028,586	—	—	4,028,586	4,055,631
Supporting services:					
Management and general	1,042,475	—	—	1,042,475	1,052,908
Fund-raising	85,483	—	—	85,483	81,763
Total expenses	5,156,544	—	—	5,156,544	5,190,302

Table header:
Job Training Now, Inc.
Statements of Activities
Years Ended December 31, 2010 and 2009

(Continued)

Table 5.3   (Continued)

	2010				2009
	UR	TR	PR	Total	Total
Increase/(decrease) in net assets:					
Unrestricted	(440,267)	—	—	(440,267)	141,960
Temporarily restricted	—	(25,877)	—	(25,877)	211,640
Permanently restricted	—	—	100,000	100,000	—
Increase/(decrease) in net assets	(440,267)	(25,877)	100,000	(366,144)	353,600
Net assets, beginning of year	586,588	211,640	—	798,228	444,628
Net assets, end of year	$ 146,321	$ 185,763	$ 100,000	$ 432,084	$ 798,228

See accompanying notes to financial statements.

Table 5.4   Statement of Activities (by restrictions method)

Job Training Now, Inc.
Statements of Activities
Years Ended December 31, 2010 and 2009

	2010	2009
Support and Revenues:		
Unrestricted:		
Government grants	$ 2,441,632	$ 2,855,000
Contributions	1,265,854	1,575,260
Program service revenue	358,875	415,920
Total before special events	4,066,361	4,846,180
Special events:		
Auction sales	15,200	18,800
Less: cost or fair value of auction items	(5,300)	(6,700)
Event-related income and support	565,000	595,000
Less: event-related direct costs	(249,111)	(231,460)
Net special events income and support	325,789	375,640
Contributions in-kind	91,000	92,00
Investment and other income	21,487	18,442
Release of restricted assets	211,640	—
Total unrestricted support and revenues	4,716,277	5,332,262
Expenses:		
Program expenses:		
Simulated on-the-job training	3,756,128	3,790,268
Corporate on-site training	272,458	265,363
Total program expenses	4,028,586	4,055,631

(Continued)

Table 5.4   (Continued)

Supporting services:		
Management and general	1,042,475	1,052,908
Fund-raising	85,483	81,763
Total expenses	5,156,544	5,190,302
Increase/(decrease) in unrestricted net assets	(440,267)	141,960
Temporarily Restricted:		
Corporate contributions	185,763	211,640
Release of restricted assets	(211,640)	—
Increase/(decrease) in temporarily restricted net assets	(25,877)	211,640
Permanently Restricted:		
Corporate contributions	100,000	—
Increase/(decrease) in permanently restricted net assets	100,000	—
Increase/(decrease) in net assets	(366,144)	353,600
Net assets, beginning of year	798,228	444,628
Net assets, end of year	$ 432,084	$ 798,228

See accompanying notes to financial statements.

receipts and cash disbursements during a specified period (e.g., one year), classified by three principal sources of use—*operations, investing,* and *financing.* As mentioned earlier, this statement is the least understood of all the required financial statements. The purpose of this statement is to assist the reader in understanding how cash (and cash equivalents to be discussed later) was generated during the year. Since financial statements are required under GAAP to be prepared on the accrual basis of accounting, this statement shows the change in cash and cash equivalents by *converting* the accrual-based amounts to cash-based amounts. An in-depth discussion of this statement is beyond the scope of this book; however, the basic elements will be covered. Table 5.5 is an example of a statement of cash flows.

The statement of cash flows groups information into five basic categories—the three principal sources of use: operating, investing, and financing; net change in cash during the period; and supplemental disclosure of noncash investing and financing activities. The first section, cash flows from operating, shows the changes in assets and liabilities from the prior year. The next section, cash flows from investing activities, shows the purchases and sales of assets, such as investments and property and equipment. The third section,

Table 5.5 Statements of Cash Flows (indirect method)

Job Training Now, Inc.
Statements of Cash Flows
Years Ended December 31, 2010 and 2009

	2010	2009
Cash flows from operating activities:		
Increase/(decrease) in net assets	$(366,144)	$ 353,600
Adjustments for noncash items included in operating activities:		
Depreciation	10,136	10,001
Changes in assets and liabilities:		
Accounts receivable	52,635	153,789
Government grants & contracts receivable	271,234	146,282
Contributions receivable	141,230	(238,383)
Prepaid expenses	(5,685)	(12,358)
Inventory	7,000	(5,500)
Security deposits and other assets	(36,563)	(15,277)
Accounts payable & accrued expenses	(121,458)	(308,994)
Refundable advances	10,000	(106,188)
Deferred income	(340,484)	(183,258)
Total adjustments	(11,955)	(559,886)
Net cash provided/(used) by operating activities	(378,099)	(206,286)
Cash flows from investing activities:		
Sale of investments	20,000	—
Purchase of property and equipment	(17,136)	—
Net cash provided/(used) by investing activities	2,864	—
Cash flows from financing activities:		
Proceeds from bank loans	—	—
Repayment of bank loans	(46,853)	—
Net cash provided/(used) by financing activities	(46,853)	—
Net increase/(decrease) in cash and cash equivalents	(422,088)	(206,286)
Cash and cash equivalents at beginning of year	671,697	877,983
Cash and cash equivalents at end of year	$ 249,609	$ 671,697
Supplemental information:		
Interest paid	$ 19,843	$ 19,772

See accompanying notes to financial statements.

cash flows from financing activities, shows cash inflows and outflows from money borrowed and repaid (e.g., loans from banks).

The term *cash and cash equivalents* was mentioned earlier. Cash is defined as currency (bills and coins) on hand and demand deposits held at banks and other financial institutions (checking and savings accounts). Cash equivalents are investments that are highly liquid, that is, they can be, or will be, converted to cash in such a short period of time that a change in their value is highly unlikely. Examples of cash equivalents include money market accounts, Treasury bills, and certificates of deposit or bonds with less than a three-month maturity period. For more detailed information on the statement of cash flows, you can read *Wiley Not-for-Profit GAAP 2010: Interpretation and Application of Generally Accepted Accounting Principles* by Richard F. Larkin.

Presentation Issues

As with the previous two statements, the heading at the top of the statement of cash flows should show the legal name of the NFP organization, the statement name, and the period covered (years ended) as shown here:

Job Training Now, Inc.

Statements of Cash Flows

Years Ended December 31, 2010 and 2009

Similar to the other statements, it is preferable to show two years together because it provides the reader with a better perspective of how well or poorly the organization is doing.

Presentation Formatting Options

There are two acceptable formats for presenting the statement of cash flows: the direct method and the indirect method (shown earlier). The direct method starts with cash receipts and then deducts operating costs and other expenses. The indirect method starts with the change in net assets and adds and subtracts noncash items (e.g., depreciation) and then changes in assets and liabilities and items related to investment and financing activities. There are other disclosures on this statement, such as the cash paid out for interest. This statement, like the others, should include a footnote that the reader should see the notes to financial statements for additional information.

Statement of Functional Expenses

As previously mentioned, GAAP does not require all NFP organizations to present a statement of functional expenses. It only requires that NFPs present information about their expenses by functional classification, such as by program activities and supporting services. It does require that voluntary health and welfare organizations (VHWO) prepare this type of statement. The statement of functional expenses is a two-dimensional report. It shows expenses by function and by natural classification. Natural classification details expenses by type of expense such as salaries, office supplies, insurance, and telephone.

This report is probably the easiest to understand. Most people, even nonfinancial individuals, understand expense categories. The most difficult part of reading this statement is ascertaining how certain joint costs get allocated between programs and supporting services, especially when it comes to allocating joint costs between fund-raising and other functional areas. The AICPA issued statement of position 98-2 *Accounting for Costs of Activities of Not-For-Profit Org. & State & Local Governmental Entities That Include Fund Raising* that gives guidance on how joint costs should be accounted for and reported. One problem that readers of NFP financial statements faced many years ago, and sometimes even today, was how to compare the financial activities of one NFP with the financial activities of another. More specifically, it is relatively easy to see how much support (e.g., contributions and grants) an NFP received in a particular year, but it is very difficult to determine how much they had to spend to receive that money. For example, NFP A reported they earned $2,000,000, and NFP B reported they earned $1,500,000 from contributions and government grants. It appears that NFP A had a better year. But what was the cost (and there is a cost) to raising those funds. Fund-raising costs can include direct costs such as the cost of hiring a director of development or an outside fund-raising firm. It can also include allocated (joint) costs such as the portion of time the ED or president spends soliciting corporate donations. It is important that these costs are properly included and reported as fund-raising expenses, so the reader of the financial statements can have a better understanding of the costs associated with receiving support. Obviously, there is an inherent bias to show fund-raising costs as low as possible. Table 5.6 is an example of a statement of functional expenses.

Presentation Issues

Similar to all other statements, the heading at the top of the statement of functional expenses should show the legal name of the NFP organization, the statement name, and the period covered (year ended) as shown below.

Job Training Now, Inc.

Statement of Functional Expenses

Year Ended December 31, 2010 with comparative totals for 2009

Table 5.6 Statements of Functional Expenses (indirect method)

Job Training Now, Inc.
Statement of Functional Expenses
Year Ended December 31, 2010 with Comparative Totals for 2009

| | 2010 | | | | | | 2009 |
| | Program | | | Support Services | | | |
	Simulated On-the-Job Training	Corporate On-Site Training	Total Program	Management & General	Fund-Raising	Total Expenses	Total Expenses
Compensation and related expenses:							
Salaries	$2,627,962	$140,901	$2,768,863	$619,716	$30,002	$3,418,581	$3,633,211
Payroll taxes	230,462	12,056	242,518	44,826	2,567	289,911	308,823
Employee benefits	307,594	15,033	322,627	56,120	3,201	381,948	363,322
Total	3,166,018	167,990	3,334,008	720,662	35,770	4,090,440	4,305,356
Advertising, brochures, and promotion	30,723	18,554	49,277	12,484	—	61,761	68,205
Bank charges and payroll service fees	1,595	271	1,866	13,470	—	15,336	15,477
Conferences, dues, and training	40,007	15,270	55,277	5,544	—	60,821	58,447
Computers and equipment purchases	22,407	5,080	27,487	5,387	—	32,874	32,888
Consultants and outside services	41,176	6,244	47,420	26,881	49,713	124,014	125,832
Depreciation	—	—	—	10,136	—	10,136	10,001
Dues, books and subscriptions	7,999	6,996	14,995	3,054	—	18,049	17,966
Equipment leases and rentals	3,000	—	3,000	12,575	—	15,575	15,476
Insurance	15,000	5,000	20,000	15,117	—	35,117	34,441

(Continued)

Table 5.6 (Continued)

	2010						2009
	Program			Support Services			
	Simulated On-the-Job Training	Corporate On-Site Training	Total Program	Management & General	Fund-Raising	Total Expenses	Total Expenses
Interest	—	—	—	19,843	—	19,843	19,772
Local transportation	5,020	10,999	16,019	2,477	—	18,496	18,315
Office security	28,189	—	28,189	11,548	—	39,737	39,796
Miscellaneous	11,002	4,995	15,997	10,899	—	26,896	35,124
Office supplies and expenses	18,172	4,553	22,725	31,278	—	54,003	52,343
Postage and delivery	4,490	997	5,487	11,477	—	16,964	16,874
Printing and reproduction	3,349	1,869	5,218	6,879	—	12,097	11,774
Professional fees	12,511	1,158	13,669	15,899	—	29,568	29,560
Recruitment and staff development	—	—	—	11,196	—	11,196	10,464
Rent and related expenses	71,756	—	71,756	30,004	—	101,760	102,225
Repairs and maintenance	7,031	1,311	8,342	9,897	—	18,239	21,177
Stipends and trainees, allowances	221,208	—	221,208	—	—	221,208	21,146
Telephone and communications	3,651	2,777	6,428	15,991	—	22,419	22,364
Temporary help	14,200	—	14,200	10,992	—	25,192	25,558
Travel, hotels, seminars and meetings	1,170	3,640	4,810	5,996	—	10,806	10,675
Utilities	11,700	—	11,700	6,893	—	18,593	23,546
Web site development and support	14,754	14,754	29,508	15,896	—	45,404	45,500
Total expenses	$3,756,128	$272,458	$4,028,586	$1,042,475	$85,483	$5,156,544	$5,190,302

You will notice that the title of the report is not for the "Years ended . . . " but rather for the "Year ended December 31, 2010 with comparative totals for 2009." This makes the report less cumbersome to read. By summarizing the prior year's figures, you get comparability on an organization-wide level without encumbering the report with so many additional columns. If a more detailed presentation is desired, two separate schedules can be presented—one for the current year and one for the prior year.

Notes to Financial Statements

To be in compliance with GAAP, certain material disclosures must be reported. There is no required format for presenting these disclosures. Including them on the face of the required financial statements would crowd the statements and make them difficult to read, especially since most of the disclosures are textual in nature. The conventional method is to include these disclosures in a document called notes to financial statements and placed behind the three (or four) required financial statements.

Typically, notes to financial statements should include a paragraph describing the organization and significant accounting policies, such as the basis of financial statements (accrual or cash) and a statement that management uses estimates and assumptions in preparing financial statements in accordance with GAAP; composition of property and equipment (office equipment, vehicles, leasehold improvements), cash equivalents (CD, money market), and investments (stocks, bonds); applicable commitments, such as office leases, and bank loans and any contingencies, such as potential lawsuits and concentration of revenue sources (i.e., all from two government grants in our example).

NFP organizations should also provide additional disclosures. Some typical NFP disclosures are as follows:

NFP Mission and Major Programs: The organization's mission is job training for inner-city youths. Its two main program areas include on-the-job training and corporate on-site training.

Recognition of Donor Restrictions: Support that is restricted by the donor is reported as an increase in unrestricted net assets if the restriction expires in the reporting period in which the support is recognized.

Tax-Exempt Status: The organization has been granted tax-exempt status by the IRS under Internal Revenue Code Section 501(C)(3) in April, 1989. Accordingly, no provision for federal, state, or local income taxes has been recorded.

Major Government Grants: The organization receives a significant portion of its income from two government grants, one from NYS

Department of Education for $1,500,000 and the other from the NYS Office of Children and Family Services for $500,000.

Functional Expense Allocation: The direct costs of providing programs and other activities have been summarized on a functional basis in the statement of activities and in the schedule of functional expenses.

Management and General Expenses: The organization classifies expenses, which are not directly related to a specific program or fund-raising, as management and general expenses.

Restricted Assets: As of December 31, 2010 and 2009, $185,763 and $211,640, respectively, in temporarily restricted contributions are restricted for corporate on-site training.

Presentation Issues

Once again, the heading at the top of the notes to financial statements should show the legal name of the NFP organization and the report name (the period covered is optional) as shown here:

Job Training Now, Inc.

Notes to Financial Statements

December 31, 2010 and 2009

The general practice among preparers of financial statements is to arrange the notes in the same order as they are listed on the financial statements. Either numbers or letters can be used (e.g., note 1 or note A). It is also general practice to reference the notes in the body of the financial statement, although the author doesn't recommend this, because this generally increases the likelihood of referencing errors.

Assets—Concepts and Data Flow

As discussed in Chapter 4, computers removed many repetitive book-keeping tasks from accounting, such as totaling up numbers from transactional journals such as accounts receivable (A/R) and accounts payable (A/P) and automatically posting (moving) data to various ledgers and reports (e.g., general ledger, trial balance, financial statements).

Computerized Data Flow: An Illustration

sales journal (A/R) → general ledger → trial balance → financial statements
purchase journal (A/P) → general ledger → trial balance → financial statements

No one would complain about the removal of manual, tedious, and repetitive bookkeeping tasks. However, as discussed in the previous chapter, if there is one downside to automating the accounting function, it is the removal of seeing, on a day-to-day basis, how financial information flows through the accounting system. The result is an initial disconnect between the knowledge acquired in a four-or-more-years accounting program at a college or university and the practical skills required of a junior staff position in an organization's accounting department. For example, every accounting student learns, in their first or second accounting course, how to perform bank reconciliations. However, very few learn how to do this on an accounting software program. It is beyond the scope of this book to discuss how to perform many accounting functions using accounting software. Nevertheless, we will briefly cover in general terms how financial information is entered into a typical program.

Entering Data

Most financial data is entered into high-cost (more expensive and powerful) accounting programs in separate components called modules. Standard modules include sales/accounts receivable (A/R), purchases/accounts payable

(A/P), inventory, general journal (G/J)/general ledger (G/L), and financial reporting/statements. Lower cost software, such as QuickBooks (Intuit) and Peachtree (Sage), don't have separate modules but rather use separate areas to enter similar data. These separate modules or areas perform a similar function as separate journals did in the old manual bookkeeping system.

Typically, NFPs, using a properly set up and functioning accounting software program on the accrual basis of accounting, would enter most financial transactions through the accounts payable or accounts receivable module/area. Transactions entered this way include all organization invoices, cash receipts, vendor bills, and cash disbursements (i.e., checks). To a lesser extent, a number of transactions are entered through the general journal module/area such as bank transfers, payroll (if using an independent payroll service), and revenue and expense allocations between programs and supporting functions. If the accounting software system is not set up and used properly, many more transactions tend to be entered as general journal entries, and a large amount of detailed financial information will have to be maintained on various Microsoft Excel or other spreadsheet files. In this case, the reporting system will be less efficient and timely.

Task-Based Accounting Scenario

Up to this point we have discussed how NFPs are formed and structured, and what the role of the board of directors is. We also discussed the NFP accounting system, applicable accounting rules under GAAP, and NFP financial statements. We are now ready for the nuts-and-bolts of what an NFP staff accountant does and how financial activity gets recorded and reported in a typical NFP organization. The approach for explaining this in this book will be different from the traditional approach. The approach used here will be to work backward from typical line items displayed on a statement of financial position and statement of activities (illustrated previously), to explaining the accounting concepts underlying related financial transactions, to understanding the transactional flow of the financial activity through the accounting system. Or, what the author likes to call the task-based accounting approach to learning. Explanations will also include a behind-the-scenes look at how transactions are typically treated (i.e., how they are they debited or credited).

It is very important to mention that *in theory* most accounting tasks are straightforward and should be handled quite easily. However, in the real world problems due to a multitude of reasons surface all the time that make recording financial activity difficult. Most have very little to do with accounting theory. Some typical reasons for difficulties in tracking and reporting financial activities (although there are probably thousands) include the following:

- Shortage of accounting staff (tasks get backed up).
- President/ED, BOD, Treasurer, and so on. make unrealistic or inconsistent demands on the accounting staff.
- Management is constantly changing accounting procedures.
- High turnover in accounting staff and constant need to retrain new people.
- Cash-flow problems due to grant reimbursements being too slow, shortage of contributions, government funding cutbacks, or nonproductive employees.
- Accounting software is antiquated or not configured properly.
- Employing inexperienced or incompetent accounting staff due to lack of desire or ability to pay proper salaries.

Most of the problems mentioned (especially the lack of qualified accounting personnel) affect smaller organizations more than larger ones because they are forced to do more with less due to shortage of funds. Despite these shortcomings, it is important to state that the majority of NFPs do an admirable job of tracking and reporting their financial activity with limited resources.

Assets—General

As previously defined, an asset is something that is owned or owed to you that will be converted to cash or some other asset in the future. Assets are listed on the statement of financial position in the order of liquidity or ability to be converted to cash.

Cash and Receivables

Accounting Concepts—Cash and Cash Equivalents

	Job Training Now, Inc. Statements of Financial Position (partial presentation) December 31, 2010 and 2009	
	2010	**2009**
Cash and cash equivalents	$ 249,609	$ 671,697

Cash is the most important area for most businesses, including NFPs. Without a healthy cash flow you cannot operate properly for any period of time. You might be able to get by on loans for a while, even a number of years, but not forever. Cash includes coins, cash on hand (petty cash), undeposited receipts, and cash on deposit with banks (savings and checking accounts). It also includes checks held but not released. Many times, checks will be written and recorded to remove them from accounts payable and show they have been paid, but held in a safe or drawer so as not to draw down the cash balances. Before preparing financial statements, these checks should be added back to cash and accounts payable.

Petty cash is bills and coins kept on hand in a box or an envelope to pay for small, incidental expenses, such as local transportation (subways, taxis), meals for staff meetings, and postage. The average amount held in petty cash should not be large or used to handle significant transactions. There are two major methods for accounting for petty cash. The first is to write and cash a check for, say, $200 and record the expense as an office expense. Then, when the money is used up, write another check and repeat the procedure. This method is okay when the amounts involved are small. If the amounts are large and the money is used to pay for a number of expenses, such as transportation and meals, recording everything to office expenses would be incorrect.

The second method is the preferable method. In this method, a fixed amount of money (e.g., $400) is withdrawn from the bank, held in a box or envelope, kept in a locked drawer or safe, and recorded to an asset account called petty cash. When money is taken out and spent, a receipt is placed in the box or envelope. Then, when funds get low, a check is written to replenish the fund and bring the amount back up to the fixed petty cash amount. The receipts are separated and totaled by the type of expense, and the replacement check is charged to the various expense accounts involved. This type of account is called an imprest fund.

Cash equivalents were previously defined as investments that are highly liquid and can be, or will be, converted to cash in the very near future. Examples include money market funds and Treasury bills.

Other Cash Considerations

- Many investment portfolios are comprised of a cash or cash equivalents portion, and those amounts should *not* be included with investments but rather with cash and cash equivalents.
- Cash that is restricted for use or has some time restriction is not a current asset and should be reported separately on the statement of financial position and not lumped in with all the other cash.
- When the dollar amount of checks written exceeds the balance in the bank account it is called an overdraft and would appear as a negative cash balance in the general ledger. A negative cash balance should *not* be shown as a negative asset on the statement of financial position, but instead should be reclassified to a liability account and shown with other liabilities. The overdraft is actually money that is owed back to the bank and, as such, it is similar to any other liability.

- It is not unusual for NFPs to have multiple bank accounts. Sometimes this is based on grantors' requirements, and sometimes it is based on operational needs (e.g., for different locations or branches or to separate payroll activities from general operating activities).
- Most cash-related transactions are recorded through the receivable or payable function of the accounting system whereas the following are typically recorded by way of a general journal entry (recording these transactions will be covered later in this chapter):
  ∘ Bank charges
  ∘ Bank interest earned
  ∘ Wire transfers between organization bank accounts

Accounting Concepts—Receivables

The word *receivables* is very broad and a generic term for amounts legally due to the NFP because of the sales of products, services, or assets or because of loans or advances made by the organization to another entity. In order for a transaction to be a receivable it must be realizable, that is, it must be probable that it will be collected. If a receivable is not legally enforceable or it is not probable that it will be collected, it shouldn't be recorded. Examples of transactions that shouldn't be recorded are tentative pledges made by donors and an approved government agency grant that is frozen indefinitely due to a budget freeze, with no expectation of receipt.

Many times different receivables are lumped together under the heading "receivables" but should be broken out into subcategories. Receivables include accounts receivable (A/R), contributions (or pledges) receivable, grants receivable, employee receivables, and notes and loans receivable. Unless immaterial, receivable subcategories should be listed separately on the statement of financial position. There is no required order for listing them, but typically they are listed in the order of largest amount to smallest. For example:

- Contributions (or pledges) receivable
- Government grants receivable
- Accounts receivable
- Loans and notes receivable
- Other receivables (from affiliates, employees, interest and dividends, etc.)

One thing that should not be reported as a receivable is the borrowing and repayment (or transfers) between an organization's own accounts. These are not true receivables or payables but rather internal cash-management transfers. An example of an incorrect entry would be when an organization transfers money from a restricted government grant bank account to its general operating account and reports the following on its statement of financial position:

Assets		Liabilities	
Due from NYC grant account	10,000	Due to general fund	10,000

Contributions (Pledges) Receivable   GAAP requires that contributions be identified as unrestricted, temporarily restricted, or permanently restricted. *Unrestricted* contributions are contributions received without a specific requirement of how they are to be used. Temporarily Restricted means the donor has imposed a restriction on how the contributions are to be used. This stipulation can be for a specific purpose (e.g., donations should be used as scholarships or to renovate a building), or to be used after a specific period of time (e.g., next year or as soon as the program starts). The first is generally known as a purpose restriction and the second as a time restriction. Restrictions can be for any legal purpose and must be complied with. If the organization doesn't like or disagrees with the restricted condition, it can always refuse the gift, although in practice this is unlikely because most organizations are in constant need of money.

A permanently restricted contribution becomes what is generally known as an *endowment fund.* In most cases the contribution must be invested in some manner and can never be used. It is held forever. Typically, the donor stipulates that either part or all of the income earned on the investment can be used either for some unrestricted or restricted purpose or a combination of both. For example, a wealthy individual donates $100,000 to a library with the stipulation that the money must be invested in a mutual fund and all of the income earned from the fund must be used to purchase only religious books. Another example is a permanently restricted donation that stipulates that the earned income can be used for operations (i.e., unrestricted).

Contributions should be recorded at their net realizable value, that is, the amount that is expected to be actually received. If the likelihood of collection is low, recognition should not be made. Let's say a telethon campaign receives 1,000 calls from individuals pledging to donate money. Experience has shown that only 80 percent of those pledges are actually received. Some people say that nothing should be recorded until money is actually received. Others say that 100 percent of the pledges should be recognized and then anything not received should be *written off* (i.e., reversed). The correct treatment is to record the full amount of the pledge ($50 × 1,000 = $50,000) because it is a legally enforceable right to receive money, but the organization should also record a reserve for the estimated amount that will not be collected. This way, the full activity can be tracked along with a reduction to adjust the receivable to the *net realizable* amount.

This would appear on the statement of financial position, assuming no other contribution receivable, as follows:

Statements of Financial Position (partial presentation)	
Contributions receivable	50,000
Less: allowance for uncollectible pledges	(10,000)
Net contributions receivable	40,000

It should be noted that although a pledge is a legally enforceable right to receive money, rarely does an organization try to enforce this right on those who renege on their promise to give.

Government Grants Receivable   Although accounting for *government grants* in theory is not difficult, in practice it often is. The reason is because government grants are accounted for differently depending on the terms of the grant. More specifically, some government grants are treated similar to contributions and can be restricted (purpose or time restriction) or unrestricted. Or, the grant can be conditional, which is very common with many government agency grants. In this situation, the grant provisions require that approved expenditures must first be made (the condition) before any grant money is received. Another type of government grant is one with elements of an exchange transaction. When the government says they will give an organization money in exchange for the organization providing a specific product or service in return, that is an exchange transaction. Examples of exchange transactions are a government contract that calls for paying $40 for each individual who receives drug/alcohol abuse counseling at a treatment center, or tuition subsidies given to an NFP for each individual enrolled in their education program.

So determining how to account for a particular government grant can be tricky. The factors to consider are the terms of the grant agreement and whether cash is first received or will be received at a later date. In some cases the entire grant is recognized immediately, and in other cases, it is not recognized until the conditions are met (e.g., NFP pays for expenses or provides a product or service). In those cases where grant money is received first, the accounting treatment can either be immediate re-cognition (contribution-type grants) or deferred recognition (i.e., recorded as a liability) until the condition is met or the product or service is provided. Many times an expense-reimbursement type government grant is recorded incorrectly and recognized immediately or prematurely. An example is a $1 million educational grant from a New York state government agency, covering the period July 1, 2009 through June 30, 2010, to pay for science textbooks that will be given to the NFP after the textbooks are purchased. In this case, it would be incorrect to recognize the entire grant when the grant is approved. The proper treatment is to record a government grants receivable only after the approved expenditures (i.e., textbooks) are made. How to record different types of government grants are covered in more detail later in this chapter.

Sometimes the collectability of a government grant is in doubt. In these cases, a provision for uncollectible receivables should be made, similar to providing for uncollectible contributions. For example, let's say a government agency grants an organization $100,000 for skills training and job placement for blind or sight-impaired workers, but the agency requires that 75 percent of these workers get jobs within two years. The government agency initially gives the organization $50,000 and owes the organization $50,000 at the end of the training program. The organization estimates at the end of the program that due to economic conditions it is unsure whether it can help place 100 percent of the trainees and estimates they will only be able to assist 75 percent in getting jobs. Since the organization already received $50,000 they should record a receivable for the balance and an estimated provision for uncollectible as follows.

Statements of Financial Position **(partial presentation)**	
Government grants receivable	50,000
Less: allowance for uncollectible grants	(25,000)
Net government grants receivable	25,000

Accounts Receivable   Most commercial enterprises on the accrual basis of accounting have receivables from customers, clients, or patients incurred in the normal course of business. These are commonly called trade receivables. NFP organizations also typically have accounts receivable generated from their normal program activities. Program service revenue generated from program activities covers every type of service or product including:

- Medical services (hospitals, clinics, counseling)
- Rent (housing)
- Tuition fees (education, training)
- Access and attendance usage fees (museum, parks, recreation, government buildings, etc.)
- Day-care and child-care services
- Assessment and user fees (use of NFP facilities)
- Sales of products (museum store, T-shirts, program material such as DVDs and CDs)
- Membership fees, dues, chapter and subscription fees

- Advertising income
- Other services (legal assistance, advisory, etc.)

Most times membership in an organization or program is optional (i.e., not forced to be a member). A common mistake is to record a receivable when invoicing the member for the upcoming membership or subscription period (i.e., for next year). So, unless a payment is required as part of employment, union agreement, or is based on a signed agreement, income should not be recognized when the participant is invoiced and no receivable should be recorded.

Loans and Notes Receivable   Loans receivable are obligations to receive payments in the future. Although not always required under state law, they should be evidenced in writing. Notes receivable are similar to loans receivable in that they are obligations to receive payments in the future (lump sum or installments). The difference is that notes are supported and evidenced by a legal document. Notes receivable are commonly created from the sale of property, such as a building or other asset, or from lending money. Unless loaning money is a part of an NFP's mission, it should avoid lending money to any individual or entity. The biggest issue related to accounting for loans and notes receivable relates to recording interest. The treatment of interest will be covered when discussing notes payable later in this chapter.

Other Receivables (from Affiliates, Employees, Interest, and Dividends)
Other receivables cover all miscellaneous receivables not material enough to be separated with its own line on the statement of financial position. Other receivables include money due from

- Affiliates (e.g., chapters, subsidiaries, or sister organizations) for dues or for expenditures it made on the affiliate's behalf.
- Employees (e.g., salary advance, flexible spending accounts, loans).
- Interest and dividends earned but not received from investments (e.g., from a nonmatured Certificate of Deposit).

Transactional Flow—Receivables

As mentioned earlier, NFPs generate revenue mostly by performing program activities, providing goods or services, receiving contributions and government grants, and from earnings generated from investments. The first assumption we make about our sample organization, Job Training Now, Inc., is that it is on the full accrual basis of accounting. As such, we record revenue when earned or, in the case of contributions, when promised. We will use the term *customer* to be encompassing and include customers, clients, grantors, and contributors. We will now discuss the following four common revenue-generating NFP activities using our sample NFP, JTN, to demonstrate how revenue is reported:

- Program service revenue (training)
- Contributions
- Government grants (conditional grants based on making approved expenditures)
- Event income (tickets)

Since each accounting software program has a different place for entering data, we will use the generic term *module/area* to describe the place where the data is entered. It is also important to note that there are many different types of NFP organizations and program activities that generate revenue, and some require different or distinct accounting treatment (e.g., hospital, day-care, education institutions). So the examples in this book are not all-encompassing and are not applicable to every type of organization or situation.

Program Service Revenue Recording *program service* (training) *revenue* and receivables is very similar to recording service revenue at a commercial business. Commercial businesses call their normal receivables from their customers trade receivables. JTN sends trainers to companies to give a one-to two-week training course to train their low-skilled employees. Each week trainers complete a time sheet that specifies the amount of time they spent on each assignment (i.e., training job). Unfortunately they do not have an automated system for tracking time. At the end of each week, the director of training (program director) takes the information from each employee's time sheet and enters it into a Microsoft Excel spreadsheet. At the end of the month, the director prepares and mails invoices to each corporation where training was performed. A copy of the invoice is sent to the accounting department to be entered into the accounts receivable system.

At some point, one of the staff accountants takes all of the invoices and enters the information in their accounting software program in the module/area used for entering accounts receivable. Since information is tracked by customer, the customer is first accessed or created by name or number and then the amount due from them is entered. Although it appears that only one side of the accounting entry is being made, actually there is a balanced entry being made behind the scene (i.e., both a debit and a credit), as follows:

Recording $15,500 in Program Service Receivable—Behind-the-Scenes

	Debit	Credit
Accounts receivable (asset)	15,500	
Program service revenue		15,500

Contributions (Pledges) Revenue   As previously mentioned, the decision to recognize a pledge (i.e., promise to make a contribution) is a complicated one. We assume for our example an unconditional and unrestricted pledge made by Mr. Goode E. Guy for $5,000 and an unconditional pledge of $25,000 made by Ms. Rebecca S. Rich that is temporarily restricted for use in the future. The staff accountant in charge of receivables received an e-mail from the fund-raising department requesting that the pledges be recorded and he/she in turn enters the information into the accounting system as follows:

Recording $30,000 in Contributions Receivable—Behind-the-Scenes

	Debit	Credit
Contributions receivable (asset)	30,000	
Contributions—unrestricted (income)		5,000
Contributions—temp. restricted (income)		25,000

Government Grants Revenue   JTN receives two government grants from New York City. One in the amount of $1,400,000 (Grant 1) for job-training skills (office assistant, data entry), and the other (Grant 2) in the amount of $1,000,000 for general work skills (resume and general writing, interpersonal and conflict resolution). Earlier in this chapter we spoke about how the terms of the grant agreement dictate how the grant gets treated in the accounting system. For our example, if both grants awarded to the organization came with no conditions, then the grant provisions have characteristics similar to a contribution and, therefore, should be recorded as follows:

Recording $2,400,000 in Grants Receivable—Behind-the-Scenes

	Debit	Credit
Government grants receivable (asset)	2,400,000	
Grant income—unrestricted		2,400,000

If the provisions of both grants said that the organization must first pay for approved, budgeted expenses before receiving grant proceeds (expense reimbursement grants), then no entry would be made at the time the grants are awarded or approved. These types of grants are conditional, with the condition being that expenditure must first be made before receiving any money. Consequently, no entry is made until the expenditures are made. Let's say that the organization spends $185,000 on salaries and allocated rent and other expenses on the first grant, and $75,000 for similar expenses on the other grant. If the staff accountant was instructed to record these receivables, the entry would appear in the general ledger as follows:

**Recording $260,000 in Grants Receivable
(Expense-Reimbursement Type)—Behind-the-Scenes**

	Debit	Credit
Government grants receivable (asset)	260,000	
Grant income		260,000

Invoicing government agencies is a little different than just issuing an invoice for program services. Usually the NFP has to prepare and submit an agency-specific request form (their format) that requests grant proceeds. With expense reimbursement-type grants, some organizations record the receivable as soon as the expenditures are made and others wait until the request form is sent to the government agency.

Loans, Notes, and Other Receivables Loans, notes, and other receivable transactions occur less frequently at many NFPs and are typically entered through a general journal entry and not through the accounts receivable module/area of the accounting software. The biggest problem associated with this area is one of not reconciling the general ledger balances to the details. This is covered more at the end of this chapter.

Transactional Flow—Cash Receipts

Organizations receive funds in a variety of forms including cash, checks, credit-card charges credited to the bank, bank wire transfers, and transfers from investment brokerage accounts. Although electronic transfers are becoming more prominent, checks are still the most prevalent method for receiving contributions and paying for program goods and services. Typically checks are received by mail and given to the accounting department for processing. There are many different approaches to entering receipts, especially among organizations that receive a large number of checks for a variety of functions or purposes. Although recording a check into the accounting system is relatively easy, many complications arise in practice. Some typical complications include the following:

- Poorly worded or nonexistent description of what the check is for.
- Check covering different income items but specific identification is unclear (e.g., membership dues and contributions or event tickets, contributions and publications).
- Corporation paying an individual's receivable or vice versa, or an individual (parent) paying for another individual's (child's) receivable.

After checks are deposited into an organization's bank account, the bank deposit slip, along with supporting documentation (e.g., copy of checks), are given to the accounting department to enter into the accounting system. When the receipt relates to an item previously recorded as a receivable, the staff accountant enters the information in the accounting software program in the module/area used for entering cash receipts (typically accounts receivable, customer, or tasks). Because receivables are maintained by customer name or number, payments received are also entered by customer name or number. Again, although it appears that only one side of the accounting entry is being made, a balanced entry is actually being made. The following is a behind-the-scenes example of recording cash receipts where a receivable was previously recorded:

Recording $390,000 in Cash Receipts—Behind-the-Scenes

	Debit	Credit
Cash (asset)	390,000	
Accounts receivable (asset)		(390,000)

Many times checks are received for something that was not previously entered as a receivable. Some people first create a receivable and then enter the cash receipt, whereas others bypass the receivable area entirely and record the cash receipts as follows:

	Debit	Credit
Cash (asset)	390,000	
Program service revenue (income)		85,000
Contributions—unrestricted (income)		125,000
Grants income		180,000

Transactional Flow—Other Accounts Receivable and Cash Issues

Accounts Receivable Reversals and Credits   Many times a receivable will not be collected or the amount received is less than the amount owed. When this happens, an adjustment has to be made to the accounting records. There are a number of ways to do this in practice. Some enter a credit memo/refund. A credit memo or refund is a reverse invoice. It has the opposite effect of entering an invoice and is entered in the accounts receivable module/area of the accounting software under the heading of credit memo or refund or similar wording. A $1,500 credit to Customer ABC Corp., would appear as follows:

	Debit	Credit
Program service revenue (income)	1,500	
Accounts receivable (asset)		1,500

The effect is to wipe out part of the receivable and associated revenue. This is the best method for recording a credit or refund. However, some accountants will simply void or erase the original entry and create and enter another invoice with the revised amount. This is not the best way to record this transaction because you lose track of what actually happened (i.e., *lose the trail*). Another method for recording the credit is to enter the credit transaction as a general journal entry and not enter it through the accounts receivable module/area. This is not a good method because all accounting software programs produce some kind of accounts receivable *open invoice report*, and if the credit is not made through the accounts receivable module/area, the receivable amount will still appear as open (i.e., not received) and the open invoice report will be incorrect.

Reclassifications, Adjustments, and Miscellaneous Transactions   Even when an organization uses its accounting software optimally (i.e., processing everything through its receivable module/area), there still will be a need to make a number of general journal entries that affect cash and receivables each month. Typical general journal entries related to receivables and cash receipts include the following:

- Reclassifications (cash recorded in incorrect bank account, reclassified to correct bank account).
- Any unrecorded transactions listed on the bank statement and bank reconciliation, such as bank charges and fees, bank wire transfers, and bank interest earned.

Prepaid Expenses, Inventory, and Collections

Accounting Concepts—Prepaid Expenses

Prepaid expenses are payments currently made for expenses that apply to a future year (hence, prepaid). Since the theory of accrual accounting is to match expenses incurred to the income generated, expenses paid in advance are not current-year expenses and should not be included on the statement of activities. As such, they are recorded on the statement of financial position as prepaid expenses. They are subsequently reclassified as an expense in the period they relate to. Common examples of prepaid expenses include the following:

- Prepaid insurance, rent, or taxes
- Prepaid consulting or other fees (e.g., down payments)
- Salary advances

Many times, there is disagreement about whether a transaction should be recorded as a prepaid expense. Sometimes this is because the transaction is ambiguous, and other times it is due to ignorance or misapplication of accounting rules. For example, a consultant requires a retainer (advanced payment) in December 2009 for consulting work to be performed the following January 2010. This is a prepayment and should be recorded as a prepaid expense in calendar year 2009 because the organization will not receive the services until 2010.

Transactional Flow—Prepaid Expenses

If an organization is utilizing its accounting software system properly, all expenses will be entered through its accounts payable module/area. Typically then, a portion or all of the expense must be reclassified through a general journal entry. For example, let's say the organization pays the consultant a $5,000 retainer in December 2009 for consulting work to be performed in 2010, and pays the annual directors, and officers, insurance premium of $6,000 in March 2009, covering the period March 1, 2009 through February 28, 2010. Assuming that both payments for the consultant and the insurance were initially recorded as expenses in the current year, the entry to adjust the expense accounts and record prepaid expenses is as follows:

Recording $5,000 (consulting) and $1,000 (insurance) of Prepaid Expenses

	Debit	Credit
Prepaid Expenses (asset)	6,000	
Professional fees (expense)		5,000
Insurance expense		1,000

The prepaid insurance expense was calculated by prorating two months of expense applicable to 2010 as follows:

$$\frac{\$6,000}{12} \times 2 \, \text{months (Jan} - \text{Feb)} = \$1,000$$

As with everything else, if the prepayment is so small that it is immaterial, it is not necessary to make any allocations to prepaid expenses. Also, an adjustment is not necessary when insurance premiums are paid on a monthly basis.

Accounting Concepts—Inventory

Inventories play a big role with retail, wholesale, and manufacturing enterprises but not with many public charities or other service-oriented NFPs, so we will not spend too much time on this area. Types of inventories that some nonmanufacturing NFPs might have are as follows:

- Donated materials including donated auction items.
- Items purchased that are sold to the public (e.g., museum/cultural institution store products).
- Items purchased to be used in performing program activities such as medical supplies at hospitals or books for educational institutions.

Transactional Flow—Inventory

The accounting treatment for inventory varies depending on whether the inventory was purchased or donated. If purchased, inventory is recorded at cost and *capitalized*, meaning it is recorded as an asset until it is sold or used, and then reclassified as an expense. For example, say the organization purchased a number of items for a future auction at one of its events and pays for it immediately (i.e., no accounts payable), the resulting accounting entry is:

Recording Inventory Purchased Costing $2,500

	Debit	Credit
Inventory (asset)	2,500	
Cash (asset)		2,500

If inventory is donated, it is recorded at its *fair value* in the period received and also capitalized. For example, a board member donates a valuable signed autographed football. The fair-market value of the football at time of donation is $50,000 even though it only cost the board member $5,000 twenty years ago to buy it (note, this is very advantageous to the board member as a personal tax deduction). The resulting accounting entry is:

Recording Inventory Donated Valued at $50,000

	Debit	Credit
Inventory (asset)	50,000	
Contribution income		50,000

Inventory remains as an organizational asset until it is sold. Using our preceding example, the organization has a fund-raising event where it auctions off all of the items it purchased and had donated. The entry to record this transaction is:

Recording Sale of the $100,000 in Inventory Purchased and Donated

	Debit	Credit
Cash (asset)	100,000	
Auction sales (income)		100,000

Cost of auction sales (expense)	52,500	
Inventory (asset)		52,500

Collections

What are collections? SFAS 116 *Accounting for Contributions Received and Contributions Made* defines collections as works of art, historical treasures, or similar assets that are:

- Held for exhibition to the public, for educational purposes, or for research in furtherance of public service and not financial gain.
- Protected, cared for, and preserved.
- Subject to a policy requiring any proceeds from the sale of collection items to be reinvested in other collection items.

There are three acceptable methods for accounting for collections that an NFP can use. Once adopted, the accounting treatment must be used consistently from year to year. These three methods are:

1. Capitalize all collection items.
2. Capitalize no collection items.
3. Only capitalize collection items acquired after adopting SFAS #116 (June, 1993).

Method 1—Capitalize All Collection Items   In this method all purchased or donated collection items are *capitalized,* that is, recorded as an asset. The amount recorded is either the *cost* if purchased or *fair value* (FV) if donated. It should be kept in mind that there is an obvious bias on the part of the donor to value their donation very high for tax-deductibility purposes. But fair value should be determined objectively, such as through quoted market price, purchase price of similar collection items, or appraisal. Unless immaterial, collections should be reported as a separate line item on the statement of financial position under one of the following headings: *collections, collectible items, art or museum collections,* and so forth.

Method 2—Capitalize NO Collection Items   Instead of capitalizing collections as an asset, collections can be reported on the statement of financial position with no amount but with a reference to see notes to financial statements. Example:

Collections   (see notes) $ —

If collection items are purchased, the expense would be included on statement of activities and reported at the bottom of the statement after all support and revenue and expenses as follows:

Museum, Inc. Statement of Activities (partial presentation)	
Support and Revenue:	
Contributions	900,000
Grants	100,000
Total support and revenue	1,000,000
Total Expenses	575,000
Less: Collections purchased	**(250,000)**
Increase in unrestricted net assets	175,000

Method 3—Capitalize Only Those Acquisitions Purchased after Adopting SFAS 116 Because it was too burdensome to go back and ascertain the value of collections acquired before 1993, a third method is allowed where only post-SFAS 116 acquisitions will be capitalized. In this case a hybrid method is used, combining both methods just mentioned.

GAAP also requires that certain information about collections be disclosed in the notes to financial statements. These include:

- Accounting policy for recognizing collection items.
- If not capitalizing or not capitalizing before SFAS 116, a description and fair value of the collectibles.

Investments

Accounting Concepts—Investments

The term *investments* is a very broad and general term. When many people think of investments they think of stocks (equity securities) and bonds (debt securities). But investments are much more. They also include other income producing assets such as real estate, mortgage notes, interest in partnerships and limited liability companies, and ownership in nonpublic corporations (subsidiaries, etc.) There is a common misconception that NFPs cannot own shares of another entity. This is not true as long as the investment activities don't become a significant or prominent activity of the NFP organization.

A number of years ago there was a great deal of confusion about the proper way to account for NFP investments, with some organizations following the same rules that commercial enterprises did, whereas others used a modified approach. To provide uniformity in the treatment of investments held by NFP organizations, the FASB issued SFAS 124 *Accounting for Investments Held by Not-for-Profit Organizations* in November 1995. This statement affects investments in equity securities (i.e., stocks) with readily determinable fair values and all investments in debt securities (i.e., bonds). Although GAAP generally requires that assets be recorded and maintained on the cost basis, SFAS 124 modified this basic GAAP tenet and required that these securities be measured at their fair value, because values of these securities are objective and readily available (e.g., current sales prices available on security exchanges).

For many NFPs, especially smaller ones, accounting for investments is not a problem. However, for many larger NFPs or those with sizable investments, accounting for investments can be very complicated. NFP investment accounting can become complex because many times investments have to be separated by restrictions placed on their use or the use of earnings received from those investments. Other times various investments are pooled together into a single investment fund or portfolio but components of the fund must be separately tracked and reported. In this chapter we will discuss components of a simple investment portfolio consisting of equity and debt securities. In Chapter 10 we will cover more complicated issues, such as pooled funds, split-interest agreements, and ownership in other entities.

Investment Components or Elements   Seven major investment components or elements to consider with regard to investments are the following:

1. Acquisition value (cost if purchased or fair value if donated).
2. Current fair value (listed value of investment at a particular point in time).
3. Unrealized gains and losses (change in fair value from one point in time to the next).
4. Realized gains and losses (difference between sales price and carrying cost of investment).
5. Other investment earnings (interest and dividends).
6. Investment expenses such as broker fees from sales of securities, performance fees, and custodial fees.
7. Allocating and properly recording investment income as unrestricted, temporarily restricted, or permanently restricted, based on donors' stipulations.

Transactional Flow—Investments

Recording Acquisition of Securities   Recording the acquisition of equity or debt securities through purchase or donation is pretty straightforward.

Recording the $50,000 Purchase of Equity or Debt Securities

	Debit	Credit
Investments (asset)	50,000	
Cash (asset)		50,000

Recording Receipt of $200,000 in Donated Equity or Debt Securities

	Debit	Credit
Investments (asset)	200,000	
Contributions—unrestricted (income)		200,000

If the donor places a restriction on the use of the investments, the contribution income would be recorded as contributions—temporarily restricted or as contributions permanently restricted.

Change in Value and Recording Unrealized Gains and Losses   GAAP requires that NFPs report their investments in marketable securities at fair value. As such, NFPs need to adjust their accounting records at least once a year (if not more frequent) to account for the change in value of these investments. This gain or loss resulting from the change in value is then included in current operations and reported on the statement of activities. The following example will illustrate. Let's say on December 31, year 1, the organization has marketable securities worth $82,500, and on December 31, year 2 the value on the stock exchange is $95,700. The organization would make the following entry to reflect the change in value as follows:

Recording $13,200 in Changed Fair Value of Investments (using only 1 investment account)

	Debit	Credit
Investments (asset)	13,200	
Unrealized gain on investments (income)		13,200

There are two acceptable methods of reporting the current fair value of investment assets on the statement of financial position. The first is to record all changes to only one account called investments (as just shown), and the second is to track all fair value changes in investments from historic cost value in a separate account called *allowance for unrealized gains and losses.* The following illustrates this method:

Recording $13,200 Change in Fair Value of Investments (using a separate allowance account)

	Debit	Credit
Allowance for unrealized gains and losses (asset)	13,200	
Unrealized gain on investments (income)		13,200

Recording Realized Gains/Losses (i.e., Earnings/Losses from Sales) Using the following example, we will demonstrate recording a realized gain from the sale of stock assuming the organization uses an allowance account to track changes in investment values. You will notice that the realized gain is calculated on the difference between the investment's sales price ($99,000 in year 3) and the carrying value (most recent value as of year 2).

Year 1 Purchase price $82,500 (660 shares at $125 per share)

Year 2 Fair value $95,700 (660 shares at $145 per share)

Year 3 Sales price $99,000 (660 shares at $150 per share)

	Debit	Credit
Cash (asset)	99,000	
Investment (asset – historical cost)		82,500
Allowance for unrealized gains or losses (asset)		13,200
Realized gain on sale of investments (income)		3,300

Investments Disclosure Certain disclosures related to investments are required to be made in accordance with GAAP. A typical disclosure would be found in the first section of the notes to financial statements as follows:

Job Training Now, Inc.
Notes to Financial Statements
(partial presentation)

Nature of Activities and Summary of Significant Accounting Policies:

Investments: The organization carries investments in marketable securities with readily determinable fair values and all investments in debt securities at their fair values in the statements of financial position. Unrealized gains and losses are included in the change in net assets in the accompanying statements of activities.

(Continued)

(*Continued*)

> Investment income and gains restricted by donors are reported as
> increases in unrestricted net assets if the restrictions are met (either
> a stipulated time period ends or a purpose restriction is accomplished)
> in the reporting period in which the income and gains are recognized.

In addition, SFAS 124 *Accounting for Certain Investments Held by Not-for-Profit Organizations* requires components of investment returns be disclosed on either the face of the statement of financial position or in the notes. To reduce crowding on the face of the statement, it is suggested that this information be put in the Notes to Financial Statements as the following illustrates:

Job Training Now, Inc.
Notes to Financial Statements
(partial presentation)

The Organization's investments are stated at fair value and consist of the following at December 31, 2010 and 2009:

	2010	2009
Mutual Fund	$ 25,000	$ 20,700
Stock	180,000	204,300
Total Investment (at fair value)	$ 205,000	$ 225,000

The Statements of Activities summarize the investment return for the years ended December 31, 2010 and 2009 as follows:

	2010	2009
Interest/dividend income	$ 11,000	$ 8,700
Gains and losses	12,000	11,300
Less investment expense	(3,800)	(2,100)
Total investment income	$ 19,200	$ 17,900

Other Investment Issues   There are a number of other accounting issues related to investments, such as accounting for restrictions, pooled investment funds, and split-interest agreements. These will be covered in Chapter 10.

Property and Equipment, Depreciation, and Other Assets

Accounting Concepts—Property and Equipment

The property and equipment (P&E) category covers many types of assets, and its significance will vary depending on the type of NFP organization and type of activities. For example, some organizations rent facilities, whereas others typically own the space they operate from, which is the case with educational and cultural institutions, hospitals, and religious organizations. Many organizations will only have office equipment consisting of a few computers and monitors, whereas those that manufacture goods will own millions of dollars worth of equipment. Those NFPs that provide recreational activities (camps and parks), distribute food or clothes, or service the elderly will have significant transportation equipment (i.e., vehicles), whereas most others will have none.

P&E can be broken down into two major categories—tangible and intangible. *Tangible* assets are those assets with some physical substance and include the following:

- Buildings and land
- Equipment (office equipment, production equipment)
- Computer equipment (hardware and software)
- Autos and other transportation vehicles
- Office furniture and fixtures
- Leasehold improvements (improvements to rented property)

Intangible assets are assets with no physical substance and are not prevalent in most NFPs except scientific, research, and literary organizations. Intangible assets include patents, copyrights, trademarks, and goodwill.

There are a number of accounting issues that must be considered with regard to P&E and these include the following:

- Classification
- Materiality and valuation (amount to record)
- Depreciation method
- Capital leases treatment
- Disposal

Classification Probably the single largest issue that arises regarding P&E is the decision about whether to capitalize (record as an asset and depreciate over a number of years) or expense in the year acquired. This issue is more important with commercial entities because how P&E is classified can significantly affect income-tax liabilities. Because most NFPs do not pay income tax, except on unrelated business activities (covered later in this book), a common question is, Why should NFPs be concerned with classification issues and not just expense all P&E in the year acquired? The answer is because property and equipment has a useful life of more than a year and is used during its useful life to generate support and revenue, and, therefore, it is required under GAAP to be capitalized. So to properly match expenses to the revenue generated, all P&E of a certain value is capitalized and only a portion is expensed each year. This allocating of a portion of each P&E asset to current year's expenses is called depreciation.

Materiality and Valuation   Should every single P&E asset be capitalized? No. The cost in time of capitalizing and depreciating every asset would outweigh the benefits. Each organization needs to determine an appropriate threshold (materiality level) for capitalizing their P&E. For example, an NFP with total net assets of $1,000,000 could choose not to capitalize any acquired P&E under $500 (e.g., a computer monitor costing $350). However, if an organization purchases 15 monitors costing $350 each, it should total them together and capitalize $5,250. There is no absolute rule to capitalizing, but once an appropriate policy is determined it should be applied consistently each year.

Valuating P&E is very similar to inventory. If purchased, the asset should be recorded at purchase price plus all associated costs such as delivery, sales tax, and setup charges. If the asset is donated, it should be recorded at the assets current fair value.

Accounting Concepts—Depreciation and Accumulated Depreciation

According to GAAP, all NFPs are required to capitalize and depreciate long-lived assets except in certain cases such as certain works of art and historical treasures or as previously mentioned, if immaterial in value. The reason for depreciating is to spread the cost of an asset over the periods that benefit from its use. To depreciate assets, two main factors must be determined—an asset's estimated useful life and an acceptable depreciation method.

Assets are depreciated over a period of time called their estimated useful life. Simply put, this is the number of years an NFP expects the asset to be useful. Each asset's useful life depends on a number of factors including the type of asset and how vigorously it will be used. To reduce the necessity of estimating each asset's useful life, organizations typically group assets into major categories and depreciate the assets in each category over a set number of years. Once the estimated useful life is chosen, it should be applied consistently unless an asset has been significantly impaired. Typical P&E categories and their respective estimated useful lives are as follows:

- Computer equipment—3 or 5 years
- Office equipment—5 years
- Furniture and fixtures—7 to 10 years
- Buildings—20 to 30 years
- Leasehold improvements—over the life of the lease

GAAP recognizes two depreciation methods for allocating an asset's cost over the period it benefits. These depreciation methods are straight line

(SL) and accelerated. There are several accelerated methods, but the most common one used is called double-declining balance (DDB).

Straight line is the simplest to use; it takes the asset cost and divides it by the asset's useful life. For example, a copier costing $10,000 with a five-year estimated useful life would be depreciated under the SL method as follows:

$$\$10,000/5 \text{ (or 20 percent per year)} = \$2,000 \text{ depreciation expense each year}$$

The DDB method assumes that the asset is more productive in its earlier years and, therefore, more should be depreciated in the earlier rather than the later years. As such, twice the straight line rate is applied until the asset balance is zero. Using the same example, the depreciation expense for the copier in years one and two is as follows:

Year 1 : $\$10,000/5 \times 2$ (double or 40 percent per year) $= \$4,000$
Year 2 : $\$10,000 - \$4,000 = \$6,000/5 \times 2$ (double or 40 percent per year)
$$= \$2,400$$

Because the DDB method is more complicated and requires the organization to switch to the SL method at some point to fully depreciate the asset to zero, we will use the SL method in this book. An example of how to record depreciation expense is covered in the "Transactional Flow" section later in this chapter.

Rather than reduce an asset for the amount of depreciation expense taken each year, a separate account is used to track the accumulation of depreciation (hence the term *accumulated depreciation*). Accumulated depreciation is reported in one of two ways. Either on the face of the statement of financial position or in the notes to financial statements. In both cases, it generally appears directly under the property and equipment categories and shown as a negative amount. The following is an example of how accumulated depreciation is reported in the notes to financial statements:

Job Training Now, Inc.
Notes to Financial Statements
(partial presentation)

Property and equipment by major class consisted of the following at December 31, 2010 and 2009:

	2010	2009
Office equipment	$ 80,136	$ 75,301
Furniture and fixtures	21,000	18,700

(*Continued*)

(*Continued*)

Vehicles	25,000	25,000
	126,136	119,001
Less: accumulated depreciation	**(10,136)**	**(10,001)**
	$116,000	$109,000

Capital Leases Treatment   Understanding what a capital lease is and how to account for it confuses a lot of people. Let's start by explaining the difference between a capital lease and an operating lease. Operating leases are basically rental agreements (e.g., rent office space). Capital leases, on the other hand, are leases (or rental agreements) in which the purchaser is actually purchasing the asset despite the fact that the agreement is called a lease agreement instead of a purchase agreement. The asset is treated as a purchase because by the end of the lease period most of the asset is *used up*. Since most lease agreements call for monthly payments to be made, a capital lease is treated as a purchase that is financed over a fixed number of years. To determine whether a lease should be treated as a capital lease, the agreement must be non-cancelable and have one of the following characteristics:

- Title (legal ownership) passes to the leasee at the end of the lease term.
- Leasee can purchase the asset at a bargain at the end of the lease term (for a nominal value such as a $1).
- Lease term is at least 75 percent of the asset's useful life (e.g., lease period is close to the asset's estimated economic life).
- Present value of lease payments equals or exceeds 90 percent of the asset's fair value.

An example of how to record a capital lease is covered in the "Transactional Flow" section in this chapter.

Disposal   When P&E is sold, the asset must be removed from the NFP's financial records. If the amount received is greater than the carrying value of the asset (i.e., the original cost less the accumulated depreciation or *adjusted basis*), then the organization would report a gain. Conversely, the organization would report a loss if the amount received is less than the carrying value. The organization would also report a loss on disposal if the asset is thrown out or given away and the carrying value is greater than zero. Examples of the sale of P&E are covered in the next section.

Transactional Flow—Property, Equipment, and Depreciation

Recording $25,000 Acquisition of P&E by Purchase or Donation   Recording P&E purchased for cash is pretty straightforward as follows:

	Debit	Credit
Equipment—Telephone (asset)	25,000	
Cash (asset)		25,000

Recording P&E that is donated is also pretty straightforward as follows:

	Debit	Credit
Equipment—Telephone (asset)	25,000	
Contribution (income)		25,000

Recording Depreciation   To demonstrate recording depreciation, we will assume the telephone equipment just mentioned has a five-year estimated useful life, the organization uses the straight-line method of depreciation, and the asset was purchased on January 1. We will ignore the application of what is called the half-year convention, which many organizations use, and we will calculate a full-year's depreciation in the first year as follows:

$$\$25,000/5 = \$5,000 \text{ per year}$$

	Debit	Credit
Depreciation Expense	5,000	
Accumulated Depreciation (contra asset)		5,000

Accumulated depreciation is called a contra account. Contra accounts are treated the opposite of other accounts in the same category, and in this case, it is a negative asset account.

Recording Capital Leases   To illustrate how to record a capital lease, let's say the organization enters into a lease agreement to lease a photocopier for five years. The terms of the lease call for paying $250 per month for 60 months and at the end of the lease the organization can purchase the machine for $100 (bargain purchase option). Since basically the organization is buying the photocopier, it should capitalize the asset and not expense the monthly lease payments. For simplicity sake, we will ignore calculating the *present value* of the 60 monthly payments. Present value is a concept in which a determination is made of the current worth today of money to be received (or paid) in the future.

First we calculate the fair value of the asset (again, ignoring present value and implicit interest) and then record the asset. Going forward, we would record the monthly lease payments and finally we would depreciate the asset as illustrated here:

Recording Capital Lease Initially:
$250 × 12 (months) × 5 (years) = $15,000

	Debit	Credit
Equipment—Photocopier (asset)	15,000	
Installment Notes Payable (liability)		15,000

Recording Monthly Lease Payments in Year 1:

	Debit	Credit
Installment Notes Payable (liability)	3,000	
Cash (asset)		3,000

Recording Annual Depreciation Assuming 5-Year Life:
($15,000/5 = $3,000)

	Debit	Credit
Depreciation Expense	3,000	
Accumulated Depreciation (contra asset)		3,000

Recording Disposal of P&E   At some point in every asset's life it must be disposed of because it is sold, destroyed by fire or some casualty, it is obsolete, or it simply is no longer productive. When the asset is disposed of, it must be removed from an organization's general ledger. If the asset is fully depreciated, the entry is very easy: the asset and accumulated depreciation accounts are simply reversed. However, if the asset is sold, there might be a resulting gain or loss from the sale. The following illustrates how to record the disposal of an asset when it is sold for less than its carrying value. Using the example of the telephone equipment mentioned earlier that was purchased for $25,000, let's say at the end of the fourth year the asset is sold for $2,000. The carrying value (*adjusted basis*) at that time is $5,000, calculated as follows:

Equipment—Telephone (asset)	$ 25,000
Less: accumulated depreciation ($5,000 × 4 years)	(20,000)
Carrying value (adjusted basis)	$ 5,000

The entry to record the sale of the telephone equipment for $2,000 is as follows:

	Debit	Credit
Cash (asset)	2,000	
Accumulated depreciation (contra asset)	20,000	

Loss on sale of asset (expense)	3,000	
Equipment—Telephone (asset)		25,000

Other Property and Equipment Points

Intangible Property   Intangible assets such as patents and copyrights are also capitalized and expensed over their estimated useful life. Instead of depreciating the asset, the allocations of costs are called amortization and the accumulated cost is called accumulated amortization. The calculation is similar to depreciation.

Government Grants   Sometimes a government grant will allow the NFP recipient to purchase equipment or other capital assets in accordance with their grant terms. Many NFPs must report actual expenditures compared to approved, budgeted expenses and want to report the purchase of the P&E as an expense to match the grant. If the amount of the expenditure is not material relative to its other assets, it is acceptable to expense the entire acquisition cost of the asset. For example, if the organization purchased five computers for a total of $10,000, it could expense this in the current year to better match the grant revenue with the approved expenditure. However, if the organization received $1 million from a government grant to purchase or improve a building, the proper treatment would be to capitalize the assets regardless of what the grant budget showed.

Other Assets

Security Deposits   Security deposits are required cash outlays that will be refunded at some point in the future. They are very similar to receivables but usually long term. Typical security deposits required to be made include rent, utilities, and equipment. The amounts are usually immaterial and lumped in with other assets

Other Assets   Other assets is a catch-all category whose content varies with each organization. It could include amounts due from an insurance company for a claim, temporary salary advances to an employee, or a refund from an overpayment. The total amount in other assets should be small relative to all other assets. This category should not be (although many times it is) used to bury or hide a transaction the organization does not wish to disclose, such as a large receivable from a terminated employee for an overpayment in salary.

Reconciliations

General

The word *reconciliation* scares nonaccountants and even accountants starting out in their profession. It sounds very technical, but it really isn't. It has a simple definition: "Reconciliation is the matching or comparing the details of two or more written statements, reports or listings and identifying all differences." When identified, differences or discrepancies should be investigated and explained. Reconciliations perform a very important function in every organization. Without it, errors can go undetected; money can go uncollected, lost or stolen; creditors can go unpaid, and financial activity can be misreported. Reconciliations perform an important internal control function and assist management in monitoring the organization's financial activities.

Cash in Bank

Overview Cash is usually the most important asset of any organization. For without it, an organization cannot operate. Cash is also the most vulnerable to manipulation because it is the most liquid (used as currency), most flexible, and many times the most accessible. In addition to restricting who can receive cash, deposit cash in the bank, or write and sign checks, one of the major ways that cash is protected is by preparing bank reconciliations on a timely basis, such as monthly. *Bank reconciliation* is the term used for comparing information reported on a bank (or other financial institution) monthly statement to the information entered in a organization's general ledger. If bank reconciliations are not performed on a timely basis, errors won't be discovered and corrected (e.g., customer deposited check bounced) or the misuse of funds might not be detected (e.g., forged checks).

In theory, preparing a bank reconciliation is straightforward and easy. The theory of how to do a bank reconciliation is taught in every introductory accounting class from high school through graduate school. Beginning accounting students are taught about deposits in transit, outstanding checks, and bank charges, but they usually lack the practical training to actually perform a bank reconciliation at their job because of real-world complications not taught in school and not anticipated. These complications include accounting for disbursements when an outside payroll service is used, working with bank statements with ending dates that are different from the organization (e.g., June 19–July 18), and trying to match receipts from credit cards that do not provide a breakdown and include credit-card processing fees. So the actual procedure for performing a bank reconciliation is usually learned on the job after a number of months of trial-and-error mistakes. Since bank reconciliations are so important for every organization, we will spend a little time in this book discussing some suggestions for improving their preparation.

Problem Everyone who performs a bank reconciliation has their own method for doing it. If the method works, great. No need to do anything different. But if there is difficulty reconciling the numbers or it takes an unusually long period to complete the task, there is a fundamental problem, and a change in the procedure is necessary. Let's start with the statement that is often made when someone has a problem: "The numbers don't reconcile." This is almost impossible. Unless there is a computational or report-generation problem with the bank or the organization's computers (computer bug), and the totals reported do not agree with the details (rare but possible), the preparer has all the information necessary to compare the two sets of finite numbers. The preparer might not know what the reason is for the difference between the two reports, but the fact that some number appears on one and not the other is definitely ascertainable. It is the author's opinion that one of the biggest reasons for not being able to reconcile a bank statement to the general ledger is because the preparer stops in the middle of the reconciling process to try to understand why there is an unidentified difference and loses track of the steps he or she has already completed. The result is confusion and then the preparer states, "*The bank reconciliations don't reconcile.*" The best way to complete a bank reconciliation is to methodically perform a number of specific procedures, identify all differences, and then go about analyzing and explaining the differences.

Procedure First we will assume that there are no computer problems and the totals and balances are correct on both the bank statement and the organization's general ledger. We also assume that the organization uses the services of an outside payroll-service company to handle its payroll.

Step 1: Lay all required documents out on a desk or table including the following:
- Last month's bank statement and bank reconciliation worksheet.
- Current month's bank reconciliation worksheet.
- Current month's bank statement (if bank uses a different period, both bank statements containing the current month's activity).
- Monthly payroll summary report if using an outside payroll service company (e.g., ADP).
- Printout of general ledger cash account with current month's detail transactions.

Step 2: Put the checks returned with the bank statement in numerical order. This might not be possible because many banks today no longer return the organization's checks with the bank statements. This isn't a problem as long as they provide a separate list on the statement showing the checks that cleared (deducted from the bank account) in numeric order. If this is not provided, it becomes more difficult to compare the checks listed on the statement with the checks listed in the general ledger since the checks listed in the general ledger almost always are listed in numeric order. Not to worry, many banks will provide a list of cleared checks in numeric order for a small fee, and it is well worth the fee to get it.

Step 3: Confirm that all outstanding items on the prior month's bank reconciliation were posted to either the bank statement or to the general ledger in the current period. If not, note all differences on current bank reconciliation.

Step 4: Compare (check off) all bank deposits and additions on the bank statement to the general ledger. Note all dollar differences on the bank reconciliation. **Do not try to find out the reason for the difference at this point**.

Step 5: Compare (check off) all bank checks and withdrawals on the bank statement to the general ledger. Note all dollar differences on the Bank Reconciliation.

Step 6: Compare (check off) the total amount disbursed for payroll and payroll taxes reported on the payroll service report to the total amount reported in the general ledger and on the bank statement. Note all outstanding checks and other differences on the bank reconciliation.

Step 7: Examine the bank statement for all unchecked items. Note the missing items on the bank reconciliation (e.g., outstanding checks, deposits in-transit, unrecorded bank charges, etc.).

Step 8: Examine the general ledger for all unchecked items. Note the missing items on the bank reconciliation.

Step 9: Go to the bank reconciliation and add or subtract all reconciling items. The ending numbers should agree (see sample bank reconciliations in the section that follows).

There are a number of common reasons that the ending numbers on a bank reconciliation do not tie or agree. These include:

- Dollar difference between deposits, additions, withdrawals, or check amounts were missed and not identified.
- Reconciling amounts on the bank reconciliation were *transposed* or reversed (e.g., amount written was $45 but should have been $54).
- Omitted a reconciling (difference) item on the bank reconciliation, such as an outstanding check or bank charge for insufficient funds.
- Net payroll doesn't tie to bank statement (payroll, payroll taxes, or employee withholdings are not properly accounted for in the general ledger).
- Credit or charge-card transactions are not properly accounted for in the general ledger.

Format There are a number of worksheet formats used to do a bank reconciliation. All are acceptable methods. There is the popular bank to general ledger (G/L) format, the general ledger to bank format used by many auditors, the general ledger to bank with current activity format, and the author's preferred format, which is the multicolumn format. All four formats are illustrated next:

Bank to General Ledger (G/L) Format

Job Training Now, Inc. Cash Operating A/C - Bank Reconciliation December 31, 2009	
Bank balance - 12/31/09	$ 99,200.50
Timing Differences:	
Plus - Deposits in-transit	5,250.00
Minus - outstanding checks	(10,100.00)
Adjustments:	
Bank charges & fees	10.00
Interests income	(5.50)
Recording errors	100.00
Adjusted G/L balance - 12/31/09	$ 94,455.00

General Ledger (G/L) to Bank Format

Job Training Now, Inc. Cash Operating A/C - Bank Reconciliation December 31, 2009	
G/L balance - 12/31/09	$ 94,455.00
Timing Differences:	
Less - Deposits in-transit	(5,250.00)
Plus - outstanding checks	10,100.00
Adjustments:	
Bank charges & fees	(10.00)
Interests income	5.50
Recording errors	(100.00)
Adjusted G/L balance - 12/31/09	$ 99,200.50

General Ledger (G/L) to Bank Format with Current Activity

Job Training Now, Inc. Cash Operating A/C - Bank Reconciliation December 31, 2009	
G/L balance - 12/1/09 (beginning)	$ 75,755.00
Plus deposits and additions in Dec.	35,600.00
Minus withdrawals and subtractions in Dec.	(16,900.00)
G/L balance - 12/31/09 (ending)	94,455.00
Timing Differences:	
Less - Deposits in-transit	(5,250.00)
Plus - outstanding checks	10,100.00
Adjustments:	
Bank charges & fees	(10.00)
Interests income	5.50
Recording errors	(100.00)
Adjusted G/L balance - 12/31/09	$ 99,200.50

Multicolumn Format

Job Training Now, Inc. Cash Operating A/C - Bank Reconciliation December 31, 2009		
	General Ledger	**Bank**
Ending balance - 12/31/09	$ 94,455.00	$ 99,200.50
Timing Differences:		
Plus - Deposits in-transit		5,250.00
Minus - outstanding checks		(10,100.00)
Adjustments:		
Bank charges & fees	(10.00)	
Interests income	5.50	
Recording errors	(100.00)	
Adjusted ending balance - 12/31/09	$ 94,350.50	$ 94,350.50

Accounts Receivable (A/R)

As discussed earlier in this chapter, most revenue-related transactions are entered into an organization's accounting system through the accounts receivable (A/R) module/area. By entering data into the system this way, certain important reports can be generated such as an open receivable report (unpaid invoices listing by customer) and an aged receivable report (unpaid invoices grouped into 30-day periods such as 30–60–90 days). In order to ensure that all appropriate detail is being accounted for, the totals on the A/R detail reports should be periodically compared (reconciled) to the total in the A/R general ledger account. Why would the total amounts be different than the details? Not all transactions were entered into the accounting program through the A/R module/area and, therefore, would not show up on the detailed A/R reports. Instead, a number of entries were entered into the system by making a general journal entry, which does not appear on the detailed A/R reports. Many times the general journal method of entering data is used because of lack of familiarity with the accounting program, such as not understanding how to enter a credit memo. Typical general journal entries include: changes in amounts owed from customers (adjustments), corrections to errors, and writing off uncollectible receivables. A/R reconciliations should be performed periodically and preferably monthly.

CHAPTER

Liabilities and Net Assets—
Concepts and Data Flow

Liabilities, as previously defined, are organizational obligations—something the organization owes to another entity. Liabilities are listed on the statement of financial position according to their nearness to maturity or need to be satisfied with cash. For example, amounts owed to vendors (i.e., accounts payable) would be listed first because they are usually paid within a number of months. The most common NFP liability categories include the following:

- Accounts payable
- Accrued liabilities
- Loans and notes payable
- Deferred revenue
- Refundable advances
- Other liabilities (e.g., scholarship payable, due to employees)

Accounts Payable and Accrued Expenses

Accounting Concepts—Accounts Payable

Accounts payable is defined as "obligations to pay for goods and services that have been acquired on open account." Processing accounts payable is one of the most basic tasks performed by the accounting department of every NFP organization. This is also one of the most understood and least complicated areas of accounting, because most people, even non-accountants, understand the concept of paying for goods and services on a timely basis. GAAP requires NFPs to maintain their accounting records on the accrual basis of accounting, which calls for recognizing all liabilities when incurred rather than when paid. At what point is a vendor invoice a liability?

When the organization is legally liable for the obligation. However, this is not always clear. Should it be?

- The date the invoice is prepared (i.e., invoice date).
- The date the invoice is received.
- The due date stated on the invoice.
- When purchases are shipped.
- When purchases are received.
- When a prepayment is required.

In most cases, the decision which policy to follow to record the liability will not be material as long as the organization is consistent and vendors receive their payments in a reasonable period of time consistent with normal business practices. Most problems arise at year end when incorrectly recognizing or not recognizing expenses could have a significant impact on the organization's bottom line (i.e., net income) for the year. The reasons vendor invoices are not recorded in the proper period varies. Some of these include the following:

- Inconsistency with applying vendor due dates (mentioned earlier).
- Not receiving vendor invoices on a timely basis (e.g., many months after the year is closed out).
- Recording nonincurred vendor liabilities to better match grant revenues and expenditures (this is understandable but not correct because products or services have not been received and no legal liability has been incurred).

Transactional Flow—Accounts Payable (A/P)

General   Any organization recognizing a liability by recording a vendor bill when received or due (as opposed to when paid) is, by definition, maintaining their financial records on either a partial or full accrual basis of accounting. As we noted in our discussion of receivables, if an organization has a fully functional accounting software program, it is preferable to have all typical liabilities and subsequent payments to vendors go through the accounts payable (A/P) module/area of the accounting program. By entering data into the system this way, as opposed to entering data by making general journal entries, additional detailed reports can be generated. As with receivables, each accounting software program has a different place for entering this data. For our purposes, we will use the generic term A/P module/area to describe the place where the data is entered.

It is also important to mention again that there are many different types of NFPs; organizational structures; and operational policies, practices, and procedures. As such, the examples in this book are not all encompassing and are not applicable to every type of organization or situation. The following should be read in the context of an acceptable guide and not as an absolute requirement.

Scenario—A/P Document Processing System   Vendor bills are typically received through the mail. They can be addressed to a specific person (e. g., the initiator or other person requesting the goods or services) or to no one in particular. Depending on the organization's policy, they will either be given to the initiator or directly to the accounting department. If the organization's accounting policy requires the preparation of a *check request form,* a form would be prepared and approved by an authorized individual first before being given to the accounting department for processing (i.e., to be paid).

Once received, vendor bills (including approved check request forms) are put into a tray or folder, and then, at some point, the liability is entered into the accounting software's A/P module/area. Because the availability of cash is an issue for many organizations, the timing of paying vendor bills is an important matter. Ideally, all bills would be entered into the accounting system within a short period after being received and paid within 30 days or shortly thereafter for good vendor relations. In practice, cash availability dictates when bills are paid.

A typical process might be to enter, at the beginning of each week, all bills received and authorized to be paid from the previous week. Then, at the end of the week, print an *open payables* report. Then, based on available cash, decide which vendor bills are to be paid (or have to be paid), and generate checks.

After processing and paying vendor bills, all related documentation must be stored and maintained by the organization in accordance with required and necessary record-keeping policies. There are several methods used to store vendor bills and copies of check disbursements, such as the following:

- Smaller organizations (e.g., those generating < 30 checks per month) might set up 12 folders, one for each month, and store the vendor bills and the copy of the organization's check in check number order (which is usually also in date order).
- Larger organizations typically maintain a separate file folder for each vendor or a file for each major vendor and a miscellaneous file folder for all other vendors.
- Some organizations maintain a dual system of vendor file folders and files for copies of all checks disbursed, and maintained in chronological order.
- A very small number are now scanning and digitizing their documents and discarding the physical documents. The general consensus is that this will be the method all organizations will use to store documents in the future.

Accounts Payable Approval System A good internal-control system requires that certain steps be performed before buying or paying for any goods or services. Larger NFPs, with more employees and activities, are more likely to institute internal-control procedures than smaller NFPs. The following is a progression of procedures that an NFP could require to provide assurance that organization funds are properly managed and protected.

- **Purchase request for ordering supplies, and so forth**—Employees complete a purchase request form, attach all necessary support, and have it signed by an appropriate staff member (e.g., supervisor or manager) before any goods or services are purchased. In smaller organizations, employees ask the person responsible for ordering supplies or the president/ED for permission to buy something and then they just order it.
- **Receipt of goods or services**—Goods or services and vendor invoices are received.
- **Check requests**—Requestor prepares a check request form, attaches the vendor bill and purchase request form (if used), and has the form signed by an appropriate supervisor. Then all documents are forwarded to the accounting department for processing.
- **Generating and signing of checks**—Accounting department staff enters vendor bills into accounting software program, selects bills to pay, prints physical checks, and forwards them to an authorized person to review and sign.
- **Mailing checks**—Checks are placed in envelopes and mailed out.

Recording A/P

- We will assume for our example that the accounting department has entered three vendor invoices to be processed—one to Mr. D. Ell in the amount of $8,000 for computer consulting, the second to Bell Tele in the amount of $300 for telephone expenses, and the third to Larry the Landlord in the amount of $2,500 for office rent. A staff accountant would typically enter these payables by going into the Enter Vendor Bills/Invoices section in the A/P module/area and picking each vendor from a list and entering the appropriate amount due and any other necessary information. If these three entries are the only amounts entered, the entry recorded in the system would be as follows:

	Debit	Credit
Consultant (expense)	8,000	
Telephone (expense)	300	
Rent (expense)	2,500	
Accounts payable (liability)		10,800

Recording Cash Disbursements

Let's say, for illustration purposes, that the preceding three payables are the only payables that need to be paid. After all approvals for payment have been received, the staff accountant would go to the Pay Bills/Invoices section in the A/P module/area and pick the three bills to be paid and print out checks. The entry recording this transaction would be as follows:

	Debit	Credit
Accounts payable (liability)	10,800	
Cash (asset)		10,800

Transactional Flow—Other A/P Issues

Errors and Reclassifications   Errors are sometimes made even among the most conscientious employees, and transactions are sometimes recorded to the wrong expense account. Or, it is decided that a transaction would be better classified in a different account than originally entered. In these cases, an adjustment is required to reclassify (move) one or more amounts to a different general ledger account. This is typically done by making a general journal entry. For example let's say the vendor bill from Mr. D. Ell for $8,000, mentioned earlier, and originally recorded in consulting was really for computer repairs. A general journal entry would be made to record the following:

	Debit	Credit
Repairs (expense)	8,000	
Consultant (expense)		8,000

Allocations   A significant number of NFPs perform several programs in addition to management and general and fund-raising activities. Typically, expenses incurred are not identifiable to any specific program or activity at the time they are entered into the accounting system and must be allocated (split) to the appropriate area at some later point in time. Other times, expenses incurred are for multiple programs and activities (known as joint costs) and also must be allocated to the appropriate account at some point in time. A prime example of joint costs is salaries. Salaries paid to NFP staff who work on various programs, projects, grants, and events must be allocated either weekly, monthly, or annually to the appropriate general ledger expense account. Many other common expenses must also be allocated, such as payroll taxes, employee benefits, rent, telephone, postage, and delivery. A great amount of time is spent allocating and reclassifying expenses at most NFP organizations. Even when the accounting software is used optimally, paper schedules, Microsoft Excel, or other spreadsheets are used to track and allocate joint costs, especially salaries. Allocations and reclassifications are usually made through general journal entries. The following is an example where salaries and payroll taxes were originally recorded to management and general and must be allocated to the program functions:

	Debit	Credit
Salaries—Simulated on-the-job training program (expense)	250,000	
Payroll taxes—Simulated on-the-job training program (expense)	23,000	
Salaries—Corporate on-site training program (expense)	85,000	
Payroll taxes—Corporate on-site training program (expense)	7,200	
Salaries—Management and general (expense)		335,000
Payroll taxes—Management and general (expense)		30,200

Accounting Concepts—Accrued Expenses

General Many people, even nonaccountants, understand the term *accounts payable* but don't have a clue what *accrued expenses* are. Accrued expenses (accrued liabilities) can be defined as estimated obligations (usually expenses) that have been incurred but aren't supported by a vendor bill or other documentation. Typical examples include the following:

- Payroll and related payroll taxes.
- Employee benefits such as vacation pay and severance pay.
- Interest payable on loans or notes payable.
- Partial or completed services received but those for which the organization hasn't received an associated bill, such as for professional or consulting services (computer, legal, and auditing).

Some organizations record accrued expenses as they would any other accounts payable (i.e., through the A/P module/area) even though there isn't an invoice. Other organizations record accrued expenses by way of a general journal entry, debiting some expense (legal fees) or asset (computer equipment) and crediting a separate liability account called accrued expenses. The problem with entering accrued expenses through a general journal entry is the possibility of entering the liability twice, the second time when the bill is actually received.

Some accrued expenses are not straightforward and must be calculated to determine the appropriate accrual amount (e.g., payroll, see the next section).

The calculation should be made in a rational and supportable manner. Many organizations don't make accrual entries during the year and only make them at year's end to ensure all required expenses are recorded in the proper year.

Transactional Flow—Accrued Expenses

Many organizations pay their employees on a biweekly basis (i.e., every two weeks) or semimonthly basis (twice a month on the fifteenth and thirtieth). If the end of the year falls in the middle of a payroll period, a calculation will need to be made to allocate a portion of the payroll to the appropriate year. For illustration, let's say JTN pays their employees on a biweekly basis that covers the pay period from Monday, December 28, 2009 through Sunday, January 10, 2010. The following calculation and accrual would be required:

Biweekly payroll = $12,400

$12,400/10 day (not 14 days) = $1,240 per day

$1,240 × 4 days (December 28 through December 31) = $4,960

Make a journal entry recording the $4,960 accrued payroll expense:

	Debit	Credit
Salaries (expense)	4,960	
Accrued Expenses (liability)		4,960

Loans and Notes Payable

Accounting Concepts—Loans and Notes Payable

What is the difference between a *loan payable* (L/P) and a *note payable* (N/P)? Both are a legal obligation to pay a specific sum of money at a specific period of time. A notes payable is a written promise to pay money at a future date. Loans or notes payable all have the following elements:

- A required amount to be repaid.
- Time period when money will be repaid (e.g., monthly or annually).
- Interest (if any) required to be paid in addition to the principal amount of debt.

Many loan or note payable agreements allow repayment (principal and interest) to be made in equal, monthly installments (i.e., installment loans). An example of how to record the note and installment repayment is shown in the following section.

Transactional Flow—Loans and Notes Payable

On December 1, JTN borrowed $24,000 from a bank to finance office renovations, with the amount going directly to the contractor. The bank requires the JTN's president to sign a note payable that states that the loan, along with 5 percent annual interest (compounded), must be paid back to the bank in equal, monthly installments over a period of five years. The monthly payment is calculated to be $452.91. The journal entry to record the $24,000 debt is as follows:

	Debit	Credit
Leasehold improvements (asset)	24,000	
Notes payable (liability)		24,000

On January 1, the installment payment of $452.91 is due. Many times an incorrect entry is made, reducing the N/P by the full amount of the payment (illustrated next). However, the payment includes an interest portion, which should be recorded as interest expense and remaining principal portion recorded in the N/P general ledger account.

Correct Recording of $452.91 Monthly Installment Payment

	Debit	Credit
Notes payable (liability)	352.91	
Interest expense	100.00	
Cash (asset)		452.91

Incorrect Recording of $452.91 Monthly Installment Payment

	Debit	Credit
Notes payable (liability)	452.91	
Cash (asset)		452.91

It should be noted that the monthly portion of principal and interest is determined based on calculating the present of future cash flows, known as the *present-value* method. A present-value table or Microsoft Excel software can be used to calculate the present value of future cash flows.

Deferred Revenue and Other Liabilities

Accounting Concepts—Deferred Revenue

What is *deferred revenue?* Simply put, it is receiving money in advance for providing goods or services in the future (i.e., received before it is earned). Basically, it is a timing issue. You will eventually earn the money as soon as you do something, which could be in a few months or in the next few years. Examples of money that might be received in advance include:

- Membership dues or publications fees received in advance.
- Tickets purchased in advance of event.
- Tuition fee or any other program service fee received in advance.
- Contract advance from a governmental agency.

Transactional Flow—Recording Deferred Income

Let's say JTN receives an advance payment in December 2009 from several corporations to perform on-site training of their employees in February, 2010.

Recording $50,000 Cash Receipts

	Debit	Credit
Cash (asset)	50,000	
Deferred revenue (liability)		50,000

Recording $50,000 Revenue Earned

Once the training is completed (in February 2010), the income can be recognized and the following entry made:

	Debit	Credit
Deferred revenue (liability)	50,000	
Program service revenue (income)		50,000

Accounting Concepts—Refundable Advances

What is a *refundable advance?* Basically, it is money that is received that might not be earned. Examples include the receipt of contributions that have a condition that might not be realized (e.g., NFP receives $1 million from a foundation to start a day-care center but must return the money if it doesn't obtain the necessary state permits and approvals; or an NFP receives a $100,000 donation from an individual to create a permanent endowment but must return the money if it doesn't raise an equal amount from other donors).

Transactional Flow—Refundable Advances

The entry required to record the receipt of the conditional donations from both the foundation ($1,000,000) and individual donor ($100,000) just mentioned is as follows:

	Debit	Credit
Cash (asset)	1,100,000	
Refundable Advance (liability)		1,100,000

Accounting Concepts—Contributions, Grants, and Scholarship Payable

Many NFPs have programs that provide subsidies in the form of cash to individuals for food, housing, transportation, and scholarships. If the organization makes a promise to contribute money to pay a scholarship but hasn't remitted the money by the end of the year, it must record a liability.

Transactional Flow—Grants and Scholarship Payable

Scenario: JTN has an incentive program for their top student of the year to receive a $5,000 scholarship to attend a community college. On December 20, 2009, the organization has selected a former participant in one of its training courses to receive the award. However it did not generate or mail out the check until January 10th of the following year. The organization should make the following entries:

Entry Made to Recognize the $5,000 Liability in December 2009

	Debit	Credit
Program scholarships (expense)	5,000	
Scholarships payable (liability)		5,000

Entry Made to Recognize $5,000 Payment Made in January 2009

	Debit	Credit
Scholarships payable (liability)	5,000	
Cash		5,000

Contingencies and Commitments

Accounting Concepts—Contingencies

What are *contingencies*? GAAP defines contingencies as "Uncertain, existing conditions that may create a possible benefit (i.e., gain) or a legal obligation in the future that are based on past transactions or events." The accountant must be aware that certain situations, activities, or events might have an effect on the current financial position, even though they will not occur until some future date. That effect might have financial consequences in the current period or just require a disclosure in the notes to financial statements, and in both cases (recognition or disclosure) the impact might be material.

The accounting and reporting of contingencies is dependent on various factors including whether the outcome will create a gain or a loss, the probability of the outcome occurring, and whether the dollar outcome of the contingency can be estimated. More specifically, these factors dictate whether an amount should be recorded on the organization's financial records, whether a descriptive disclosure should be added to the notes to financial statements, or a combination of both. The likelihood of the outcome (probable, possible, or remote) must be determined as well as an estimation of the monetary effect of the contingency. Therefore, there is a degree of subjectivity in making a determination. The following general rules apply with respect to contingencies:

- Contingencies that result in a *gain* should NOT be accrued. Under conservatism rules, contingent revenue shouldn't be recognized because it has not been earned until the future event has occurred. However, if material, it should be disclosed in the notes to financial statements.
- If the following two conditions exist, contingencies that can result in a *loss* should be accrued and recorded in the organization's general ledger by debiting an expense account and crediting a liability account:
  - Based on information available prior to issuing financial statements, it is *probable* that an asset has been impaired or a liability has been incurred.
  - The amount of the loss can be reasonably estimated.
- If either or both of these conditions are not met and it is reasonably *possible* that a loss will be incurred, information about the nature of the contingency and an estimate of the loss (or a range) should be disclosed in the notes to financial statements.
- If NO estimate can be reasonably made, the notes should reflect this.
- If likelihood is remote, do not accrue and do not disclose.

Typical loss contingencies include the following:

- Litigation, claims, or assessment threatened or pending (i.e., lawsuits). These types of contingencies usually require a legal opinion from an attorney.
- Unreimbursed loss due to a casualty (e.g., fire, flood, storm). Estimation of loss should exclude any estimated insurance reimbursements.
- Losses due to theft or a business closing. Included in this area are losses from the bankruptcies of banks and other financial institutions.

- Noncompliance with a donor or government grantor restriction on use of contributions. If an NFP does not comply with the restriction placed on the funds received, it might have to pay back some or all the money received, which might have to be accounted for or disclosed.
- Nonfulfillment of terms of government contracts (e.g., the organization did not achieve certain results or meet certain time or other requirements, such as train or service a minimum number of individuals, and, therefore, must return the money received).

Significant Risks and Uncertainties

GAAP requires an organization to disclose certain future situations or events that might have a material impact on the future operations of the organization (i.e., significant risks and uncertainties). The purpose of this disclosure is to provide the reader of financial statements with additional information about an organization. Without this, a prudent person would assume that the future results of operations would be similar to past operations and base their decisions accordingly. For example, if the NFP has offices in several locations, the closing of one of the offices in the future might have the effect of lost revenue and possible penalties for breaking a lease and write-off of leasehold improvements.

Many organizations have concentrations in areas of support or activities and as such are vulnerable to even a single loss in that area. For example, a loss of a major donor, government grantor, supporter, or discontinuation of a major program, activity, or event could significantly reduce income. Nonrenewal of important contracts or other agreements could greatly increase future expenses (e.g., expiration of below-market-rate office lease). Loss of rights (e.g., license, charter, etc.) could also have a major effect. Then there is the daddy of them all—the *going-concern* issue. If there is substantial doubt about whether the organization can meet its future obligations (i.e., pay all bills) without disposing of its assets or significantly curtailing its activities, it might be necessary to disclose this fact. Obviously this is a very sensitive issue faced by NFP accountants since the mere disclosure of a going-concern issue might actually precipitate, accelerate, or cause the demise of the organization. Who wants to donate money to an organization that might be closing, and what bank would want to loan that organization money? Great care should be taken in making this disclosure. However, this disclosure *cannot* be omitted if circumstances require it.

Accounting Concepts—Commitments

Commitments are contractual obligations that require a future expenditure. Disclosure of commitments might be required because of their effect on future changes in net assets. No amounts are accrued and recorded in the financial records, but the amount of the commitment and the period when payments will be made should be disclosed in the notes to financial statements. The following are some typical commitments that require disclosure:

- Long-term leases and bank loans that require payment over several years.
- Contracts with employees or outside contractors for services spanning several years.
- Agreements to make grants, contributions, or scholarship payments over several years.
- Agreements to purchase goods or any other long-term commitment.

Illustrative Disclosure in Notes to Financial Statements

The following are examples of disclosures for contingencies and commitments in the notes to financial statements.

Job Training Now, Inc.
Notes to Financial Statements
(partial presentation)

Contingencies:

Insurance coverage: The Organization maintains its bank accounts, money market funds, mutual funds, and certificates of deposit with financial institutions. The combined balances that exceed the Federal Deposit Insurance Corporation's (FDIC) and Security Industry Protection Corporation's (SIPC) insurance coverage are as follows:

	2010	2009
Institutional balances	$ 325,100	$ 571,412
Less: amount covered	(300,000)	(350,000)
Uninsured amounts	$ 25,100	$ 221,412

Commitments:

The Organization has several non-cancelable operating and capital leases for rent, office equipment, and software.
As of December 31, 2010, the minimum future aggregate annual rentals and lease payments for office space, equipment, and software are as follows:

Year ended	2011	$ 371,789
	2012	356,940
	2012	363,252
	2012	390,735
Thereafter		957,523
		$ 2,440,239

Net Assets

What are *net assets?* In the simplest terms, net assets are the difference between what an organization owns (its assets) and what it owes (its liabilities). GAAP (previously SFAS 117) requires that the net assets of NFPs be separated and classified within the following three categories: unrestricted, temporarily restricted, and permanently restricted. The amounts for these three categories are required to be reported on the face of the statement of financial position. Certain information is also required to be reported for temporarily restricted and permanently restricted net assets (see the JTN statement that follows). The amount of change in each category is required to be reported in the Statement of Activities.

It's important to note here that restrictions, by definition, can only be placed by an external party making the donation (i.e., donor restricted). It can't be internal. However, many NFP boards want to show their stewardship by imposing their own restriction on the use of their funds. These *board-restricted* funds should not be commingled with externally restricted funds since they are technically unrestricted, but they can be presented on a separate line in the statement of financial position, under unrestricted net assets, as follows:

Job Training Now, Inc.
Statements of Financial Position
(partial presentation)
December 31, 2010 and 2009

	2010	2009
Net Assets:		
Unrestricted		
General	$ 96,321	$ 536,588
Board restricted	50,000	50,000
Total unrestricted	146,321	586,588
Temporarily restricted	185,763	211,640
Permanently restricted	100,000	—
Total net assets	$ 432,084	$ 798,228

Illustrative Disclosure of Restricted Net Assets in Notes to Financial Statements

Job Training Now, Inc.
Notes to Financial Statements
(partial presentation)
December 31, 2010 and 2009

As of December 31, 2010 and 2009, contributions are restricted for the following activities:

	2010	2009
Temporarily restricted:		
Classroom training equipment	$ 150,600	$ 60,750
Training instructional material	35,163	50,890
Total	$ 185,763	$ 21,640
Permanently restricted:		
Endowment	$ 100,000	$ —

Reconciliations

Just as reconciliations are performed for certain asset accounts such as cash (bank reconciliations) and accounts receivable, reconciliations of certain liability accounts should also be performed to ensure that transactions are properly recorded and to provide a level of oversight. One of the main accounts that require analysis and reconciliation is A/P. As mentioned earlier, most vendor bills are entered through the A/P module/area of the accounting software. This allows the generation of various reports such as the open payables report (unpaid bills) and the A/P aging report. However, just as with accounts receivable, some transactions are entered as a general journal entry and not through the A/P module/area and, therefore, they will not show up on the detailed A/P reports. As such, in order to ensure that all appropriate detail is being accounted for, the totals on the A/P detail reports should be periodically compared (reconciled) to the total in the A/P general ledger account. By periodically comparing these reports, errors such as double posting (recording a transaction twice) or missing transactions can be discovered and corrected.

In addition to A/P, other liability account reconciliations should be periodically performed, such as employee *flexible benefits* accounts (e.g., medical savings) and employee contributory retirement accounts.

CHAPTER

8

Accounting for Support and Revenue

The *support and revenue* an organization earns within a discrete period of time (usually a year) is reported on the statement of activities. *Revenue* is something that is generated by engaging in some type of activity, such as selling goods or providing services (e.g., medical, educational, counseling, etc.). It can also be generated by receiving a return on some type of investment (e.g., investment income) or from gains created from incidental transactions or activities such as gains on the sale of equipment or investments. *Support* is income that is not generated through an exchange transaction (i.e., by providing a product or services). It includes contributions, grants, and contributed facilities and services.

Major categories for support and revenue for many NFPs are contributions, government grants, and program service revenue. A discussion of income generated from these activities was covered in Chapter 6, while discussing receivables. In this chapter we cover some additional material with regard to these activities, as well as other major categories including contributions in-kind, special events and auctions, membership dues, and investment income.

Contributions and Release of Restricted Funds

Accounting Concepts—Contributions

Contributions are defined as voluntary, unconditional transfers of assets to an entity (or cancelation of a debt). They are nonreciprocal. They can take the form of cash, nonmonetary tangible and intangible assets, and unconditional promises to give in the future. Many times, accounting for contributions is straightforward. Donations received or pledges made are recorded as cash or contributions receivable and contribution income. Problems surface when contributions have donor imposed restrictions, are conditional, or are combined with other income. Additional problems arise when the terms of the contribution are vague or convoluted or communicated orally and not documented. Organizations should make every attempt to clarify a donor's wishes to ensure compliance. One practice many NFPs do is to send a follow-up letter or e-mail thanking the donor for their contribution and stating the organization's understanding of donor's restriction or condition.

Classifying contributions properly is very important because misclassifying them can have a material effect on misreporting financial activities in the current and subsequent years (e.g., misclassifying a temporarily restricted contribution as deferred income and not recognizing the income in the current year). When income includes both contributions and other revenue, misclassifications can distort fair presentation of financial statements and other financial reports. A common example is the receipt of a combined payment for a fund-raising event (i.e., tickets) and a contribution. It is important to understand the difference between a contribution and an exchange transaction. Contributions, as recently stated, are nonreciprocal. Exchange transactions, on the other hand, are really purchases of goods or services and are not contributions.

GAAP requires that contributions be measured at fair value and reported in the period received or promised, even if the organization cannot use the funds until a future period because of a restriction placed on its use by the donor. Fair value is not always easy to ascertain especially when the donations are certain kinds of noncash assets (e.g., collectibles or antiques). Because most NFPs are not expected to be valuation experts, a third-party valuation (i.e., appraisal) should be sought to determine an appropriate value. Appraisals are also required by the IRS to substantiate tax deductibility by a donor. See Chapters 5 and 7 for examples on how to record unrestricted and conditional contributions.

Accounting Concepts—Agency Transactions

Some NFP organizations are set up or occasionally act as a go-between for a donor and the end-receiver or beneficiary of the contribution. In these cases, the NFP does *not* recognize the contribution as income but rather as liability.

Whether an NFP organization is an agent, a third-party beneficiary, or something in between, is not always clear-cut and can contain elements of both. For example, an NFP would recognize the receipt of funds as a contribution if it has the right to determine which organization to give the funds to (i.e., who the beneficiary is), if it can redirect the funds to a different beneficiary than the one named by the donor (power of variance), or if the NFP and the beneficiary are financially interrelated.

There are three participants in *agency transactions*—the resource provider (i.e., donor/contributor), the recipient organization (agrees to do something with the assets such as transfer or invest), and the specified beneficiary (recipient of funds). The recipient organization can be an *intermediary* (doesn't receive funds but acts as a broker or conduit), *trustee* (holds or manages assets for a beneficiary), or an *agent* (receives assets and agrees to use assets in accordance with donor's wishes for the beneficiary specified by the donor).

Many transactions appear to be agency transactions, but they aren't. For example, it is not an agency transaction when the transfer is revocable, or when the resource provider specifies itself or an affiliate as the beneficiary, or when the resource provider has variance power (previously mentioned) to redirect the funds to another beneficiary.

Accounting for Agency Transactions

If an NFP received $250,000 in funds as an agent, it would record the transaction as follows:

	Debit	**Credit**
Cash (asset)	250,000	
Due to beneficiary		250,000

If a portion of the funds received, say $50,000, does not qualify as agency funds because the NFP (recipient organization) has the right to redirect the funds to a recipient of their choice, then the transaction would be recorded differently, as follows:

	Debit	**Credit**
Cash (asset)	250,000	
Due to Beneficiary (liability)		200,000
Contribution income		50,000

Accounting Concepts—Restricted Contributions

As previously mentioned, donors can impose restrictions on how or when their donations can be used. The restriction can be for a stipulated purpose (purpose restriction), such as to fund a specific activity or purchase assets, or allowed to be used at a specific time (time restriction). These are considered temporarily restricted (TR) contributions. A donor can also stipulate that their donation must be invested in, say, marketable securities and can never be touched. And can allow the income earned on the invested donation to be used in any way the organization desires. These are considered permanently restricted (PR) contributions, which create what is known as an endowment fund.

Restricted contributions are required to be recognized in the period received even if a condition imposed by the donor prohibits the recipient organization from using those funds until some future date. Although this violates one of the basic accounting concepts, known as matching, the accounting rule-making bodies felt that it was more important to be consistent than to allow NFPs to decide how to treat restricted contributions, which they found were historically reported inconsistently by different NFPs on their financial statements.

Recording Restricted Contributions and Release of Restricted Contributions

For illustrative purposes let's say JTN received $185,763 in temporarily restricted contributions. GAAP allows temporarily restricted contributions to be recorded in a specific year in one of two ways: (1) record all temporarily restricted contributions received during the year in a separate general ledger account and release them to unrestricted (UR) at the time the restriction has been met, or (2) at year's end record only those contributions for which the restrictions have not been met as temporarily restricted. The second method requires fewer entries in the accounting system, but the organization still needs to track temporarily restricted contributions somewhere (e.g., Microsoft Excel) in order to know which restrictions haven't been met by year's end.

To illustrate, we will use the second method just mentioned. Facts: on December 25, 2010, a corporate donor gave JTN $185,763 to be used in 2011 (i.e., temporarily restricted) and $200,000 to be used for general operations in 2009. To record both the unrestricted and temporarily restricted contributions, the following entry is made:

	Debit	Credit
Cash (asset)	385,763	
Contributions—unrestricted (income)		200,000
Contributions—temporarily restricted (income)		185,763

Release of Restrictions   In 2009, JTN received $211,640 in contributions that was restricted for use in 2010. In 2010 the restriction has been met and the $211,640 can be released to unrestricted. The entry to record the release of restricted contributions in 2010 is as follows:

	Debit	Credit
Release of Restricted—Contributions (TR income)	211,640	
Release of Restricted—Contributions (UR income)		211,640

Financial Statement Presentation   The following partial presentation of JTN's statement of financial position illustrates how temporarily restricted contributions, release of temporarily restricted contributions, and permanently restricted contributions are reported. Note two things. First, the release of temporarily restricted contributions is both an increase and a decrease, so the net effect in the current year (2010) is zero. Second, this presentation is the one preferred by the author. As mentioned in Chapter 5, there are several acceptable presentation methods for statements of activities.

	2010	2009
Job Training Now, Inc.		
Statements of Activities		
(partial presentation)		
Years Ended December 31, 2010 and 2009		
Support and Revenues:		
Unrestricted:		
Government grants	2,441,632	2,855,000
Corporate contributions	**1,265,854**	**1,575,260**
Release of restricted assets	**211,640**	—
Temporarily Restricted:		
Corporate contributions	**185,763**	**211,640**
Release of restricted assets	**(211,640)**	—
Permanently Restricted:		
Corporate contributions	**100,000**	—

Contributed Goods, Facilities, and Services

Introduction

Many NFPs receive a significant amount of contributed goods, facilities, and services, and without this they could not operate and perform their mission. Contributed goods can include office supplies; equipment; food; clothes; furniture, collectibles (e.g., autographed football), collections (painting), jewelry; inventory; long-lived assets, such as a building; and any other asset that has a useful value. Contributed goods can be used by an NFP for internal operations, to perform program services, or to sell at auction or to the general public to generate income. Many NFPs also receive the free use of facilities to run their operations, perform program services, or for fund-raising events. And most NFPs couldn't survive without the free services provided by volunteers (including board members) and professionals.

GAAP requires that donated goods, facilities, and some services be recorded at *fair value* at the time of receipt. Fair value could be defined as the amount a prudent person would pay for obtaining an asset or transferring a liability in an arm's-length transaction. Some donated goods and facilities are restricted for a specific purpose or are restricted for use at a particular time. When restrictions are placed on contributed goods or facilities, they must be recorded as restricted contributions until the restriction is met, and then the contribution should be released to unrestricted.

Accounting Concepts—Contributed Goods and Facilities

Determining the value of some goods is easy whereas others are much more difficult. For example, the cost of tickets to shows or events or the value of inventory or supplies is generally easy to obtain. Other goods such as advertising (e.g., TV, radio time, or print space), buildings (market value can vary significantly), collectibles (coins, autographs, sports memorabilia) and collections (e.g., rare books) are more subjective and can fluctuate over time and geographic area. To determine fair value, an NFP should try to find the cost of similar goods. If there is variation in the marketplace, then the average or lowest amount should be used to be conservative (not the highest). To determine the fair value of donated facilities, the organization should find the cost of renting or leasing space of a similar size and location. The NFP should be careful not to accept without question the valuation provided by the donor of the goods and facilities. There is an obvious inherent bias on the part of donors to inflate the value of donated goods and facilities for egotistical reasons, as well as for tax benefits the donation might provide.

Accounting Concepts—Contributed Services

Services provided by volunteers are unique to NFP entities and many NFPs depend, and could not survive, without receiving these free services. In the past, organizations accounted for volunteer services in so many different ways that it was hard to compare the benefits between one organization and another. GAAP (formerly SFAS 116) specifies how contributed services should be valued and accounted for. It requires that the fair value of donated services be recognized in the financial statements if the services (1) create or enhance a nonfinancial asset; or (2) require specialized skills, are provided by entities or persons possessing those skills, and would need to be purchased if they were not donated. If either of these criteria is not met, the donated services should not be recognized. Simply put, the accounting rule states that only some donated services get recognized whereas others do not. Let's break the rule down.

The first criteria, *create or enhance a nonfinancial asset* includes constructing or making major improvements to property and equipment (e.g., contractor work or software design). These donated services should be recognized. Services that are related to a financial asset would *not* be included, such as those provided by investment brokers and fund-raisers. The second criteria, "Require specialized skills, and provided by entities or persons possessing those skills and would need to be purchased if they were not donated" is more ambiguous and is often debated by management, board members, and accountants alike. Nevertheless, *specialized* or *skilled* is generally interpreted to mean attorneys, teachers, accountants, licensed mechanics, and so forth; *provided by entities or persons possessing those skills* means someone can't just say they are an accountant or nurse but must actually possess the skills necessary to perform the services (i.e., have experience or knowledge); and finally, *would need to be purchased if not donated,* means that the organization would have to pay for the needed services if they were not donated. The last criteria is the most ambiguous because it could be said that every donated service would have to be paid for if it were not donated. Materiality must also be considered. How material is the service provided to the accomplishment of the organization's mission? The more material, the more recognition should be considered in light of the other criteria.

It is generally understood that the services provided by volunteers who assist with events or program activities, answer telephones at telethons, assist with collection or distribution of food and clothes, drive, assist with office duties, and even serve as board members do not qualify for recognition.

Valuation and Recording Contributed Services

GAAP (formerly SFAS 116) requires that *contributed services* be valued at the normal market rate that it would cost to purchase the service—not the rate that the donor assigns to the services provided but the rate similar services would cost. Some donors place a high value on their services for egotistical reasons. Others are under the mistaken impression that their contributed services are a tax-deductible item (which it isn't).

With the exception of long-lived assets, such as buildings, the recognition of contributed goods, facilities, or services does *not* have an effect (positive or negative) on the NFP's results of operations (i.e., increase or decrease in net assets). The income recognized from these contributions are offset by an expense that would have been incurred had the organization paid for the contributed goods, facilities, or services. For example, if a clinic had to pay for the services of several doctors and nurses, instead of receiving those services for free, it would recognize the payments as expenses. In the case of contributed services, it is as if someone donated money to the organization to pay for these services, only no cash has been exchanged. The result is the recognition of both revenue and expense, and it is important that these activities get recognized in the financial records in order to accurately depict the true cost of providing the services the NPF provides. The following example illustrates how the contributed services of two doctors and three nurses worth $40,000 would be recorded:

	Debit	Credit
Professional services (expense)	40,000	
Donated services OR contributions in kind (income)		40,000

Recording Contributed Goods and Facilities

Once a fair value is determined for the contributed goods and facilities, recording the transactions is straightforward and similar to the recording of contributed services. Let's say a corporation donates the use of office space for one year and the normal rent for that office is $120,000. The entry to record the receipt of free facilities is:

	Debit	Credit
Rent (expense)	120,000	
Donated Facilities OR Contributions In-Kind (income)		120,000

When long-lived assets, such as a building are contributed to an NFP, the assets must be capitalized the same way similarly purchased assets would be accounted for. And similar to purchased assets, a depreciation expense would be recorded each year over the assets' estimated useful live. The recording of the contribution and first-year depreciation for a building donated on January 1, with a fair value of $2,000,000 and an estimated useful life of 20 years, is as follows:

	Debit	Credit
Building (asset)	2,000,000	
Donated facilities OR contributions in kind (income)		2,000,000
Depreciation (expense)	100,000	
Accumulated depreciation (contra asset)		100,000

Government Grants

Accounting Concepts—Grants

Accounting for *government grants* (or grants) is less straightforward than contributions and has its own set of complications. The biggest complication is determining whether a particular grant has attributes similar to a contribution, in which case the accounting treatment is the same as contributions, or whether it has attributes similar to *fee-for-service* (or exchange transactions) or is a *refundable advance*, in which case different accounting rules apply. To complicate matters further, some grants have more than one attribute. To determine the attributes applicable to a specific grant, one must read the grant contract or agreement very carefully. Even when being careful, the terms of the agreement can be ambiguous, and how grant funds are actually distributed can be different from what is called for in the agreement, which makes accounting for a transaction very difficult. For example, let's say the terms of a grant agreement state that funds will be disbursed only after approved grant expenditures are incurred, but then the granting agency advances the organization $10,000 to assist them with their cash flow. How do you treat the advance? As income? As a liability? Before answering this question, let's review some accounting definitions.

Contributions are voluntary, unconditional, and a nonreciprocal transfer of assets from one entity to another. *Fee-for-service* or *exchange transactions* are basically the purchase of goods or services from another entity and *refundable advances* are the receipt of funds in advance of providing goods or services. Usually (but not always) when the agreement says "Contract," it has fee-for-service attributes and is treated accordingly. When the agreement says "Grant Agreement," it can have one of several different attributes depending on the agreement's terms. If the terms call for the general use of grant funds to support a program or the general mission of the organization, the funds are treated as either a temporarily restricted or unrestricted contribution. However, if the terms of the agreement require that approved expenses must first be incurred before the receipt of funds (*expense reimbursement*-type grants), the grant takes on the attributes of a conditional grant until expenditures are made. A typical mistake with these types of grants is to book the entire grant upon approval. Now the answer to the previous question: The $10,000 should be recorded as a refundable advance.

As you can see, accounting for grant-related income can be difficult at times. Correct treatment requires careful analysis of each agreement, knowledge of existing accounting rules, judgment about application of accounting rules, and appropriate configuration of the accounting software to capture all necessary information to report grant income properly. Several scenarios are provided in the next section to illustrate the different accounting treatments of government grants based on different grant provisions. All are based on the receipt of $100,000 in cash from a federal governmental agency.

Recording—Grants

Illustration 1
Receipt of funds to support JTN, Inc. training program.

	Debit	Credit
Cash (asset)	100,000	
Grant Income—Unrestricted		100,000

Illustration 2
Receipt of funds to purchase computers in the future.

	Debit	Credit
Cash (asset)	100,000	
Grant Income—Temporarily restricted		100,000

Illustration 3
Receipt of funds for the training of 100 students @ $1,000 per student (based on a $1,000,000 contract to train 1,000 students).

	Debit	**Credit**
Cash (asset)	100,000	
Contract income or program service income		100,000

Illustration 4

Same as Illustration 3 except the government advanced the NFP funds before they trained the 100 students and JTN, Inc. is unsure whether it will be training the students this year.

	Debit	**Credit**
Cash (asset)	100,000	
Refundable Advance		100,000

Illustration 5

Same as Illustration 1 except the agreement requires that expenses be incurred first before receiving funds, but no expenditures were made prior to receipt of funds.

	Debit	**Credit**
Cash (asset)	100,000	
Refundable Advance		100,000

Table 8.1 summarizes the treatment of government grants with different provisions. The following abbreviations are used: Dr. = Debit, Cr. = Credit,

Table 8.1   Treatment of Government Grants with Different Provisions

Transactions	Contribution Type	Fee-for-Service Type	Expense Reimbursement Type
Awarded grant	Dr. Grant Rec. (OR) Cash Cr. Grant Income (UR or TR)	Nothing	Nothing
Provide products/ services	Nothing	Dr. Grant Rec. (OR) Contract Rec. Cr. Grant Income (UR or TR)	Dr. Expenses Cr. Cash AND Dr. Grant Rec. Cr. Grant Income
Receive cash after providing products/ services	Nothing	Dr. Cash Cr. Grant Rec. (OR) Contract Rec.	Dr. Cash Cr. Grant Rec.
Receive cash before providing products/ services	Nothing	Dr. Cash Cr. Deferred Income (OR) Refundable Advance	Dr. Cash Cr. Due to Grantor (OR) Refundable Advance

Rec. = Receivable, UR = Unrestricted, and TR = Temporarily restricted, and OR means either entry is acceptable.

Program Service Revenue and Membership Dues

Program Service Revenue

As discussed in Chapter 6, program service revenue covers a multitude of activities, such as medical services in hospitals and clinics; day-care or elder-care services; camp fees; tuition fees at educational and training institutions; fees for legal and advisory services; rent; entrance fees at museums, parks, and cultural institutions; library fees; sales of products; advertising income; and almost any other fees charged for any products or services provided by an NFP organization. Accounting for program service revenue is relatively straightforward most of the time, especially when compared to contributions and government grant income. Generally speaking, if program service revenue pertains to the current year, it is recorded as revenue in that year. If program service revenue is received in the current year but is prepaying for something that will be provided in the future, it isn't current-year income so it is recorded as a liability called *deferred income*. To illustrate, let's say JTN didn't invoice, but received a check in the amount of $20,000 in November 2009, for training that will be performed the following February 2010. The entry to record this transaction would be as follows:

	Debit	Credit
Cash (asset)	20,000	
Deferred income (liability)		20,000

Then, the following year when the training services are provided, JTN would record the earned revenue as follows:

	Debit	Credit
Deferred income (liability)	20,000	
Program service revenue (income)		20,000

Membership Dues

Many NFPs, especially those classified under Internal Revenue Codes 501(c)(4) (civic leagues and local associations of employees) and 501(c)(6) (membership organizations, business leagues, chambers of commerce, real estate boards, and economic development corporations), receive revenue in the form of membership dues. In addition, many NFPs receive dues from related organizations, such as affiliates or chapters. Often, recording membership dues is straightforward, but sometimes it is more complicated.

There are a number of accounting issues that could affect the way membership dues are accounted for. By definition membership dues are exchange transactions; that is, they are payments for inclusion in some group or entity that provides some tangible or intangible benefits to the member (such as access to facilities or information or receipt of some publication). Accounting for dues invoiced or received in the year the membership period applies is relatively easy, as illustrated next:

	Debit	Credit
Cash (asset) or accounts receivable (asset)	16,000	
Membership dues (income)		16,000

It is not unusual for organizations to send out membership renewal notices several months before the membership period begins. Since in most cases there is no mandatory requirement that an existing or prospective member become a member and pay a membership fee, the NFP's invoice is more like an offer to be a member rather than a notice to pay a legal obligation. As such, the invoice should not be recorded as a receivable in the organization's financial records. Furthermore, if the organization receives membership dues in advance of the membership period it should not be recorded as revenue but rather as a liability, similar to receiving program service revenue in advance of providing any products or services. The receipt of say $5,000 in membership dues in advance of the applicable membership period would be recorded as follows:

	Debit	Credit
Cash (asset)	5,000	
Deferred income (liability)		5,000

Then, the following year, when the membership applies, the organization would record the earned revenue as follows:

	Debit	Credit
Deferred income (liability)	20,000	
Program service revenue (income)		20,000

Sometimes the amount paid for membership dues exceeds the fair value of the benefits received. In these cases, an allocation is required separating a portion of the dues to membership dues for the fair value of the benefits received and the balance to contributions. For example, let's say an NFP charges a membership fee of $200 for which a member will receive a quarterly newsletter and a T-shirt with the organization's logo. The fair value of the newsletter and T-shirt is estimated to be $125. The $75 balance ($200–$125) is a contribution. The NFP would record the receipt of a single membership fee as follows:

	Debit	**Credit**
Cash (asset)	200	
Membership Dues (income)		125
Contribution Income		75

Fund-Raising (Special) Events

Accounting Concept—Fund-Raising (Special) Events

Fund-raising events (sometimes referred to *as special events*) are a major source of revenue for many NFP organizations. Many charities hold one or two large events a year, where they sell tickets, hold raffles or auctions, and sell merchandise to raise money. Under GAAP (formerly SFAS 117), the statement of activities must report the gross amount of revenue earned from fund-raising events separately from related direct expenses (i.e., can't only show a net amount). Only direct expenses should be included, not allocated expenses such as salary or other management and general expenses. Also, if an event includes an auction (live, silent, raffle, etc.) where either purchased or donated items are sold, both the gross sales income and the cost or fair value of the donated goods sold should be presented (again, it should not be netted). There are several presentation methods for reporting income and expenses from fund-raising events and these are illustrated in the next section.

Statement of Activities Presentation Methods

The two most common presentation methods are (1) to show both the gross revenue and related direct expenses in the support and revenue section or (2) include only the gross revenue in the support and revenue section and show expenses in the expense section under the functional category of programs or fund-raising expenses.

The author suggests the first method, presenting both the gross revenue and related direct expenses in the revenue and support section of the statement of activities.

Investment and Other Income

Accounting Concept—Investment income

Income from investments includes income earned on various types of investments, including marketable securities (e.g., stocks, bonds, Treasury

Revenue and Support Section Presentation Method

Job Training Now, Inc.
Statements of Activities
(partial presentation)
Years Ended December 31, 2010 and 2009

	2010	2009
Support and Revenues:		
Unrestricted:		
Government grants	$2,441,632	;2,855,000
Contributions	1,265,854	1,575,260
Program service revenue	358,875	415,920
Total before special events	4,066,361	4,846,180
Special events:		
Auction sales	**15,200**	**18,800**
Less: cost or fair value of auction items	**(5,300)**	**(6,700)**
Event-related income and support	**565,000**	**595,000**
Less: event-related direct costs	**(249,111)**	**(231,460)**
Net special events income and support	**$ 325,789**	**$ 375,640**

Separate Revenue and Support and Expenses Section Presentation Method

Job Training Now, Inc.
Statements of Activities
(partial presentation)
Years Ended December 31, 2010 and 2009

	2010	2009
Support and Revenues:		
Unrestricted:		
Government grants	$2,441,632	$2,855,000
Contributions	1,265,854	1,575,260
Program service revenue	358,875	415,920
Total before special events	4,066,361	4,846,180
Special events:		
Auction sales	**15,200**	**18,800**
Event-related income and support	**565,000**	**595,000**
Total special events income and support	**580,200**	**613,800**

Expenses:		
Program Expenses:		
Simulated on-the-job training	3,756,128	3,790,268
Corporate on-site training	272,458	265,363
Special event—costs of auction and events	**254,411**	**238,160**
Total program expenses	$ 4,282,997	$ 4,293,791

Notes), real estate ventures, partnership interests, and equity in nonpublic corporations. We will discuss investment income earned from marketable securities such as stocks and bonds. We will not discuss income earned on other types of investments, which is beyond the scope of this book.

Investment income is a generic description and can include interest, dividends, realized gains and losses (from sales of securities), and unrealized gains and losses (changes in market value from one period to the next). Some accountants also include investment expenses in this category instead of separately reporting it with other expenses. Accounting for investments is relatively straightforward for many NFPs, because the size of their investment portfolio is not large or there are no external restrictions placed on how the investment income is to be used. If the income earned on investments is very small, it will be combined and included with other income as illustrated:

Job Training Now, Inc.
Statements of Activities
(partial presentation)
Years Ended December 31, 2010 and 2009

	2010	**2009**
Support and Revenues:		
Unrestricted:		
Government grants	$2,441,632	$2,855,000
Corporate contributions	1,265,854	1,575,260
Investment and other income	**21,487**	**18,442**

For many other NFPs, accounting for investment income is quite complex. There are many reasons for the complexity, such as having many different types of investments that are pooled together but must be accounted for separately or have investments with different external restrictions placed on the use of related investment income. Accounting for restricted and pooled investment income will be covered in more detail in Chapter 10.

Other Income

Other income is a catch-all category used for reporting support and revenue received or earned that doesn't fit into any other category. The total dollar amount reported in other income should not be large. A rule of thumb is it shouldn't be greater than 5 percent of total revenue and support. If greater, one or more of its components should be identified and separately stated on the statement of activities.

Examples of items included in *other income* include incidental income earned on sales of assets, insurance proceeds received in excess of the value recorded in the general ledger (i.e., basis), rental or royalty income, and advertising income. Sometimes transactions are grouped together and included in this area purposely to avoid disclosing their nature. Common examples include income earned from advertising in an NFP's membership directory or publication or income earned from an activity not typically provided by the organization. The reason an organization might not want to disclose this revenue is the potential tax liability for earning *unrelated business income* (UBI). UBI will be covered in Chapter 14.

Accounting for Personnel Costs and Other Expenses

Personnel and related costs (also known as salaries and fringe benefits) are one of the largest expense areas for a significant number of (if not most) NFPs. Many times this area is difficult to account for because of a number of reasons, such as a lack of knowledge of proper classification of service providers or payroll tax reporting rules, or the need to allocate and track personnel costs by program, activity, government grants, fund-raising event, and so forth.

For discussion purposes, accounting and reporting personnel and related costs will be separated into three areas: classification of service providers (employee vs. independent contractor), payroll processing and reporting, and accounting for payroll and related costs.

Employee Classification

Misclassification of service providers as independent (outside) contractors instead of as employees is a significant and consistent problem that the IRS and many State Department of Labor agencies have been trying to correct for years. This problem exists in both NFP organizations and commercial entities alike. The reason for misclassification varies from blatant disregard to ignorance of the rules, with ignorance of the rules being the paramount reason. There is also a widespread misbelief that if found to be in non-compliance there are no repercussions other than doing the right thing going forward. This is a false assumption. If audited by the IRS or a state agency and found to be in noncompliance, an organization could be held responsible for any and all unpaid payroll taxes as well as subjected to huge fines and penalties. The problem is so persistent that in 2007, New York's Governor Eliott Spitzer signed an Executive Order creating an interagency strike force to address the problem of employers who inappropriately classify employees as independent contractors or pay workers off the books as part of the underground economy (*New York Times*, Sept. 2007).

One frequently asked question is, "Where can I find the rules for proper classification of service providers." Unfortunately there is no one place to find an all-encompassing rule because there is no one set of criteria to use. Rather, classification determination is based on characteristics of the relationship. That being said, the IRS and U.S. Department of Labor web sites do provide guidance. For example, on the IRS web site you will see that the IRS applies both a common-law and statutory approach to classification and uses a 20-factor test as a guide. Generally speaking, under common-law rules, anyone who performs services for you is your employee *if you can control what will be done and how it will be done.* This is so even when you give the employee freedom of action. What matters is that you have the right to control the details of how the services are performed.

One common misconception is the belief by the organization (payer) and/or individuals (payee) that they can decide among themselves which classification applies to their situation. Unfortunately classification is not optional if the characteristics of the relationship support a specific classification. In the majority of cases the misclassification is not properly classifying the service provider as an employee. Over his more than 30-year career, this author has heard numerous reasons why an individual should be classified as an independent contractor and not an employee. Although some of these reasons might support this conclusion if other factors exist, in and of itself these reasons are not justification. Some of the reasons given include the following:

- Service provider works only part-time.
- Service provider is an intern.
- Service provider works flexible hours.
- Service provider works on an hourly basis.
- Position is only temporary (e.g., only until project is completed).
- Service provider doesn't have a degree or is not technically qualified.
- Service provider and payer have an agreement (i.e., contract).
- Service provider doesn't want to be paid as an employee.
- Organization doesn't want to pay benefits.
- Organization can't afford to pay all required taxes, insurances, or benefits.
- Organization is too small so they are not required to follow employment rules.
- Service provider uses his or her own computer or car.
- Service provider is young (e.g., college student).
- Service provider is not required to complete a time sheet.
- Payment is a stipend and not salary (Stipends should be nominal, not material).
- Payment is for reimbursed expenses (*can't* be $300 per month).
- Board member said it was alright (owns a business and is a smart person).

To repeat, these reasons are not justification for independent-contractor classification unless other factors exist and support this classification.

Statutory Employees and Nonemployees

As previously mentioned, the IRS applies both a common-law (degree of control) and statutory approach (rules embodied by statute) to classify workers. The IRS uses the terms *statutory employee* and *statutory nonemployee* to categorize specific workers.

Those deemed employees by statute include the following:

- Officers (common for NFPs).
- Full-time traveling salesperson who solicits orders from wholesalers, restaurants, or similar establishments on behalf of a principal.
- Full-time life insurance agent whose principal business activity is selling life insurance and/or annuity contracts for one life insurance company.
- An agent-driver or commission-driver engaged in distributing meat, vegetables, bakery goods, beverages (other than milk), or laundry or dry cleaning services.
- A home worker performing work on material or goods furnished by the employer.

Those deemed nonemployees (i.e., independent contractors) by statute include the following:

- Directors of a corporation or board members (common for NFPs). If an exempt organization pays its board members to attend board meetings or otherwise compensates them for performing their duties as directors, the organization should treat them as independent contractors.
- The director fee is reported on Form 1099-MISC. This is the most common type of statutory nonemployee that may apply to an NFP.

Employment Eligibility

Prior to hiring someone as an employee or paying someone as an independent contractor, the employer/payer must first obtain all necessary information and required documents. This ensures that the prospective workers are who they say they are and that they are legally allowed to work in the United States. *Form I-9 (Employment Eligibility Verification)* must be completed by all prospective employees. The purpose of this form is to document that each new employee (both citizen and noncitizen) hired after November 6, 1986 is authorized to work in the United States. Section 2 of the form requires the employer to sign that they have reviewed various documents (e.g., passport, green card, drivers license) to ensure that the individual is legally allowed to work in the United States. Form W-9 (Request for Taxpayer Identification Number and Certification) should be completed for individuals providing services as an independent contractor.

Payroll and Payroll-Tax Processing and Reporting

General

NFP organizations that pay individuals to perform services are subjected to the same rules and regulations regarding wages, payroll, and payroll-tax withholding and reporting that other payers of wages are subjected to with a few minor exceptions or modifications. This includes mandatory coverage of certain types of insurance and benefits, nondiscrimination rules, required notification and reporting rules, and compliance with numerous other federal, state, and local laws. One exception that applies to public charities is the exemption from paying Federal Unemployment Tax (FUTA). This exemption cannot be waived. Another exemption applies to churches and qualified church-controlled organizations. Churches can elect to be exempt from paying employer Social Security and Medicare taxes (FICA) by filing Form 8274, Certification by Churches and Qualified Church-Controlled Organizations Electing Exemption from Employer Social Security and Medicare Taxes.

Terminology

There is a lot of confusion, especially among new accountants, about what exactly are payroll taxes. Technically speaking, payroll taxes are only federal, state, and local income taxes; and Social Security and Medicare taxes (FICA) withheld from wages paid to employees along with the employers' portion of FICA. Other payroll-related employee withholdings and employer payments such as for federal and state unemployment tax, State Disability, and Workers Compensation are actually insurance and not payroll taxes. However, since these insurance expenditures are related to payroll, they are frequently combined with other employer payroll taxes and recorded as payroll taxes.

Reporting Requirements

Employers and other payers for services are required to prepare and submit annual wage or compensation statements to both recipients and the federal government if the payments during the year meet requirements. If payments are made to employees, *employers* must file Form W-2 (Annual Wage Statement) for wages paid to each employee from whom income, Social Security, or Medicare tax was withheld during the calendar year. For payments made to independent contractors, payers must file Form 1099-MISC (Miscellaneous Income) for each person who was paid at least $600 during the year for rents, services (including parts and materials), prizes and awards, other income payments, medical and health-care payments, crop insurance proceeds, cash payments for fish (or other aquatic life), and gross proceeds to an attorney. *W-2* forms are filed with the Social Security Administration (not the IRS) to substantiate Social Security withholdings; 1099 forms are filed with the IRS. One of the most common reasons for not filing these and other required payroll-related forms is that the payer did not have the necessary payee information needed to complete the forms, such as Social Security number or current address. Even if true, this excuse is invalidated because the rules require that all employers and other payers first obtain all necessary information from the payee before making any payment, and if they don't, they are held responsible.

Who Handles Payroll and Payroll-Tax Processing and Reporting?

Payroll and payroll-tax processing and reporting can be handled either internally by an organization's staff accountant or externally by an accounting firm or payroll service company such as ADP or Paychex. If performed *internally*, the person handling the function has to be knowledgeable about payroll and payroll-tax rules, withholding and reporting rules, and has to understand how to account for payroll transactions in the organization's general ledger. The organization's accounting software should also include a separate payroll module to allow for tracking detailed payroll information.

If the payroll processing and reporting function is handled *externally*, the organization's accounting department needs to be mostly concerned with only how to account for payroll transactions on the organization's books and not as concerned with knowing all the technical payroll rules.

Accounting for Payroll and Related Expenses

As mentioned in the previous section, payroll processing (i.e., generating wage payments, withholding payroll taxes, and payroll reporting) can be handled either internally by an organization's accounting staff or externally by an accountant or payroll service. Because of the complexities involved, we will not cover performing payroll processing and related reporting functions internally, which is beyond the scope of this book. For our purposes, we will assume that this function is handled externally by a payroll service company. However, recording payroll and related expenses in an organization's financial records is obviously still necessary even when the processing and reporting function is handled externally.

Components of Payroll and Payroll-Related Withholdings

Components of a noncomplex, typical payroll include wages paid to employees, employee payroll-tax withholding (federal, state, and local income; and

FICA), employer's portion of FICA, employer's liability for federal and state unemployment taxes (FUTA & SUI), employee's contributory portion of SUI or disability insurance (which is minimal), and other employee with-holdings, such as retirement contributions (e.g., 403(b), 401(k) or SIMPLE IRA), flexible benefits account (e.g., FSA), medical savings account (MSA), and court-ordered mandatory wage garnishment.

Recording Payroll and Related Expenses—General

Even when using the services of an external payroll service company, there is a significant amount of tracking and accounting that must be performed by an organization's internal accounting staff. Tasks include recording in the organization's general ledger all payroll-related expenses (e.g., salaries, employer payroll taxes, and employee withholdings for fringe benefits), reconciling general ledger payroll transactions to bank-statement activity, and managing all employee-related benefits, such as health insurance.

Some organizations make all payroll disbursements through their general operating bank account, whereas others have a separate bank account used solely for making payroll-related disbursements. There are pros and cons to both approaches. Separate payroll bank accounts have the benefits of making it easier to reconcile payroll transactions and identifying recording errors, but the drawback is requiring more cash transfers between bank accounts.

There are several methods for recording payroll transactions in an organization's general ledger when an external payroll service is used to process payroll. One method is to record every transaction handled by the payroll service, such as gross wages, payroll tax and benefits withholdings for each employee, and all remittances made to government agencies. Another method is to summarize the weekly, biweekly (every two weeks), or semi-monthly (twice a month) payroll activity and enter this information as a summarized transaction in the general ledger. The author suggests using a summarized approach, because all payroll service companies provide detailed reports that can be used for reconciliation purposes.

Recording Payroll and Related Expenses—Illustration

For our example, we will assume that the organization has four employees, pays their employees on a biweekly basis, and uses an external payroll service company. The organization has a flexible spending account (FSA) that allows employees to contribute up to $2,600 in pretaxed earnings into a separate account to be used to pay for personal medical-related expenses. The payroll elements to be accounted for include gross wages, income and other payroll taxes withheld from each employee, net cash payments made to each employee (check or direct deposit), payments made to government agencies (IRS, state) for withheld employee payroll taxes and employer's portion of payroll taxes, payroll-tax-service processing fees, and payments made for medical expenditures. As previously mentioned, there are several methods for recording payroll transactions, two of which are the transactional method and the summary method. An example of both entries is provided here:

Transactional Method
Journal Entry 1 (Record Payroll Expense)

	Debit	Credit
Gross Wages—Employee 1	3,000	
Gross Wages—Employee 2	2,000	
Gross Wages—Employee 3	1,500	
Gross Wages—Employee 4	1,300	
Employer Payroll Taxes (FICA, FUTA, SUI)	1,014	
Payroll Processing Expense	85	
Federal Income & Payroll Taxes Payable		2,450
State Income & Payroll Taxes Payable		1,014
Flexible Benefits Payable		400
Net Wages Payable—Employee 1		1,900
Net Wages Payable—Employee 2		1,250
Net Wages Payable—Employee 3		950
Net Wages Payable—Employee 4		850
Due to Payroll Service Company		85

Journal Entry 2 (Record Cash Disbursed)

	Debit	Credit
Net Wages Payable—Employee 1	1,900	
Net Wages Payable—Employee 2	1,250	
Net Wages Payable—Employee 3	950	
Net Wages Payable—Employee 4	850	
Federal Income & Payroll Taxes Payable	2,450	
State Income & Payroll Taxes Payable	1,014	
Cash		8,414

Note: Payments are made for medical expenses as incurred. Because no medical payments were made, no entry was required in journal entry 2.

Summary Method   Under the summary method, only one transaction is made. The justification for making only one entry is because payroll service companies typically require payroll-related withdrawals to be made within a few days of the payroll period. Therefore, the liability is so short-lived it becomes immaterial. Also, you will notice that in the summary method, individual employees' wages (gross and net) are not recorded because the payroll service company reports provide this detail. It is duplicative and not necessary to record this information in the general ledger as well.

Journal Entry (Record Payroll Expense)

	Debit	Credit
Gross wages	8,814	
Employer payroll taxes (FICA, FUTA, SUI)	1,014	
Payroll-processing expense	85	
Flexible benefits payable		400
Cash (checks or direct bank withdrawals)		9,513

Accounting for Employee Benefits and Related Activity

In addition to accounting for payroll and payroll taxes, employee benefits must also be tracked and accounted for. Typical benefits include employee with-holdings for employees' portion of health-insurance premiums; employee retirement contributions (e.g., 401(k), 403(b), IRA-SIMPLE, etc.); employee withholdings for health savings accounts (HSA), medical savings accounts (MSA), transit checks and other flexible savings accounts (FSA), and payments made by former employees for health insurance coverage (COBRA). The organization's accounting department must also make all required payments to external parties for monies withheld from employees for the benefits just mentioned and periodically analyze and reconcile their employee-receivable and vendor-payable records to ensure that all proper amounts are received, disbursed, and recorded.

Since many NFPs, especially smaller ones, do not have a separate human resources department or personnel that handle just personnel matters, this responsibility usually falls on the accounting department. Therefore, in addition to handling all disbursements for payroll, payroll taxes, and employee benefits, the accounting department will be required to maintain employee files that include: employee time cards/sheets (if used); schedule of employees personal time off (PTO) that tracks vacation, sick time, and so forth taken; and other documents such as employee job application forms, employee identification forms (e.g., drivers license), performance evalua-tions, and salary-history schedules.

There is no one perfect method used for tracking employee benefits and personnel information. Methods range from no system of tracking personal time off and receivables owed from employees, to using Microsoft Excel spreadsheets and manila file folders, to using sophisticated human-resources software. Those organizations that have no or inadequate tracking and document retention procedures could be leaving themselves open to negative financial consequences from lawsuits from current and former employees and from regulatory bodies because of poor record keeping and the problems that this can create.

Compensated Absences

General   Compensated absences are another type of benefit organizations give their employees. Unless required by contract or state or local law, most organizations are not required to pay employees for time not worked (i.e., time off). This includes weekends and days not worked due to holidays, vacation, or illness. However, common practice is to pay employees their normal daily salary for a certain number of nonworked days due to holidays, vacations, and illness.

When an organization's policy is to pay employees for future absences (i.e., vacation time) GAAP (formerly SFAF 43, *Accounting for Compensated Absences*) requires that an organization accrue for this obligation if all the following exist:

- The obligation to the employee is attributable to services already rendered.
- The obligation is based on rights that are vested or accumulated. *Vested* means the right can't be revoked even if the employee is terminated, and *accumulated* means it can be carried over from one year to the next (no use-it-or-lose-it rule applies).
- Payment is probable.
- Amount can be reasonably estimated.

Compensated absences typically include vacation and personal time earned. Sick time is generally not earned but allowed when needed. If the amount of time owed and not taken at the end of the year is not material, nothing needs to be done. If the amount is material but can't be calculated, it should be disclosed in the notes to financial statements. And, if the amount is material, the liability should be accrued and accounted for.

Accounting for Compensated Absences   There are two general methods for calculating and accruing compensated absence expenses—the exact method and the estimation method. The exact method requires that the accounting department calculate the liability on an employee-by-employee basis, which is very time consuming, especially if specialized personnel or human-resources software is not used. The estimation method is much easier and sufficient if performed consistently and conservatively. The following steps illustrate how an estimated accrual is calculated:

- Total all eligible employees' annual salaries.
- Divide the total by the eligible work period (e.g., 50 or 52 weeks).
- Multiply the result by the period of paid time allowed (e.g., 2 or 3 weeks).
- Subtract from this result, the amount of time off taken by employees.

Using this method, a calculation can be made to determine a reasonable amount to accrue for compensated absences. For example, if an organization allows three weeks paid vacation and employees are allowed to carry over to the following year up to two weeks unpaid vacation time, and experience suggests that, on average, one week of vacation time is not taken at the end of each operating year, the organization can make an easy calculation to determine how much to accrue for unpaid vacation time at year's end. The following example of an NFP with gross annual salaries totaling $520,000, illustrates this calculation:

Gross salary (per year)		Average weeks of unpaid vacation time	Accrual amount
$\dfrac{\$520,000}{52}$	$\times$	1	$10,000

The general journal entry that would be made to reflect this transaction is as follows:

	Debit	Credit
Salaries or employee benefits (expense)	10,000	
Accrued expenses (liability)		10,000

Expense Allocations, Fund-Raising Activities, and Joint Costs

Expense Allocations

It was mentioned in an earlier chapter that GAAP requires that NFPs separate, track, and report expenses by function (i.e., by program and supporting services). NFPs also need to many times separate, allocate, and report expenses by location, project, department, grant, event, restricted contributions to comply with external mandates, or simply to manage their resources more efficiently. Certain expenses are easy to track because they only pertain to one area (e.g., rent for facilities for a fund-raising event or supplies for a specific program). For many NFPs, a significant portion of expenses have to be allocated to various functions and/or activities in order to properly account for the total costs involved with providing or performing those functions or activities. Allocations are usually made at the end of a month, quarter, before preparing a grant reimbursement request, before a board or budget/finance committee meeting, and at the very least, at year's end. Microsoft Excel or other spreadsheets are frequently used to calculate and tabulate allocated expenses.

Because the largest expense category for most NFPs is salaries and related expenses, these costs typically get allocated. A majority of organizations do not require that their employees prepare and submit time cards or sheets documenting how their time was spent, so organizations must base their allocations on estimates. There is no uniform methodology for determining allocations and no requirement that detailed records be kept except that the method used for making estimates should be reasonable, rational, consistent from year to year, and justifiable in some way. This doesn't mean that amounts can't fluctuate. It means that NFPs shouldn't just allocate expenses to a particular area simply because they want to present results of operations in some predetermined way (although many times it is done for this reason).

Table 9.1 is an example of a spreadsheet used to determine the amount to allocate to each functional area at year's end. Once the amounts are calculated, a general journal entry can be made to record these allocations.

It was mentioned in Chapter 5 that the statement of functional expenses present expenses by function (e.g., programs and supporting services) and natural classification (type of expense) but only volunteer health and welfare organizations are required to present this statement. If the statement is

Table 9.1   Allocation of Expenses

							Mgmt &		Fund-	
	Total		Program 1		Program 2		Gen.		Raising	
Expense Category	%	$	%	$	%	$	%	$	%	$
Salaries:										
Executive director	100	150,000	60	90,000	20	30,000	15	22,500	5	7,500
Office staff	100	100,000	60	60,000	20	20,000	15	15,000	5	5,000
Payroll taxes/ benefits	100	25,000	60	15,000	20	5,000	15	3,750	5	1,250
Rent	100	60,000	70	42,000	15	9,000	10	6,000	5	3,000
Office supplies/ expenses	100	22,000	40	8,800	20	4,400	25	5,500	15	3,300
Printing	100	50,000	35	17,500	15	7,500	30	15,000	20	10,000
Telephone	100	30,000	60	18,000	20	6,000	15	4,500	5	1,500
Total	100	437,000		251,300		81,900		72,250		31,550

Header of table: **Helpful NFP, Inc. / Allocation of Expenses / Year Ended December 31, 2010** presented, a footnote should be included in the notes to financial statements that reads as follows:

Job Training Now, Inc.
Notes to Financial Statements
(partial presentation)
December 31, 2010 and 2009

Functional expense allocation:

The direct costs of providing programs and other activities have been summarized on a functional basis in the statement of activities and in the statement of functional expenses. Accordingly, certain costs have been allocated among the programs and supporting services benefited.

Fund-Raising Activities

Fund-raising activities are those activities engaged in solely to raise revenue and support. Fund-raising expenses are the costs associated with obtaining those funds. GAAP, government regulatory bodies (e.g., IRS), grantors, and other funders all require that costs associated with raising funds be reported on an organization's financial statements. The reason is to better inform the reader about the effectiveness of time spent (i.e., portion of salaries) and other expenses incurred to generate support. For example, one organization might show current year contributions and government grants of $300,000 and fund-raising expenses of $125,000, whereas another might show contributions and government grants of $250,000 but only $50,000 in fund-raising expenses. With this information, it appears the second organization is doing a better job of raising funds ($250,000 − $50,000 or $200,000 in net receipts) versus the first organization ($300,000 − $125,000 or $175,000). However, if the second organization were less than forthright in its allocation of expenses, the conclusion reached would be incorrect.

Joint Costs—Defined

As just mentioned, GAAP requires that fund-raising costs be identified and reported in the financial statements. As a practical matter, fund-raising activities include both direct costs and allocated *joint costs*. Direct costs are obvious, but what are joint costs? Simply put, joint costs are expenditures (or costs) that have elements of both fund-raising and either programs or management and general, or both. GAAP (previously statement of position (SOP) 98-2 *Accounting for Costs of Activities of Not-for-Profit Organizations and State and Local Governmental Entities That Include Fund Raising*) provides guidance on this issue by specifying how NFPs should account for these combined costs. The rules state that in the case in which expenditures include a fund-raising component, the entire cost should be reported as fund-raising costs (instead of allocated to program or management and general, or both) except when *all three* of the following criteria exist. These criteria seek to validate that the expenditures were not made just to raise funds but for some other purpose.

1. **Purpose Criteria**—There is a specific purpose (action) other than to raise funds or educate the general public about the organization.
2. **Audience Criteria**—Expenditures were incurred for an audience other than donors.
3. **Content Criteria**—The expenditures will "help accomplish the organization's mission," not just give information to entice prospective donors.

If these criteria are met, costs can be allocated or split between fundraising and other functions. When joint costs exist, the notes to financial statements should include information about the components of the allocation. An illustrated example of this note is provided next:

Job Training Now, Inc.
Notes to Financial Statements
(partial presentation)

Fund-Raising Activities:
The Organization conducted activities that included direct solicitation for contributions from individuals, foundations, and governmental agencies. The costs of personnel conducting those solicitation activities included fund-raising, program, and administrative expenses (collectively defined as joint costs). The total joint costs for the years ended December 31, 2010 and 2009 are as follows:

	2010	2009
Program	$ 86,067	$ 83,092
Management and general	18,834	18,076
Fund-raising	35,770	33,552
Total	$140,671	$134,720

The total amount charged/allocated (direct & joint costs) to fund-raising activities was $85,483 in 2010 and $74,552 in 2009.

Problems with Reporting Fund-Raising Costs

There are inherent problems with reporting fund-raising costs, as there are with reporting management and general expenses. Most organizations don't want to state that there is a cost to raising funds or that the organization is spending a lot of money on administration expenses, especially if the amounts are high. This might show that management is inefficient and, in turn, scare away contributors. Donors want to know that their donations are going directly to accomplishing the NFP's mission and not paying staff salaries. This is exactly why the accounting rule-making bodies (and the IRS) feel that this information is relevant and should be reported. To be in compliance with the rules for full disclosure, every NFP should present this information and present this information as accurately as is reasonably possible.

Rental Expenses Related to Operating Leases

General

Organizations can either purchase or rent property to run their operations. When property is purchased it is capitalized as an organization asset and depreciated over a period of useful years. When property is rented, the rental expenses are recognized in the period the expense relates to. Rental agreements typically cover several years and can contain many different provisions that lessors (landlords) use to entice lessees (i.e., tenants) to rent property. These can include giving free rent for several months as an enticement to enter into the agreement or giving free rent because the lessee will be making improvements on the property (i.e., leasehold improvements). These enticements are usually offset by increasing rent in later years to offset lower rents in the earlier years.

Because of all the possible variations that can exist with operating leases, the accounting regulatory bodies felt there was a need to provide some guidance on how to properly account for them. As such, GAAP (formerly SFAS 13—*Accounting for Leases*) requires that rent expense under operating leases be recognized on a straight-line basis over the lease period. The justification for this is that the same property is being used in the same way over the term of the lease and changes in prices during the term of the lease do not change the property's fair value for use. The straight-line method is only valid if there is no change in access and use of the same property throughout the lease period

Illustration

To illustrate how to account for an operating lease, we will assume that the lease period is 10 years, and the NFP receives four months of free rent in year one and two months free rent in year two (based on year 1 and year 2's annual rent). The calculation requires that all rent payments and escalations are totaled, all rent abatements (i.e., free rent) or discounts are deducted, and the result is divided by the total number of months covered by the lease period. A comparison between actual rent payments made and the calculated straight-line (St. Line) amounts is performed, and any differences between the two are recorded as either prepaid rent (an asset) or deferred rent (a liability) on the statement of financial position. Table 9.2 is an example of a spreadsheet calculating the amount of rent to be charged to rent expense each year.

For 2008, the entry to record the total cash rent payment of $133,900 and proper recognition of rent expense is as follows:

	Debit	**Credit**
Rent expense	214,893	
Deferred rent (liability)		80,993
Cash (asset)		133,900

For 2009, the entry to record the total cash rent payment of $171,559 and proper recognition of rent expense is as follows:

	Debit	**Credit**
Rent expense	214,893	
Deferred rent (liability)		43,334
Cash (asset)		174,559

Table 9.2 Sample Lease Commitment—Deferred Rent Schedule

Helpful NFP, Inc.
Sample Lease Commitment—Deferred Rent Schedule
2008 to 2017

As of 12/31	Annual Rent	Less Rent Abatement	Net	Cash Payments Per Lease	St. Line	Annual Deferral	Cumulative Deferral
2008	200,850	66,950	133,900	133,900	214,893	80,993	80,993
2009	205,871	34,312	171,559	171,559	214,893	43,334	124,327
2010	211,017		211,017	211,017	214,893	3,876	128,203
2011	216,292		216,292	216,292	214,893	(1,399)	126,804
2012	221,700		221,700	221,700	214,893	(6,807)	119,997
2013	227,243		227,243	227,243	214,893	(12,350)	107,647
2014	232,923		232,923	232,923	214,893	(18,030)	89,617
2015	238,747		238,747	238,747	214,893	(23,854)	65,763
2016	244,715		244,715	244,715	214,893	(29,822)	35,941
2017	250,834		250,834	250,834	214,893	(35,941)	—
	2,250,196	101,262	2,148,934	2,148,934	2,148,934	—	

Straight-line Annualized Amount	$ 214,893

Pension and Retirement Plans

Introduction

Accounting for certain pensions and similar plans can be quite complicated and often requires the assistance of actuaries to determine funding and payout requirements. A detailed discussion of this topic is beyond the scope of this book, but certain general definitions and concepts will be covered. Although there are many different types of retirement plans, many fall into three major classification groups: *defined benefit plans, defined contribution plans,* and *defined compensation plans.* Defined benefit plans are those in which specific benefit amounts are calculated to be received in the future, based on employees' age, years of service to the organization, or salary earned. Defined contribution plans are those plans in which individual accounts are setup for each participant, and benefits are based on a combination of contributions made, earnings on contributions invested, and any other participants' forfeitures allocated to individual accounts. Examples of a defined contribution plan are 403(b) and 401(k) plans, and they can be contributory or noncontributory. Noncontributory plans are those in which the employer (i.e., the NFP) does not make any annual contributions to the plan, and the plan is only funded by withholdings from employees' salaries. Defined compensation plans are usually based on compensation contracts with highly compensated individual employees.

Accounting for Pension Plans

For defined benefit plans, GAAP (formerly SFAS 158, *Employers' Accounting for Defined Pension and Other Postretirement Plans*) requires NFP organizations to recognize the funded status of their pension plans in the statement of financial position and recognize changes in the funded status through changes in unrestricted net assets. If projected benefits exceed fair value of plan assets, the organization should recognize a liability. If the fair value of plan assets exceeds the projected benefits obligation, the organization should recognize an asset. Certain information is required to be disclosed in the footnotes for these types of plans, such as general information about the plan (e.g., who is covered, criteria for calculating contributions, etc.), obligations and funded status, and amounts recognized in the statement of activities. The footnotes can be quite lengthy—from one to two pages long.

Accounting for defined contribution plans is a little less complicated. The organization doesn't have to estimate future benefits and make constant adjustments. Basically, the NFP organization would record an expense equal to the calculated amount of the pension expense (i.e., allowable salary multiplied by approved rate). Any difference between the amount calculated and the amount deposited in the plan would be recorded as an accrued liability (if underdeposited) and as a prepaid expense (if overdeposited).

GAAP also requires that certain information be disclosed in the footnotes. A typical footnote for an organization with a 401(K) defined contribution plan is as follows:

Helpful NFP, Inc.
Notes to Financial Statements
(partial presentation)

Retirement Plan:
On January 1, 2007 the organization adopted a salary reduction, 401(K) retirement plan that is funded by voluntary employee contributions, with a maximum limit based on 6 percent of an employee's annual compensation, and discretionary employer contributions. Organization contributions to the plan amounted to $55,850 and $50,275, for the years ended December 31, 2010 and 2009, respectively.

CHAPTER 10

Investments, Pooling, and Split-Interest Agreements

If an organization has excess cash from operations, it is prudent for them to invest that cash in some type of investment to earn additional income. In this case, the income earned is unrestricted, and it can be used for any legitimate purpose that the NFP's board or management deems appropriate. Many times donors donate investments or cash to purchase investments, and they require that the investments be held for a specific period of time or indefinitely and that the income earned from those investments be used in a specific way or for a specific purpose. When a donor specifies that their gift be invested for a long period of time or in perpetuity, the permanently restricted fund is called an endowment fund. Complications arise about how to treat earnings from these funds, especially when the donor isn't clear about how those earnings should be used.

Restricted Investments

In the absence of donor stipulations, income from permanently restricted or endowment funds are considered unrestricted and can be used as deemed appropriate by the organization. However, if the donor stipulates that the income must be reinvested until a future date or future occurrence, then the income would be treated as temporarily or permanently restricted income. Let's say for example, a donor gives $100,000 to an NFP with the stipulation that it create an endowment and invest the funds in marketable securities. The donor further stipulates that all earnings from the investment must be reinvested until this endowment fund reaches $200,000 in value. After that, the organization can use the income earned from the investments for any purpose (i.e., unrestricted). The entry to record the initial contribution, and $6,000 in investment income earned in the first year (that is reinvested in the permanently restricted fund), would be similar to the following:

Year 1

	Debit	Credit
Investments (asset)	100,000	
Contributions—Permanently restricted (income)		100,000
Investment (asset)	6,000	
Investment income—Permanently restricted		6,000

Now, let's say that in year 12 the endowment has reached $201,000 in fair value, in year 13 the organization would record the $14,000 in earnings from this fund as unrestricted as follows:

Year 13

	Debit	Credit
Investment (asset)	14,000	
Investment Income—Unrestricted		14,000

Unrealized Appreciation and Depreciation of Donor Restricted Runds

As you might recall from Chapter 6, GAAP requires that investments in equity securities (i.e., stocks) with readily determinable fair values and all investments in debt securities (i.e., bonds) be measured and maintained at their fair value. So each year, organizations are required to adjust in their financial records the carrying value for these investments. With unrestricted investments, all increases or decreases in fair values are reported as current period, unrestricted gains or losses on their statement of activities. Problems arise, however, with permanently restricted endowment funds when the value of the fund decreases below the initial stated restricted amount (i.e., historic dollar value). When a donor doesn't stipulate what to do in this situation, the organization's board must consider the most prudent approach to complying with the donors' wishes. Many states have adopted laws governing fiduciaries, responsibilities for managing institutional funds. Many of these laws are based on the *Uniform Management of Institutional Funds Act* (UMIFA) of 1972 and the revised *Uniform Prudent Management of Institutional Funds Act* (UPMIFA) of 2006. These acts state that public charities should act to preserve the principal (i.e., to maintain the purchasing power of the amounts contributed to the fund). Therefore, NFPs with permanently restricted funds should at the very least maintain the fund at the historic dollar value (original contribution) if not maintain the fund at a higher amount to account for changes in monetary value (i.e., inflation).

This means that if the value of the permanently restricted (PR) endowment falls below the historic restricted amount and it appears that the decrease is not temporary, then the organization must use or allocate unrestricted funds to bring the balance of the PR fund back up. To illustrate this situation, let's say an NFP received a permanently restricted contribution of $100,000 in 1990. The value of this fund declined over the five years between 2004 and 2008 and had a fair value as of December 31, 2008 of $85,000. The organization should allocate and record earnings from unrestricted funds to restricted funds. If the NFP earned $5,000 in permanently restricted investment income and $35,000 in unrestricted investment income (total $40,000) in 2009, the NFP should allocate some of the unrestricted investment income (i.e., $10,000) to the permanently restricted income account to bring the value of the permanently restricted fund back up as follows:

	Debit	Credit
Investment—Permanently restricted (asset)	15,000	
Investment—Unrestricted (asset)	25,000	
Investment income—Permanently restricted		15,000
Investment income—Unrestricted		25,000

Many board members, officers, and management find this concept perplexing and question its veracity; especially when the results of unrestricted operations in a current year are not good and this reallocation make the results even worse. But board members and officers are trustees of their organization's assets (in this case, investments) and as such must ensure that they comply with all donors' restrictions.

Allocation of Pooled Funds and Donor Advised Funds

Pooled Investments

Frequently, NFP organizations pool or combine their investments into one single portfolio fund. This is done for a number of reasons, including earning a larger return or reducing investment management fees. However, when investments are pooled together, they lose their specific identification, which can make it difficult to track and report funds with different donor restrictions, such as on the use of investment income. One popular method for accounting for pooled investment funds is to use a weighted market value to determine allocable investment values.

To illustrate how investments in a pooled investment fund are accounted for, we will use the example in which, on January 1, 2008, an NFP invests $15,000 in unrestricted excess cash in a pooled investment portfolio along with donations it just received from two foundations in the amount of $25,000 and $35,000. The foundations' funds come with a restriction that they are permanently restricted (endowment) and can't be used, but the investment income earned is unrestricted and can be used for any purpose deemed appropriate by the organization. On January 1, 2010, the NFP receives another permanently restricted endowment of $25,000, which it immediately invested in the pooled investment portfolio. The value of each fund at the end of each year is based on each component's prorated, weighted, fair value compared to the total fair value of the fund. The calculation of the value of the additional $25,000 investment in 2010 is based on its relative fair value compared to the total value of all other investments immediately preceding the addition of this amount or $25,000/ $118,750 = 21.05 percent. This is illustrated in Table 10.1.

Donor-Advised Funds

A donor advised fund is a charitable giving vehicle wherein an individual, family, or corporation makes an irrevocable, tax-deductible contribution of personal assets to a charity, and at any time thereafter can exercise a right to make a recommendation on either uses of the account, such as providing advice about how to invest, or distributions from the account, such as providing advice about how to make expenditures. The key word here is *recommend,* as opposed to *dictate* or *demand* how the funds are to be used. The IRS is increasing its focus on making sure these types of arrangements are not abused.

The benefits of a donor-advised fund are the donor gets an immediate tax benefit when the fund is set up and the donor can decide at a later date (by suggestion) how the money should be distributed. It's important to note that many donor-advised funds are pooled investments in which many donors make contributions to a single investment portfolio.

Split-Interest Agreements

Introduction

Sometimes an NFP receives assets (or rights to those assets) where only a part of those assets or income earned from those assets are to be used by the NFP and treated as contributions. These types of "split" benefit situations are called Split-Interest Agreements (SIAs).

An SIA is created when a donor contributes assets directly to an NFP or places assets in a trust for the benefit of the NFP organization, but the NFP is not the sole beneficiary of the assets or the income generated from the assets. Why wouldn't a donor just donate a specific sum of money or assets directly to the NFP? There are a number of reasons why. Some have to do with long-term estate tax planning, such as pulling assets out of an individual's estate to avoid probate (court review). Others have to do with the need to receive income while alive but the donor wants to give away money to one or more charities after death. Or conversely, the donor wants to donate

Table 10.1   Calculation of the Value of Additional $25,000 Investment

Fund Type	Fair Value at December 1, 2008		Fair Value at December 31, 2008		Fair Value at December 31, 2009		Additional $25,000 January 1, 2010	
	$	%	$	%	$	%	$	%
Unrestricted	15,000	20.00%	16,500	20.00%	18,750	20.00%	18,750	15.79%
Endow 1	25,000	33.33%	27,500	33.33%	31,250	33.33%	31,250	26.32%
Endow 2	35,000	46.67%	38,500	46.67%	43,750	46.67%	43,750	36.84%
Endow 3							25,000	21.05%
Total	75,000	1.0000%	82,500	1.0000%	93,750	1.0000%	118,750	1.0000%

money to a charity while alive but wants the residual to go to an heir or another beneficiary after the donor dies.

Terminology

To account for SIAs, one must first understand the terms applicable to these types of agreements. The following are short definitions of common terms that apply to SIAs

- Grantor (or Donor)—Entity donating assets and creator of trust or arrangement.
- Trust—Agreement with an individual or entity to take title to property owned by a grantor (donor) and to protect or conserve it for either the grantor or the trust's beneficiary or beneficiaries.
- Trustee—Empowered to manage the trust and ensure in most cases that the trust investments earn an appropriate return.
- Beneficiary—Individual or entity that will receive benefits from trust or other financial arrangement.
- Annuity—Series of payments or receipts over a period of time.
- Present Value (PV)—Current worth (value) of future sums of money, calculated by discounting future amounts at an appropriate interest rate (opposite of compounded interest).
- Discount Rate—Interest rate (i.e., **percent**) used to calculate PV.
- Amortization of Discount—Periodic adjustments made to account for differences between initial recorded discount value (PV) and current value.

Accounting for Split-Interest Agreements—General

Accounting for split-interest agreements can become complicated and is based on provisions of the agreement and some external factors. Certain factors should be considered before making any accounting entries because, based on these factors, the accounting treatment will be different. Five factors to consider include:

1. Who is the trustee of the assets (i.e., who is responsible for managing assets)? It could be the NFP organization or another trustee (e.g., another NFP, bank, individual, etc.).
2. Who are the beneficiaries of the SIA? The NFP and the donor, several NFPs, NFP and donor heirs, or another beneficiary?
3. What are the benefits? Fixed-dollar distribution, percent of investment income earned, or percent of fair value of assets held by trustee?
4. When will the benefits be received? During the donor's life only, only for a specified number of years, in perpetuity, based on the

occurrence of a certain event, such as after the donor dies, and so
forth?

5. Is the donation revocable or irrevocable?

Revocable versus Irrevocable Split-Interest Agreements

With a *revocable* SIA, donors can change their mind at any time. This is
evident by the fact that the grantor has control over the trust and can dissolve
it at any time or the grantor only promises to set up the SIA in the future with
no guarantees that it will actually be set up. In these cases in which the
grantor only makes a promise to set up an SIA, no entries are required in the
financial records because no funds have been actually given to the NFP. If,
however, assets are in fact transferred to the NFP under a revocable SIA, or
no agreement exists, then the transaction is recorded as a liability and not a
contribution as follows:

	Debit	Credit
Assets held in revocable trust (asset)	100,000	
Refundable advances (liability)		100,000

With an *irrevocable* SIA, a donor cannot cancel the arrangement, and
the NFP will need to record some amount of contributions at inception.
How this transaction is recorded will depend on who the trustee is (i.e., NFP
or third party), whether there are any temporary or permanent restrictions
on the gift, and what the fair value is of the asset and benefits involved.
Determining what is the fair value is not always straightforward. Factors to
consider include estimating the return on the investments (i.e., earnings
over a period of time) and the life of the donor or beneficiary (which is
actuarially determined). Fair value is measured at the present value of the
estimated future distributions the organization or other beneficiaries
expect to receive over the SIA term or upon termination of the agreement.
Entries to the financial records are usually made annually and include the
annual investment income earned, distributions made to beneficiaries
(NFP and other parties), changes in value of the trust, and amortization
of discount.

As a general rule, and in accordance with GAAP (formerly SFAS 116),
contributions received under a SIA should be classified as temporarily
restricted because assets will be received in the future and there is an
implicit time restriction on their use.

As mentioned previously, the organization will record the SIA differently
depending on whether they or another third party are the trustee. There are
five common types of irrevocable split-interest agreements that will be
covered shortly. They are:

1. Charitable lead trust
2. Perpetual trust held by third parties
3. Charitable remainder trust
4. Charitable gift annuities
5. Pooled (life) income fund

Charitable Lead Trust

In a *charitable lead trust* the donor establishes a trust naming an NFP as the beneficiary until the agreement terminates (e.g., donor or spouse dies), at which time the plan's assets revert either to the donor (less usual) or to another beneficiary of the donor, such as the spouse or heir (more common). The donor can restrict use of funds and either the NFP or another entity can be trustee.

There are two types of charitable lead trusts: a *charitable lead annuity trust* (CLAT), in which the NFP periodically receives a specific dollar amount, and a *charitable lead unitrust* (CLUT), in which the NFP periodically receives a distribution of a percentage of a trust's fair market value each year.

To illustrate how to account for these types of trusts, we will assume Mr. Lott Adough (donor or grantor) establishes an irrevocable charitable lead annuity trust valued at $1,000,000 and naming Lucky NFP, Inc. as lead beneficiary. The terms state that Lucky is to receive $75,000 per year. Upon Mr. Lott Adough's death, the assets are to go to his daughter, Ms. Wanna B. Richer. The present value of the estimated distributions of $75,000 to be received each year is $650,000. If Lucky NFP is the trustee, they would record this transaction as follows:

To Record Contribution Benefit (initial entry)

	Debit	Credit
Assets held in charitable lead trust (asset)	1,000,000	
Contributions —Temporarily restricted (income)		650,000
Liabilities for amounts held for others (liability)		350,000

To Record Investment Income Earned in Year 1

	Debit	Credit
Assets held in charitable lead trust (asset)	85,000	
Liabilities for amounts held for others (liability)		350,000

To Record Annual Distributions in Year 1

	Debit	Credit
Cash (asset)	75,000	
Assets held in charitable lead trust (asset)		75,000

To Record Release of Restrictions in Year 1
(from Temporary to Unrestricted)

	Debit	Credit
Release of temporarily restricted assets—TR (revenue)	75,000	
Release of Temporarily Restricted Assets—UR (revenue)		75,000

To Record Amortization of Discount in Year 1

	Debit	Credit
Liabilities for amounts held for others (liability)	38,000	
Change in value of split interest		38,000

To Record Termination of Agreement (in a future year)

	Debit	Credit
Liabilities for amounts held for others (liability)	1,120,000	
Assets held in charitable lead trust (asset)		1,120,000

Perpetual Trust Held by Third Parties

To illustrate this type of trust, we will assume Mr. Lott Adough (donor or grantor) establishes an irrevocable perpetual trust held by third parties in the amount of $1,000,000, naming a bank (Best Bank, USA) the trustee and funds manager, and Lucky NFP, Inc. as the recipient of distributions of income forever (in perpetuity). This type of transaction is similar to receiving a permanently restricted endowment fund.

To Record Contribution Benefit (initial entry)

	Debit	Credit
Beneficial interest in perpetual trust (asset)	1,000,000	
Permanently restricted contribution (income)		1,000,000

To Record Annual Distributions in Year 1

	Debit	Credit
Cash (asset)	75,000	
Investment income—Unrestricted (income)		75,000

Charitable Remainder Trust

If Mr. Lott Adough wanted to remove assets from his estate (and from probate) and wanted to give money to Lucky NFP, Inc. but also suspects that either he or his wife will need the income from his assets for a specific period of time (e.g., while he or his spouse is alive), he can set up one of two types of trusts, either a charitable remainder annuity trust (CRAT), in which distributions are for a specific dollar amount, or a charitable remainder unitrust (CRUT), in which distributions are based on a percentage of trust's fair market value each year. The accounting for these types of trusts is similar to accounting for charitable lead trusts.

Charitable Gift Annuity

Charitable Gift Annuities are similar to charitable remainder trusts in that a donor contributes assets to an, NFP in exchange for receiving distributions for a specific period of time, and upon termination (e.g., donor or other beneficiary), the assets remain with the NFP. The only difference between this type of arrangement and charitable remainder trusts is no actual trust is set up. The entry to record this type of arrangement is as follows:

	Debit	Credit
Cash or investments (asset)	1,000,000	
Annuity payment liability (liability)		294,000
Contributions—Unrestricted (income)		706,000

Pooled (Life) Income Fund

Pooled (life) income funds are similar to charitable gift annuities, except the NFP receives funds from many donors and pools the donations together into one large investment fund. And similar to a charitable gift annuity, when the agreement terminates (donor or other beneficiary dies), the balance goes to the NFP. The value of the donors' contributions and the amount of allocable income to be distributed to beneficiaries is accounted for similarly to the accounting of pooled investments mentioned earlier in this chapter.

Subsidiaries and Interrelated Entities

Many NFP organizations have material relationships with other entities or organizations. Some have partial or total ownership in commercial for-profit entities; some are related as affiliates, branches, or chapters of larger, national organizations; and some are related based on some economic or controlling criteria such as board control or sharing of management, staff, and facilities. There is a common misbelief that an NFP organization cannot own or have interest in a for-profit, commercial enterprise. This is based on the fact that NFPs are not in the business of making a profit, so how can they own a business with a profit motive? The answer is that there is nothing wrong with an NFP owning a part or all of a commercial business as long as there is no improper shifting of expenses from the NFP (a tax-exempt entity), to the commercial, tax-paying entity.

Many NFPs purchase an interest in, or create a new for-profit entity for a variety of reasons, such as the activity is significantly different from the Organization's mission; the goal is to generate profit (revenue maximization); to avoid conflict with mandatory requirements from governmental agencies, donors, or external parties (e.g., noncomingling of assets, or nonadherence of required ratios or nonsanctioned activity); or for income tax considerations (corporate tax rates and rules are more advantageous than unrelated business tax rates and rules.).

Accounting for Investments in For-Profit Entities

Equity Method

How investments in for-profit entities are accounted for depends on several factors such as the NFP's ownership interest and the degree of influence it has over the for-profit entity. GAAP (formerly APB 18, *The Equity Method of Accounting for Investments in Common Stock*, requires that investors (i.e., the NFP) use the equity method of accounting to account for their investment over another entity if "they have the ability to exercise significant influence over operating and financial policies of the investee." What determines *significant influence* is based on facts and circumstances. As a general rule, significant influence is presumed to exist if ownership exceeds 20 percent of the common stock of the commercial entity, but not more than 50 percent (i.e., between 20 percent and 50 percent).

In simple terms, the equity method of accounting requires that the NFP record the purchase of the shares of the commercial entity at its *fair value* and recognizes investment income each year based on the percentage interest the NFP has in the invested company. With other, smaller equity investments (i.e., <20 percent), income is only recognized when a dividend is declared or a distribution is made. The reason for recognizing the percentage interest regardless of whether it is received is based on the presumption that an entity with a greater than 20 percent interest can control the timing of income distributions and manipulate its financial reporting. When ownership exceeds 50 percent, recognition of income is based on the consolidation method of accounting, which is discussed in the next section.

To demonstrate the equity method of accounting for an investment in a for-profit entity, we will assume that in 2009, Helpful NFP, Inc. purchases 1,000 shares of ABC Corporation, representing 25 percent of it's total outstanding stock (i.e., Helpful owns 25 percent of ABC) for $255,000. In 2010, ABC Corporation had net income of $160,000 and issued a dividend of $5,000. The entries to record the investment in ABC Corporation and subsequent income is as follows:

To Record Purchase of 1,000 Shares of ABC Corporation at $255 per share in 2009

	Debit	Credit
Investments (asset)	255,000	
Cash (asset)		255,000

To Record Pro-Rata Share of ABC Corporation $160,000 Income in 2010

	Debit	Credit
Investments (asset)	40,000	
Investment income (income)		40,000

$160,000 × 25 percent = $40,000

To Record $20,000 Dividend Declared By ABC Corporation in 2010

	Debit	Credit
Cash (asset)	5,000	
Investment (asset)		5,000

$20,000 × 25 percent = $5,000

Consolidation Method

When the ownership interest exceeds 50 percent, GAAP requires another method of accounting for investments in other entities (subsidiaries) called the consolidation method. More specifically, GAAP (formerly ARB 51 and SFAS 94, *Consolidation of All Majority-Owned Subsidiaries*) requires that an NFP consolidate the financial results of the for-profit entity with the NFP's financial activities if the NFP has a controlling financial interest in the for-profit entity. A controlling financial interest is deemed to exist if ownership exceeds 50 percent of common stock. The justification is that because one entity had the ability to control the other, the likelihood of manipulation of financial activity between the two becomes very high, so separate reporting becomes less meaningful.

When consolidated financial statements are required, GAAP requires that all interorganizational transactions are eliminated and all balances combined. The result is basically presenting the two entities as one. Interorganizational transactions that are eliminated include all receivables and payables that are due to and from each entity and any revenue or expenses received or incurred by one with regard to the other. There are two general methods for presenting consolidated financial statements. The first is to show only the consolidated amounts on the statements of financial position, activities, and cash flows (known as consolidated financial statements). The other method is to show each entity in a separate column, show eliminations in another column, and show the consolidated totals in a third column. This method is known as consolidating financial statements and usually only used with the statements of financial position and activities but not the statement of cash flows.

GAAP requires that the basis of consolidation be disclosed in the notes to financial statements as follows:

Helpful NFP, Inc.
Notes to Financial Statements
(partial presentation)

Summary of Significant Accounting Policies:

Principles of Consolidation:

The consolidated financial statements include the accounts of Helpful NFP, Inc. and its wholly owned subsidiary, ABC Corporation. All material interorganizational transactions have been eliminated.

Accounting for Interrelated NFP Entities

Consolidation

Some NFPs own or control other NFPs. If certain conditions exist in their relationship, GAAP requires that the two NFPs consolidate their financial statements. Whether consolidation is required is based on facts and circumstances. Two determining factors are controlling financial interest similar to an NFP's ownership of for-profit entities or control and economic interest. As discussed in the previous section, controlling financial interest exists when an NFP owns more than 50 percent of the common stock of another NFP corporation. Control and economic interest exists when one NFP controls the resources or is liable for another NFP's liabilities and has control through holding a majority of seats on the board of the other NFP. In some cases, the opposite is true, and financial statements are not consolidated even if an NFP owns more than 50 percent of another NFP but it doesn't have control of that NFP (e.g., others hold a majority of board seats or another entity has control of finances or activities). A situation in which lack of control exists could be a chapter of a national organization.

Combined/Combining Financial Statements of Commonly Controlled Organizations

Sometimes two NFPs are interrelated but neither controls the other; instead there exists some degree of common control. When two organizations have common control it becomes more meaningful to present their financial information together. When the financial statements of commonly controlled organizations are presented together it is called combined or combining financial statements.

GAAP is not specific about whether combination is required. The decision to combine financial statements requires judgment, and many accountants disagree about whether presenting the combined is more informative than presenting them separately. Questions should be raised about what the common elements are and whether the combined statements are more meaningful. Common elements include sharing the same facilities (office space, equipment), staff, management, or having the same officers or board of directors. There is no requirement that the two NFPs have the same exempt status, so one can be a 501(c)(3) public charity and the other a 501(c)(6) membership organization.

Combined or combining financial statements are very similar to consolidated or consolidating financial statements in appearance with the exception of the terms. In both cases all interorganizational transactions are eliminated, such as receivables and payables and all revenue or expenses received or incurred by one with regard to the other. And similar to consolidation, when all accounts are shown as one amount on the financial statements, the statements are called combined, and when both NFPs are shown in separate columns with all necessary eliminations, the statements are titled combining. The following is a partial presentation under the combining presentation method where two NFPs have the same management and share the same facilities. For simplicity, we will assume in our example that there aren't any eliminating accounts or transactions.

Helpful NFP, Inc.
Doing Good Things NFP, Inc.
Combining Statements of Activities
(partial presentation)

Years Ended December 31, 2010 and 2009

	2010			2009
	Helpful	Doing Good	Combined	Combined
Support and Revenues:				
Unrestricted:				
Government grants	$ 2,441,632	$ 250,000	$ 2,691,632	$ 2,855,000
Contributions	1,365,854	257,800	1,623,654	1,575,260
Program service revenue	358,875	185,000	543,875	415,920
Total support and revenues	$ 4,166,361	$ 692,800	$ 4,859,161	$ 4,846,180

Budget Development and Applications

What is a budget? There are a number of technical definitions but basically it is a monetary plan, guide, and tool to assist an organization's management in allocating existing and future resources (goals element), and also to assist them in evaluating deficiencies and accomplishments in operations based on financial results (evaluation element). Basically a budget is a self-created measure to provide direction and help monitor operations. Budget development is more of an art than a science. The ability to create a budget is based more on experience than accounting acumen. It's easy to put together a bunch of numbers and call it a budget. It is much more difficult to develop a good (realistic) budget.

Who uses budgets? In a nutshell, everyone. Management and board of directors (to manage resources and activities); department and program managers and directors (to manage programs and activities); accounting department (to prepare financial reports and explain fluctuations in financial performance); external parties (to evaluate an organization's performance); government agencies (to evaluate performance and approve payments), and donors (to ensure proper use of donated funds).

Why are budgets important? Budgets are important to all entities from sole proprietorships to large multinational corporations. All need a financial roadmap in order to operate efficiently. Commercial entities need budgets to maximize their profits and NFPs need them to determine the best uses of funds to accomplish their mission. It can be said that budgets are even more important to NFPs because they tend to have limited resources and must be very careful how they use those resources. Budgets assist them in being as effective and efficient as possible. Budgets can be on an annual basis or broken down by month or quarter.

Budget Preparation

Who creates, prepares, and approves budgets?

Budgets are not typically prepared by only one person. It is usually a collaborative effort of two or more people. Smaller NFPs might have only two or three people involved, whereas larger organizations might have five, ten, or even more. Typically, the primary individuals who are responsible for preparing budgets might include the ED, President, or chief executive officer who oversees and has the most overall knowledge of operations; one or more members of the board of directors (e.g., chairperson, treasurer, budget and finance committee members); one or more department heads (e.g., program director) and the accounting department.

The budget approval process varies, and the number of people involved usually correlates to the size of the organization. For example, with smaller NFPs maybe only the ED and a few board members approve the annual budget, whereas larger NFPs have several levels of approvals from managers to the full board.

Ten Factors to Consider Before Creating a Budget

Before creating or developing a budget, certain factors should be considered. They include the following:

1. Who will be responsible for preparing part or the entire budget?
2. When will the budget be prepared?
3. Who will approve the budget?
4. When will the budget be approved?
5. What is the basis for developing budget (accrual, cash, modified cash)?
6. What is the frequency for reviewing activity (monthly, quarterly, annually)?
7. What is the required budget level (by program, project, department, grant, location, event, activity, etc.)?
8. What format will be used for presenting budget and variance (column, summary, etc.)?
9. In what reports will the budget be included or presented (e.g., included in Auditors' report, in published annual report, etc.)?
10. Who is responsible for comparing actual amounts to budget and explaining variances (controller, president, etc.)?

Nine Practical Steps to Developing an Annual Budget

Budget preparation should be performed in a systematic and organized manner if it is to be useful. The following nine steps can be used as a practical guide to preparing a typical NFP's annual budget. These procedures are only a guide and should be modified as deemed necessary to accomplish a particular organization's budgetary goals. The nine steps are as follows:

1. **Timely Budget Preparation**—Assemble the individuals responsible for preparing the annual budget at a similar time and place each year. Consistency is important for discipline purposes. If possible, hold the budget meeting off-site (i.e., not in the office). This will reduce distractions and allow the participant to give their full attention to budget amounts.

2. **Starting Point**—Start with the prior year's actual financial activity. Review amounts on various levels (program, revenue sources, expenditures, etc.). Note all nonreoccurring activities or transactions and related dollar amounts. Also note all noncash items, like depreciation and capital items.

3. **Current Year Changes**—Make a list of all known current year changes, such as new or discontinued programs, grants, major income, or expenditures. Assign dollar amounts to all new items.

4. **Support and Revenue**—Estimate current support and revenue based on current available information by combining reoccurring prior-year amounts with current-year additions. Amounts should be conservative, not optimistic. Assume the most realistic donation level and government grants that are assured or very likely to be received. It is better to underestimate than to overestimate. It is easier to explain positive variances than negative ones.

5. **Expenditures**—Estimate current expenses and capital purchases based on current available information by combining reoccurring prior-year amounts with current-year additions. Review current support and revenue budgeted amounts to ensure that all expenditures related to generating income are included. Be liberal with expense estimates. Again, don't base expenditure decisions on overly optimistic assumptions. It is better to overestimate than underestimate.

6. **Compare income to expenditures**—Determine whether adjustments are needed to expenditures to arrive at desired level of net income. Consider prior-year surplus if current-year loss exists or consider creating a surplus for unexpected occurrences in the future.

7. **Preparation of monthly budgets**—If preparing monthly budgets, use one of the three methods: exact method—for each month, go line by line for each revenue and expense category and estimate amount (this method is not recommended because it is very time consuming); straight-line method—take annual budget and divide line by 12 (easiest method but not realistic because most NFPs do not receive or spend money evenly throughout the year); and hybrid method—first calculate budget using a straight-line method. Then, starting with revenue and support, because it is easier to project, modify the months when significant receipts are expected (e.g., revenue will be received in December from annual dinner dance). Next, modify the months when major expenditures are known to have to be made

(e.g., major leasehold improvements are expected to be made in June or the paying of rent on a facility needed for an event in December).

8. **Separate expenditures**—Separate budgeted expenditures into current operating and capital expenditures. This is needed to explain variances between the budget and actual amounts reported on the statements of activities and functional expenses, which do not include capital expenditures.

9. **Review and discuss budget**—A draft budget should be reviewed and discussed with all appropriate management, officers, and board directors before approval to ensure nothing is omitted, to reduce future surprises, and to improve accountability. Once reviewed, the budget should be approved by the executive committee or full board and documented in the board minutes.

Budget Format

Developing a financial budget doesn't necessarily require someone with an accounting degree. However, accounting knowledge or experience is very helpful in understanding prior financial activity and designing a budget report. The budget report should not be so detailed that it is overwhelming to read, nor should it be so general that the numbers become meaningless. Although budget worksheets can be configured in any way desired, the final budget report should be designed with the reader in mind.

There are no perfect or correct formats for presenting budgets. The format used should be one that is the most appropriate for a particular NFP. However there are certain general concepts that, if followed, will make the budget report easier to read and understand.

The first concept can be termed the multilevel or drill-down approach. This concept requires that the budget report consist of several pages with the first page providing summary or general information and each subsequent page providing more detailed information. For example, the first page (top sheet) could include four columns: current year actual, next year budget, change (i.e., increases or decreases) and reference for explaining change, and the body of the report showing only the major revenue/support and expense categories. Table 12.1 illustrates this.

If the next year's budget is prepared before the end of the current operating year, two more columns should be added after the actual column, one with projected amounts for the months in which actual figures are unavailable, and the other with a combined total for the current year. All other columns would remain the same. This is illustrated in Table 12.2.

The second page in the budget report could provide detailed amounts by program and natural expense category (e.g., salaries, office expense, etc.), and the one after that could provide even more detail by grant or project or event. It is very important that explanations are provided for all

Table 12.1 Support/Revenue and Expense Budget

	Job Training Now, Inc. Support/Revenue and Expense Budget 2011			
	Actual 2010	Budget 2011	Ref.	Increase/ (Decrease)
Support and Revenues:				
Government grants	$3,378,416	$3,547,337	1	$168,921
Contributions	1,864,058	1,957,261	2	93,203
Program service revenue	492,172	516,781	3	24,609
All other income	786,837	826,179	4	39,342
Total support and revenues	6,521,483	6,847,558		326,075
Expenses:				
Program Expenses:				
Simulated on-the-job training	4,485,150	4,709,408	8	224,258
Corporate on-site training	314,013	329,714	9	15,701
Total program expenses	4,799,163	5,039,122		239,959
Supporting Services:				
Management and general	1,245,941	1,308,238		62,297
Fund-raising	96,753	101,591		4,838
Total expenses	6,141,857	6,448,951		307,094
Increase/(decrease) in net assets	$ 379,626	$ 398,607		$ 18,981

	Reasons for increase/(decrease)
1	Reason, Reason, Reason, Reason . . . .
2	Reason, Reason, Reason, Reason . . . .
3 to 9	Reason, Reason, Reason, Reason . . . .

major changes (i.e., increases or decreases) between the next year's budget and the current year's actual. By using reference numbers or letters, explanations can be made on the bottom of the report or on a separate page instead of on the face of the report, which makes the report easier to read.

Variance Reporting

Budgets are useful if they are used as a tool to monitor and report on current financial activity and to assist management in taking appropriate correctable action when possible. What good is a budget if no one looks at it? As such, budgets need to be compared to actual results on a periodic basis to be

Table 12.2 Support/Revenue & Expense Budget

Job Training Now, Inc.
Support/Revenue and Expense Budget
(partial presentation)
2011

| | 2010 (Current Year) | | | | | |
	Actual 01/01/10– 10/31/10	Projected 11/1/10– 12/31/10	Combined Total	Budget 2011	Ref.	Increase/ (Decrease)
Support and Revenues:						
Government grants	$2,855,000	$528,417	$3,383,417	$3,547,338	1	$163,921
Contributions	1,575,260	293,798	1,869,058	1,957,261	2	88,203
Program service revenue	415,920	81,252	497,172	516,781	3	19,609
All other income	697,722	94,115	791,837	735,086	4	−56,751
Total support and revenues	$5,543,902	$997,582	$6,541,484	$6,756,466		$214,982

beneficial. These types of reports comparing actual results to budgetary amounts are called variance reports. There is no set rule about how frequently variance reports should be prepared, analyzed, and discussed, and the frequency depends on the size of the organization, board involvement, and how much the financial activity fluctuates. For many NFPs, especially larger ones, monthly reports are necessary. For others, this might be unrealistic or unnecessary. Minimally, it should be done quarterly so that corrective steps can be taken to remediate any correctable problems (e.g., cut back on expenses, terminate staff, or increase fund-raising efforts).

Similar to problems of preparing budgets, variance reports are prepared many times with too much information presented on one page. And similar to preparing budget reports, the ideal method would be to use a multilevel, drill-down approach, to presenting information (i.e., more detailed information on each subsequent page). Again, a reference column should be used to cross-reference variance explanations provided at the bottom of the report or on a separate page.

Many organizations like presenting monthly budget and variance reports in addition to annual ones. The author does not believe monthly comparisons are useful and can even be more confusing because of all the possible timing differences that can occur. For example, it is not uncommon for activities to take place or donations received at a different time than originally planned. Then, a lot of unnecessary time has to be spent explaining these timing issues instead of addressing core variances in revenue and expenses.

Table 12.3 is an example of a variance report showing the variance between actual and budget along with the variance between actual and prior year. This dual presentation provides the reader with two comparisons on one report in an easy-to-read format. Again, summary explanations should be provided on the bottom of the report with more elaboration on a separate page if necessary.

Other Budget Preparation and Reporting Issues

Because of other pressing demands on the NFP's chief accountant, ED, and so forth, not enough time is allowed in many cases to prepare a thought-out budget and easy-to-read budget report. Poorly designed budgets will haunt the organization throughout the year, so any time that was saved by rushing will be spent many times over in analyzing and explaining variances. Here are some don'ts.

Don't try to have the budgeted income equal the budgeted expenses creating a zero change in net assets (i.e., zero net income). Some people incorrectly believe that NFPs can't show a profit, so they create this zero budget. Yes, NFPs are not in business to make a profit, but it is a fallacy that they *can't* make a profit. Furthermore, it is highly unlikely that actual results

Table 12.3   Functional Expense Budget Variance Report

Job Training Now, Inc.
Functional Expense Budget Variance Report
(partial presentation)
Year-to-Date as of June 30, 20xx

| | Actual vs. Prior | | | Actual vs. Budget | |
	2007	Variance		Actual	Budget	Variance
2008						
Support and Revenues:						
Government grants	$—	1 $—		$—	$—	4 $—
Contributions						
Program service revenue						
$—	$—	$—	Total Support & Revenue	$—	$—	$—

Reasons for Increase/(Decrease)

Ref #	Explanation
1	Reason, Reason, Reason, Reason . . . .
2	Reason, Reason, Reason, Reason . . . .

will actually net out to zero. So why create a budget that is almost guaranteed not to be accurate.

Don't wait until well into the next operating year to prepare and approve a budget. Some organization's wait until the fifth or sixth month of the year to approve that year's budget. The argument for waiting so long is that information about grants, events, and so forth isn't available at the end of the prior year so the budget is postponed until concrete information is available. Yes, there will be fewer budget variances if the budget is prepared much later, but that defeats the whole purpose of having a budget to begin with. There is nothing wrong in explaining a budget variance caused by unforeseeable events at the time the budget was prepared.

Don't create an overly optimistic budget and inflate income in order to appease board members or others and tell yourself you will worry about it later. Later will come sooner than you think, and lost credibility is difficult to regain.

Don't allow the budget/finance or executive committees or board to *rubber-stamp* or quickly approve a budget without first having a general understanding of what the numbers signify. Blame will not be in short supply even if the budget is close to target, because some people look to find fault in others for their lack of diligence when financial results are less than rosy. Board members need to be enlightened that a budget is a *best guess* of the future, not a promise or guarantee. Variances will exist and should be expected.

Explaining Variances

Calculating variances (differences) is relatively easy—simple subtraction. Actual amounts less budgeted amounts equal variance. Explaining variances on the other hand is much harder. Many times explanations are not presented properly. Either too much information or not enough information is provided on the report. If too much information is given, the reader gets bogged down with immaterial items (e.g., Why did we purchase a computer for $1,500? I bought mine from Dell and only paid $1,000!). If too little information is given about large variances, or if explanations are too vague, the reader becomes suspicious and uncomfortable with management's stewardship of the organization's finances. And, as previously mentioned, explanations should be short, simple, and to the point on the report, with more elaborate answers provided on a separate page.

Some problems that arise when explaining variances are due to a different classification basis used to prepare budgets versus the basis used to report actual financial information. For example, many budgets are prepared on the cash basis because it is easier to understand. However, the organization's financial records are maintained on the accrual basis of accounting. This difference automatically creates budget variances. Budgets should be prepared on the same basis as the financial records.

Other differences include comparing budgeted expenses that include capital expenditures (e.g., office equipment) with actual expenses that exclude capital purchases, and comparing actual results that include non-cash transactions such as depreciation expense with a budget that doesn't. Or, comparing a budget that is detailed by program, grant, or activity with actual results when allocations are not made on a timely basis or not until the end of the year, which makes comparison difficult.

Finally, budget/finance/audit committee members or any other board member who is authorized to monitor financial activity should document in their meeting minutes their review and understanding of the variance reports presented by management. This will reduce misunderstandings at a later date and provide documentation that board members are performing their fiduciary responsibilities of oversight.

CHAPTER

13

Special Types of NFP Organizations

W hen many people think of an NFP organization, they typically think of a public charity whose mission is to help the needy and less fortunate with medicine, clothing, and food (e.g., American Red Cross or Salvation Army). However, there are literally hundreds of other types of NFPs that provide a wide spectrum of beneficial services to society. These include membership organizations (chambers of commerce, professional associations, etc.); economic development and civic organizations; social clubs; schools, colleges, and other educational institutions; churches and other religious organizations; museums and cultural institutions; libraries and literary groups; performing arts, research, and scientific organizations; hospitals, clinics, and drug-treatment facilities; amateur sports and recreation groups and foundations, to mention a few. Although all are exempt from paying some or most income taxes, not all can receive tax-deductible contributions, and some must pay certain other taxes such as excise, use tax, and unrelated business taxes. And, although there are some similarities between many different types of NFPs, there are significant differences among many others in the services or products provided, sources of revenue and support received, methods used to achieve their mission, and the accounting policies and procedures used to report their operational and financial activities. We will discuss some of these different types of organizations and their unique characteristics in the rest of this chapter.

Membership Organizations (Professional and Business Associations and Leagues)

These organizations are formed to provide one or more services to a distinct or specific group of individuals and businesses. The composition of the group can be based on any legal criteria such as professionals (accounting, legal), industry (real estate, insurance) or local chapters of international groups (New York chapter of the Rotary Club). Most are classified under

Internal Revenue Code section 501(c)(6), which means they cannot receive tax-deductible donations.

The major sources of revenue for these NFPs are membership dues, ticket sales for events, and sales of publications or other products and services. One typical accounting issue has to do with accounting for membership dues invoiced or received in advance of the membership period covered. Since in most cases (unless there is a contract) there is no legal obligation to be a member, invoices are not true obligations to the recipient. Rather they are more like a solicitation or request to be a member. These types of invoices should never be recorded as a receivable in the organization's financial records. Also, if membership dues are received at the end of an operating year (e.g., December, 2009) but relate to the next operating year (e.g., 2010) the receipt should not be recorded as revenue but as deferred revenue (a liability). For example say an NFP membership organization receives $20,500 from its members in December 2009 for the 2010 membership year. The entry to record this transaction would be as follows:

	Debit	Credit
Cash (asset)	20,500	
Deferred revenue (liability)		20,500

Civic Leagues, Local Development Corporations (LDCs), and Business Improvement Districts (BIDs)

Civic Leagues and Local Development Corporations (LDCs) Generally speaking, these types of NFPs are formed by individuals or groups who want to improve the living, working, or business environment in a specific geographic area. Some LDCs are formed and operated as a governmental agency. Many others operate as an IRS Code section 501(c)(4)—Civic League, or a 501(c)(3)—Public Charity.

Business Improvement Districts (BIDs) Business improvement districts typically have operational elements of LDCs (property development and improvement) and governmental services (security and sanitation). Many BIDs are created because local governments lack the resources to improve the business climate or working conditions in their jurisdiction. Some BIDs also have elements of other types of organizations including chambers of commerce (business attraction and promotion) and public charities (e.g., social services such as homeless shelters and public and health assistance). A BID's general goal is to improve the business environment in a specific geographic area. BIDs have become very popular and have grown exponentially over the last 20 years. According to an article by Seth A. Grossman entitled "The Case of Business Improvement Districts: Special District

Public—Private Cooperation in Community Revitalization" (*Public Perform-ance & Management Review*, 32, December 2, 2008, M.E. Sharpe, Inc. publisher), there were more than 650 BIDs in the United States in 2008 and an estimated 1,500 worldwide. Many business improvement districts are concentrated in the most populated cities and states in the country. By some estimates and reports, New York, California, and New Jersey each have over 100 BIDs (with New York City having about 65 and Los Angeles about 37) and Wisconsin greater than 65.

Every state has its own laws specifying how BIDs are formed, and many cities and jurisdictions have their own rules governing the operations of BIDs. In New York City, as in many other places, BIDs are formed when a certain percentage of business owners in a demarcated geographic area (e.g., Times Square, downtown Los Angeles) vote to form a BID, prepare a BID plan, and submit it to an authorized government agency for approval.

Revenue sources and methods of receiving revenue vary by state and locality. In New York City for example, the major source of revenue comes from a special assessment levied on and paid by property or business owners based on some criteria such as square footage or fair market value of property owned. Assessment payments are first sent to the New York City Department of Finance and subsequently remitted to the appropriate BID.

Churches (includes synagogues and mosques)

The First Amendment (which prohibits making laws regulating churches) protects churches (as generally defined) from having to report their financial or other activities to the IRS or other regulatory bodies. Some choose to report voluntarily, but many others do not, so comprehensive data is not available. Churches rely very heavily on volunteers to perform most program and administrative services including the accounting and trea-surer functions. Because of this, and the lack of regulations and required oversight, many churches do not allocate significant resources to account-ing for financial activity. Therefore, many times the financial statements and IRS Form 990s that are prepared are not accurate or materially correct. Even if churches do report their financial activities, they tend to use the cash basis of accounting because of its simplicity. Since the cash basis of account-ing usually only recognizes cash transactions, many do not properly recog-nize important transactions, such as noncash contributions (buildings and vehicles) and related depreciation expense. These omissions significantly misrepresent a church's true cost of operations.

Museums and Cultural Institutions

The major source of support and revenue for museums and other cultural institutions are unrestricted and permanently restricted contributions (i.e., endowments), entrance fees, ticket sales to events, investment income, and store sales. Entrance fees can be mandatory or voluntary. The unique accounting issues these NFPs face are how to account for collections (previously covered) and contributed or free use of buildings.

Libraries (Nongovernmental)

The major sources of revenue and support for libraries are contributions, government grants, and access or user fees. One unique accounting issue these NFPs face is whether to expense or capitalize book purchases. It is preferable to capitalize book purchases and depreciate a portion each year using a 5- to 10-year estimated life or longer (if justified). Since capitalizing the cost of each book separately could be burdensome, an acceptable method is to assign a standard cost to each book (unit cost), rather than track each book separately. To illustrate, if a library purchased 200 books at various prices for a total cost of $5,000, the unit cost of each book would be $25 (not the actual cost of each book). This reduces tracking and accounting time. An exception would be made for those books that are valuable collections. These purchases should be tracked separately at cost.

Social Clubs

NFPs that are classified as social clubs range in size from small, intimate groups (checkers or dance clubs) to large multimillion-dollar organizations. Unlike all other NFPs, where there are no shares or ownership, clubs require members to purchase capital shares representing equity in the organization. However, unlike ownership in a commercial enterprise, club shares do not entitle the members to earn dividends or distributions from profits earned by the club. Rather, share ownership is more of a mechanism to control membership and to ensure that members have an inherent interest in the viability and success of the club in accordance with the club's charter, rather than to earn a return on the investment.

When shares of the corporation are purchased or sold they are not treated on the NFP's financial records as revenue or expenses but as additions and reductions to net assets (i.e., capital). The major source of revenue for social clubs are initiation fees, annual dues, usage, and other fees. Large clubs could have significant tangible assets, such as land and buildings, and should use appropriate accounting capitalization and depreciation methods to properly reflect current-year expenses.

Chapters, Branches, and Affiliates of National or Larger NFPs

Many public charities (e.g., American Lung Association), membership (professional and business associations), and other organizations (sports leagues, advocacy groups) have local or regional chapters, branches, or affiliates. Their relationships with related national organizations can vary significantly and, therefore, accounting for interorganizational transactions will be different. For example, many chapters or branches are not incorporated and, therefore, not separate legal entities. Their financial activities are usually combined with the parent organization. Other chapters, branches, or affiliates, even if formed as a separate corporation or limited liability company, are so integrated with their parents that their operations are consolidated or combined. Many others must maintain their own financial records, and as such, must account for all revenue or expenses received or paid to their related national organizations.

A significant number of chapters have their own board members that oversee the chapters operations. Typically there is a chapter agreement that allows a chapter to use the name of the national organization but also specifies the rules that a chapter must follow. These rules might include the number of required board meetings, activities that are permitted and not permitted, rules for electing and removing officers and board members and so on.

Common interorganizational transactions include the collection and remittance of *dues and contributions*. When all dues are received by the national organization, and a portion of those dues are given back to the related entities, the national organization should recognize these liabilities or payments. For example, let's say the National Organization of Helpers (NOH) receives all dues and gives back 40 percent of the dues it receives from a particular area to the local affiliated NFP. In 2010, NOH collected $10,000 in dues related to the New York City chapter. NOH's entry to record this transaction, and the amount due to the NYC affiliate, would be as follows:

	Debit	Credit
Cash (asset)	10,000	
Dues (income)		6,000
Due to local chapters (liability)		4,000

Colleges and Universities

Many colleges and universities are formed as NFPs. Their major source of revenue is student fees. They also receive support and revenue from contributions (mostly in the form of permanently restricted endowments); research grants; investment income; sales of publications; and income from seminars, use of facilities, research materials, and patents.

One unique accounting issue is the recording of *financial aid* and *tuition discounts*. The accounting treatment is different if discounts or subsidies are paid out to a third party or absorbed by the institution itself. When paid out to third parties, the accounting is straightforward as follows:

	Debit	Credit
Student Assistance—Housing (expense)	105,000	
Student Assistance—Books (expense)	45,000	
Cash (asset)		150,000

When the college or university gives tuition or other discounts to students directly, they need to recognize and report the discount separately in their financial records. The proper way to present the discounted amount is to show both gross tuition revenue and the tuition discount (a contra account) in the revenue section of the statement of activities. The tuition discount would be shown as a negative amount. An example of the entry to record the tuition fee and discount offered by the institution is as follows:

	Debit	Credit
Cash (asset)	950,000	
Tuition Fees (income)		1,590,000
Allowance for Tuition Discounts (income)	640,000	

Other Specialized Not-for-Profit Entities

There are many other NFP organizations that have unique operations and activities, and, therefore, must comply with different accounting and reporting rules. A sampling includes hospitals, other religious organizations, performing arts groups, research and scientific organizations, private elementary and secondary schools, and foundations.

Regulatory Reporting
(990, 990-T, and 990-PF)

Most governments function by raising money through various taxes, tariffs, and fees. Even before the formation of the United States, taxes existed in some fashion and were imposed on different segments of society by the controlling colonial powers (e.g., Britain, France). There were tariffs on imports, property taxes, and taxes on the sale of certain goods. The first income tax laws in the United States were instituted in 1862 to support the Civil War and later found to be unconstitutional by the Supreme Court. In 1913 the 16th Amendment was passed, making income taxes permanent. Taxes have been imposed ever since.

Regulatory Reporting Requirements

Going back centuries, certain organizations were spared the burden of paying taxes. In the colonial period, certain organizations, mostly religious, were exempt from the burden of paying taxes. It was believed by the ruling authorities that they provided needed assistance or services to individuals or groups not able to get these things from anywhere else. Exemption from taxation continued to be allowed and was incorporated into the federal tax code of 1913. In 1924 the Supreme Court issued a ruling supporting the exemption of charitable entities from taxes by recognizing the benefit the public derives from their activities, which are not conducted for private interest or gain. They basically said that, because certain organizations serve the community, they should be granted certain privileges. Other courts have upheld the constitutionality of NFPs tax exemption by stating that they perform a public service or they benefit society as a whole. One federal court justified the exclusion by saying that NFP activities relieve the government of the burden of meeting public needs that would otherwise fall on the government if not provided by these entities.

There was no incentive to support the activities of exempt organizations other than personal benevolence, so in 1917 the government granted a deduction against income taxes for contributions made to these entities. This created an economic/financial incentive to individuals and corporations to support exempt organization activities in addition to their desire to be benevolent. However, with more privileges comes more scrutiny, which means more reporting and disclosures. In general terms, the overriding concerns of the government is that no one receives a private, profit-motivated benefit from an organization's exemption from income taxes, and that the public is ensured their donations are being used for their intended purpose and not being misappropriated.

A major change in the regulations occurred in 1969 when restrictions were placed on private foundations whose goals typically are not to provide services but rather to give out funds for benevolent purposes. The restrictions included prohibitions from acts of self-dealing, from making certain types of investments, and from accumulating income. They also created the presumption that all public charities (i.e., 501(c)(3) organizations) would be classified as private foundations unless they could substantiate that they fell within one of three public charity classifications (charitable, religious, and educational).

Reporting and Auditing—General

As previously mentioned, with more benefits comes more scrutiny and that means more reporting. Over the years, NFP organizations have been subjected to more and more reporting requirements by more and more external entities. The federal government and most state governments require the filing of an annual information return for all organizations that meet certain gross-income tests. Most government agencies, along with some foundations and contributors who give money to NFPs, require that the NFPs submit periodic reports to them to ensure that the funds are being used in accordance with the stated purpose for receiving the funds. Sometimes these reports are required before any funds are disbursed, as is the case with expense-reimbursement-type grants and contracts, and sometimes the reports are submitted after funds are disbursed and the project is completed. Many times NFPs are required to have their financial records and financial statements audited by government Auditors or an independent certified public accountant (CPA) to provide assurance that financial reporting is materially correct, not misleading, and in compliance with all applicable rules and regulations. For example, New York state requires all NFPs registered in the state (except those exempted), with revenues over $250,000 to have an audit of their financial records performed annually by an independent auditor.

Internal Revenue Service (IRS)

The Internal Revenue Service is the agency responsible for regulating tax-deductible contributions and for granting exemption from paying federal income taxes and ensuring that NFPs operate in a manner consistent with their stated mission. Most states follow the federal exemption and once approved by the IRS, allow exemption from many state and local taxes (e.g., income, sales, property). After approving the exemption, it is left to the IRS to ensure that NFP activities comply with their reported mission. They ensure this compliance by requiring the submission of annual information returns (i.e., Form 990s), sending requests for additional information (i.e., notices), and performing desk audits, for which information is sent to the agent, and field audits, for which auditors examine documents at the organization's place of business.

Imposition of Taxes

Most NFPs, especially 501(c)(3) Public Charities, are exempt from paying income and other taxes. However, there are times when taxes are required or imposed, as is the case with most private foundations. Many of these imposed taxes are actually penalties or fines for engaging in some type of unacceptable activity. Most of the time these taxes are paid by the organization but sometimes they are paid by other individuals (managers), other entities, or both. Examples of taxes or penalties related to activities engaged in by *public charities* include unrelated business income (UBI) taxes (taxes on income derived from activities not related to the organization's exempt purpose, covered shortly); political expenditures (2 tier tax, 10 percent excise taxes imposed on the organization and 2.5 percent tax on the knowledgeable organization manager); prohibited tax shelters (100 percent income tax on net income derived from the transaction); excess benefit transactions (2 tier tax, 25 percent excise tax of excess benefit imposed on disqualified person and 10 percent tax on the knowledgeable organization manager); and taxable distributions from donor advised funds (20 percent tax on donor advised funds sponsoring organization and 10 percent of the amount of the benefits imposed on the fund manager making the distribution).

Private foundations typically pay a 2 percent excise tax on their organization's net investment income for the tax year. The percentage is reduced to 1 percent if the foundation makes certain charitable distributions, and it is eliminated altogether for certain qualifying private operating foundations. These are not penalties but requirements under the federal tax code. However, penalties or fines will be imposed on private foundations for failure to perform some action or in certain circumstances. Examples of penalties include failure to distribute income (initial tax of 30 percent of

income based on minimum investment return for nonoperating foundations that fail to distribute its income for a tax year by the end of the *next*
year); excess business holdings (initial tax of 10 percent on any excess
business holdings based on their value on the day during the tax year when
those holdings were the greatest); and self-dealing transactions (10 percent
of the amount of each transaction).

Unrelated Business Income and Reporting (IRS Form 990-T)

Introduction

Most NFPs are exempt from paying income tax and can receive unlimited,
nontaxable income and support for activities related to the organization's
exempt purpose. However, activities deemed to be unrelated to the organization's exempt purpose are classified as unrelated business income
(UBI) and subject to unrelated business income tax *(UBIT)*. As a reminder,
NFPs are exempt from paying income taxes because of the beneficial
services they perform for society. If the activities they engage in are not
directly related to their mission, they are acting in a manner similar to
commercial enterprises and, therefore, should be subjected to the same
income taxes as any commercial enterprise would. UBIT applies to most
exempt NPFs, and over the last 10 years the IRS has significantly increased
its scrutiny of activities that might be classified as UBI. The search for UBI is
part of almost every IRS audit.

Definitions and General UBIT Concepts

Because the IRS is the agency authorized to approve tax exemption and
regulate tax-exempt organizations, they are the arbiters of what constitutes
UBI. The IRS issued publication 598 (*Tax on Unrelated Business Income
of Exempt Organizations*), which provides information on what is and isn't
a UBI activity. The following are definitions and concepts found in that
publication.

   Unrelated Business Income (UBI)—UBI is income from a trade or business
that is regularly carried on by an exempt organization and that is not
substantially related to the performance by the organization of its exempt
purpose or function (except that the organization uses the profits derived
from this activity). The argument that the income derived from unrelated
business activities is used to pay for exempt purpose activities is *not*, repeat
not, justification for exemption from paying UBIT.

   Trade or Business—UBI applies to any activity carried on for the production of income, from either performing a service or selling goods, that is
regularly carried on (i.e., a continuous activity held throughout the year or
every year) and engaged in a way similar to the way a commercial enterprise
would manage the activity and is not substantially related to accomplishing

the exempt purpose of the organization. As you see, these definitions are very general and allow a good deal of subjective interpretation.

Exclusions—According to IRS Code sections 512, 513, and 514, there are some specific exclusions to UBI such as income substantially generated by unpaid volunteers, sale of merchandise donated to the organization, investment income from marketable securities (e.g., interest and dividends), royalties, sale of property, and real property rental income.

Reporting—An exempt organization is required to file Form 990-T (*Exempt Organization Business Income Tax Return*) if it has $1,000 or more in gross income from unrelated business activities. All unrelated activities are combined on one Form 990-T. UBIT is based on net income (i.e., gross UBI minus allowable deductions that are directly connected with carrying on an unrelated trade or business). Deductions cannot be connected with excluded income. Net income from UBIT is taxed at the regular corporate rates. The due date for filing Form 990-T is the fifteenth day of the fifth month after the end of the organization's fiscal year (e.g., May 15th for calendar year-end NFPs). A six-month extension can be requested. Many states also require the filing of returns. For example, New York state requires the filing of form CT-13 *(Unrelated Business Income Tax Return)* and payment to the state of any unrelated business tax due at the state's corporate-income-tax rate.

Excluded Trade or Business Activities

According to IRS regulations, certain activities are not deemed trade or business activities and as such are not subjected to UBIT. This includes activities in which the work is performed substantially by volunteers without compensation (e.g., bake or candy sale), when the activity is engaged for the convenience of members (e.g., employee cafeteria, student laundromat), sponsorship income related to fund-raising events, sale of donated merchandise (e.g., clothes in a thrift shop), exchange or rental of member lists to other NFPs, and income from a convention or trade show if it is carried on for an exempt purpose.

In most cases, the following income is also not considered UBI: dividends, interest, annuities, and other investment income from securities or loans; royalty income from trademarks, trade names, or copyrights (exception are royalties earned from personal services such as for interviews or appearances); income from research is excluded for certain NFPs such as colleges, universities, or hospitals; gains and losses from disposition of property (e.g., sale of equipment); and rental income from renting real property. There are a few exceptions to the rental income exclusion. Rental income is subject to UBIT if rents are based on net profits or if rental income includes a portion (>50 percent) from the rental of personal property (i.e., property other than real property).

Table 14.1 Summary of Exempt and Nonexempt Classification Status

Activity	Exempt	Subject to UBIT
Sale of exempt products or services	—	If based on sales commissions
Sales of membership lists	Sales to other NFPs	Sales to commercial firms
Rental of facilities (plus utilities & security)	Use related to exempt activities (e.g., hospital florist)	—
Membership directory	If given to members	—
Advertising space in publications	—	Yes
Museum or institutional store sales	If educational or related to mission	—
Other product sales	If immaterial	If material
Transportation services (e.g., bus, parking, trolleys)	Exempt if provided by Local Development Corps & similar type organizations	—
Product endorsements	—	Performed by scientific or other organizations

Table 14.1 summarizes the exempt or nonexempt classification status of certain activities.

Advertising Income

The IRS regulations clearly state that income derived from regularly executed advertising activities (e.g., advertising in an NFP publication such as membership directory or monthly journal) is considered exploitation of exempt activities and, therefore, is treated as unrelated business income. Advertising income from incidental activities, such as a fund-raising event booklet or banners, is not deemed to be UBI. The key factor of whether advertising is incidental is whether the advertising information presented is only general information (e.g., company name, address, and specialty, or congratulating an award recipient), or whether the advertisement provides detailed information on the various products and services the advertiser has to offer.

The taxability of advertising income is a very contentious area for many exempt organizations. In a significant number of audits, the IRS has ruled the exempt organizations to be noncompliant for not reporting or under-reporting advertising income, and in turn the organizations were assessed back taxes and related penalties.

Calculating UBIT on advertising sales in publications or periodicals can become complex because it involves separating advertising income and expenses from the total income and expenses related to selling the print material. Further complications are involved when a portion of membership dues include the receipt of printed material that includes advertising. Before performing the calculation to determine the income that is subject to UBIT, the following amounts should be determined: gross advertising income, total circulation income, allocable membership receipts, direct advertising costs, direct readership costs, and joint (allocable) costs. Because of the complexity, the calculation should be performed by someone with experience in this area.

Table 14.2 was extracted from IRS publication 598 (*Tax on Unrelated Business Income of Exempt Organizations*) and summarizes the rules for allocating joint costs between circulation and advertising activities.

Table 14.2   IRS Publication 598

IF gross advertising income is . . .	THEN UBTI is . . .
More than direct advertising costs	The excess advertising income, reduced (but not below zero) by the excess, if any, of readership costs over circulation income.
Equal to or less than direct advertising costs	Zero. Circulation income and readership costs are not taken into account. Any excess advertising costs reduce (but not below zero) UBTI from any other unrelated business activity.
IF . . .	THEN the amount used to allocate membership receipts is . . .
20% or more of the total circulation consists of sales to nonmembers	The subscription price charged to nonmembers.
The preceding condition does not apply, **and** 20% or more of the members pay reduced dues because they do not receive the periodical	The reduction in dues for a member not receiving the periodical.
Neither of the preceding conditions applies	The membership receipts multiplied by this fraction: Total periodical costs ÷ Total periodical costs + cost of other exempt activities (i.e., all other non-UBTI expenses)

History of Federal Form 990 (Return of Organization Exempt from Income Tax)

Tax-exempt organizations were also exempt from any reporting until 1942 when the Treasury Department (IRS) required tax-exempt organizations to file a two-page annual information return covering the 1941 tax year.

Many exempt organizations protested the new reporting and resisted complying with the requirement, so in 1943 there was a provision included in the Revenue Act of 1943 requiring that Form 990 be filed. The 1943 form was also two pages and consisted of three yes/no questions, an income statement, and balance sheet plus some line items requiring attached schedules. All individuals who were paid more than $4,000 in salary were required to be listed on a schedule showing their names, addresses, and amount they were paid. Contributions received from any one person exceeding $4,000 were required to be reported on the form.

In 1947, the form partly illustrated above in Figure 14.1 increased to four pages (with instructions), but some portions only applied to certain types of organizations such as farmers' cooperatives. More detailed information was required such as a separate line item for reporting compensation of officers. Over the next 30 years, Form 990 changed only slightly, and by 1976 it consisted of two main pages, three-and-one-half pages of

10,148 T. D.'s and Rulings *Form 990* Number 9—58 2-12-47

[¶ 6092] Form 990, Revised January, 1947.

Form 990
TREASURY DEPARTMENT
INTERNAL REVENUE SERVICE
(Revised Jan. 1947)

PAGE 1

UNITED STATES
ANNUAL RETURN OF ORGANIZATION EXEMPT FROM INCOME TAX UNDER SECTION 101 OF THE INTERNAL REVENUE CODE, OR UNDER CORRESPONDING PROVISIONS OF PRIOR REVENUE ACTS
(Statement of gross income, receipts, disbursements, etc., as required under Section 54 (f) of the Internal Revenue Code, as added by Section 117 of the Revenue Act of 1943) (See Instruction 1)

For Calendar Year ....

or Fiscal Year Begun ...., and Ended ....

PRINT PLAINLY NAME AND ADDRESS OF THE ORGANIZATION

This return must be filed on or before the 15th day of the 5th month following the close of the annual accounting period. Return must be filed with the Collector of Internal Revenue for the district in which is located the principal place of business or principal office of the organization.

....
(Give name in full)

....
(Street and number)

....
(Post office) (County) (State)

Have you been advised by Bureau letter of your exemption?.............. (Yes or no) If so, state date of letter and subsection of section 101 under which you are exempt...........

....

State nature of your activities ....

....

File Code ....

Serial No. ....

District ....

Figure 14.1 Top Section of Form 990

instructions, and a Schedule A consisting of four pages plus four pages of instructions.

Over the next 30 years, there were periodic changes made to the form by adding sections, questions, two schedules, and attachments. By 2007, Form 990 consisted of 9 pages, 11 parts, Schedules A, B, and D, and many attachments (if applicable). The problem with all the changes over the years was that many of the additions were placed on the form in illogical spots or just added to the end of the form, which made the form difficult to prepare, read, and understand.

The IRS has known for a while that Form 990 needed to be significantly revised. They also knew that any change had to be for the better and had to include all required information in a more logical format and instructions that provided a great deal more guidance. Mission accomplished. The 990 revision took five years of research, analysis, internal discussions, and public comments before it was released at the end of 2007. The end result was a radically redesigned form, consisting of 11 pages (broken down into 11 parts) with 16 schedules. The new form was to be used for all operating years ended with or within 2008.

Reason for Revised Form 990 and Revision Process

The federal Form 990 had not been significantly and structurally revised since 1979, and it was generally believed not to reflect all the changes in exempt organization laws and regulations and the increasing size, diversity, and complexity of the exploding tax exempt sector. The number of exempt organizations has grown exponentially to almost two million today from one million in 1996 and from a fraction of that number in 1979. In addition, the number of federal grants to NFPs has grown from millions to billions from the 1960s to the present. Furthermore, Form 990 is used by governmental agencies, foundations, and others to ensure tax compliance, perform regulatory oversight, provide transparency, and give everyone the information they need to make informed decisions about reporting exempt organizations. Lastly, according to general data provided by the IRS, the number of 990 returns has increased from approximately 100,000 in 1985 to approximately 400,000 in 2004 and is estimated to be as high as 500,000 in 2012.

On June 14, 2007, the IRS released the first draft of the redesigned Form 990 for public comment, and after receiving hundreds of comments, released the redesigned Form 990 on December 20, 2007. On April 7, 2008, the IRS released a draft of the 990 instructions for public comments and, after considering and incorporating some of the suggestions made, released the final instructions on August 19, 2008. Most of the suggestions centered on making the form easier to understand, and the IRS responded by including a glossary of terms, a sequencing list, and ample space on the form for narratives and explanations.

The *New* Form 990

Reporting Requirements

In the past, certain exempt organizations whose gross receipts were under $100,000 and whose total assets were less than $250,000 could file a simpler, less detailed version of Form 990 called 990-EZ. Other exempt organizations whose gross receipts were less than $25,000 were not required to file at all. With the new Form 990, came new reporting threshold requirements, which benefited smaller organizations. In addition, the IRS allowed a phasing-in of the new threshold reporting requirements over a two-year period, which allowed many organizations to file the easier 990-EZ form and gave them a little more time to become familiar with the new disclosures required on the new Form 990. Table 14.3 is extracted from the IRS instructions and shows the transitional filing rules based on gross receipts and total assets. The three reporting forms are Form 990, Forms 990-EZ, and Form 990-N. Form 990-N is known as the e-postcard because it is a short, electronically filed form.

All exempt organizations, except certain religious, governmental, political, and private foundations are now required to file one of the 990 forms

Table 14.3   Extract from IRS Instructions

Gross Receipts &/or Total Assets	2007 Tax Year	2008 Tax Year	2009 Tax Year	2010 Tax Year & >
≤ $25K	990-N	990-N	990-N	
≤ $50K				990-N
> $25K & < $100K/<$250K	990-EZ or 990			
> $25K & < $1M/<$2.5M		990-EZ or 990		
> $25K & < $500K/<$1.25M			990-EZ or 990	
> $50K & < $200K/<$500K				990-EZ or 990
≥$100K/≥$250K	990			
≥$1M/≥$2.5M		990		
≥$500K/≥$1.25M			990	
≥$200K/≥$500K				990

based on the aforementioned gross-income and total-asset tests. Private foundations are required to file Form 990-PF.

Returns are due by the fifteenth day of the fifth month after the organization's accounting period ends (extended to the next business day if it falls on a weekend or legal holiday). For example, organizations with December 31 calendar year ends would be required to file by May 15 and organizations with June 30 fiscal year ends would have to file by November 15. An organization can request an automatic three-month extension and an additional three-month extension after that if they show cause.

Summary of Changes to Form 990

Generally speaking, the biggest change to the new form is its drill-down approach to reporting information. As you go through the pages of the form, you will notice that summary information is first required, with more detailed information or elaboration given on subsequent pages and schedules. For example, page one of the form provides a snapshot of financial, governance, and operational information. The new form also rearranged all parts, sections, and questions for improved clarity, and it added numerous schedules and questions to increase disclosure and transparency.

Significant changes on the new form include the requirement that more exempt organizations complete applicable sections, schedules, and questions; the addition of a checklist indicating which schedules need to be completed; a new governance section consisting of three parts—composition of an organization's governing body, its governance, management policies, and disclosure practices; increased reporting of compensation of officers, directors, trustees, key employees (abbreviated as DOTKEY), and independent contractors; requirement to use information on Forms W-2 and 1099 for compensation reporting; many new schedules from C to R (no schedule P and Q) requiring significantly more information for certain types of exempt organizations (see upcoming list); and expanded instructions totaling 75 pages (Form 990); 39 pages (Form 990-EZ) that include a glossary defining important terms; and an appendix of special instructions that provides additional reporting guidance.

Other areas of significant change include determination of public charity status and public support (Schedule A has been revised to emphasize reporting of public charity status and public support and has replaced the five-year "advanced ruling period" requirement; see Chapter 2 for more information); supplemental financial statement reporting; more information on fund-raising, special events, and gaming; and the requirement of more information on organizations maintaining collections of works of art (Schedule D), foreign activities (Schedule F), hospitals (Schedule H), tax exempt bonds (Schedule K), noncash contributions (Schedule M), and related organizations (Schedule R).

General Instructions for Filing Form 990

Who Must File   Most organizations exempt from income tax under Internal Revenue Code section 501(a) (except those that are exempt, such as religious organizations) must file an annual information return (Form 990 or Form 990-EZ) or an annual electronic notice if they meet gross-receipts and total-assets tests (previously discussed). The instructions state that all organizations must file, even if they didn't file Form 1023 or 1024 and received an IRS determination letter recognizing its tax-exempt status.

Accounting Method   The new form now allows organizations to use the same accounting method on the return to report revenue and expenses that it regularly uses to maintain its financial records. It is suggested that the organization use the accrual method of accounting. Organizations should keep a reconciliation of any differences between its financial records and information reported on Form 990. Organizations with *audited financial statements* are required to provide such reconciliations in Schedule D, Parts XI through XIII.

Amended Return   To change or *amend* an organization's return for any year, an organization must file a new return including any required schedules. The same version of Form 990 applicable to the year being amended should be used. The amended return must provide all the information called for by the form and instructions, not just the new or corrected information. The Amended Return box in the heading of the return should be checked. Schedule O should be used to describe all changes. If a federal Form 990 is amended, all related state returns should also be amended.

Late Filing Penalties   The IRS (and states) will impose stiff penalties for filing a return late. Penalties against the organization equal $20 a day, not to exceed the smaller of $10,000 or 5 percent of the gross receipts of the organization, unless the organization can show that the late filing was due to reasonable cause. Organizations with annual gross receipts greater than $1 million are subject to a penalty of $100 for each day the failure continues (with a maximum penalty with respect to any one return of $50,000). Penalties can also be levied against responsible person(s). If the organization does not file a complete return or does not furnish correct information, the IRS will send the organization a letter that includes a fixed time to fulfill these requirements. After that period expires, the person failing to comply will be charged a penalty of $10 a day. The maximum penalty on all persons for failures with respect to any one return shall not exceed $5,000. There are also penalties (fines and imprisonment) for willfully not filing returns and for filing fraudulent returns and statements with the IRS (IRS code sections 7203, 7206, and 7207). States may impose additional penalties for failure to meet their separate filing requirements.

Other Requirements   All information on Form 990, including schedules, attachments, and notices (along with application for recognition of exemption and Forms 990-T after August 17, 2006) must be available for public inspection without charge (other than a reasonable fee for reproduction and actual postage costs) for a period of three years. Anyone can receive a copy of Form 990 either from the IRS by submitting Form 4506-A to request a copy, or by requesting a copy directly from the organization. They can request this in writing or to be viewed without charge at the NFP's principal, regional or district offices during regular business hours.

List of Form 990 Schedules A through R   The new form now includes the following 16 schedules. Not all schedules apply to all organizations.

Schedule A	Public Charity Status or Public Support
Schedule B	Schedule of Contributors
Schedule C	Political Campaign and Lobbying Activities
Schedule D	Supplemental Financial Statements
Schedule E	Schools
Schedule F	Statement of Activities outside the United States
Schedule G	Supplemental Information Regarding Fund-Raising or Gaming Activities
Schedule H	Hospitals
Schedule I	Grants and Other Assistance to Organizations, Government, and Individuals in the United States
Schedule J	Compensation Information
Schedule K	Supplemental Information on Tax Exempt Bonds
Schedule L	Transactions with Interested Persons
Schedule M	Noncash Contributions
Schedule N	Liquidation, Termination, Dissolution, or Significant Disposition of Assets
Schedule O	Supplemental Information to Form 990
Schedule R	Related Organizations and Unrelated Partnerships

Appendix of Special Instructions to Form 990   To assist the preparer, the Form 990 instructions include an appendix with helpful information and other requirements. The following appendixes are available:

A	Exempt Organizations Reference Chart
B	How to Determine Whether an Organization's Gross Receipts are Normally $25,000 (or $5,000) or Less

C   Special Gross Receipts Test for Determining Exempt Status of
         Section 501(c)(7) and 501(c)(15) Organizations
D   Public Inspection of Returns
E   Group Returns; Reporting Information on Behalf of the Group
F   Disregarded Entities and Joint Ventures; Inclusion of Activities
         and Items
G   Section 4958 Excess Benefit Transactions
H   Forms and Publications to File or Use
I   Use of Form 990, or Form 990-EZ, to Satisfy State Reporting
         Requirements

990 Sections (Part I–XI) and Schedules (A–R)

Summary or Purpose of Each Part on Form 990

Page 1—Heading Section   Information in this section identifies the organization and includes key information, such as tax-exempt status, year of formation, operating year, and type of entity (e.g., corporation).

Part I—Summary, and Part II—Signature Block   Part I provides a quick *snapshot* of the organization's key financial, governance, and operational information. This part should only be completed after other parts of the return are completed. Part II easily identifies who the responsible person is. For NFPs that are corporations, only legal officers should sign the return.

Part III—Statement of Program Service Accomplishments   Part III describes the NFPs mission and their three largest program services classified by total program expenses. It also provides revenue information that is directly related to the listed programs and more space for narrative.

Part IV—Checklist   This part is new and requires answering 37 questions. It will assist preparers in determining which schedules must be completed and provided to the IRS and other users, with a snapshot of various types of activities or relationships the organization might be involved in, such as public-charity status, contributors, political-campaign or lobbying activities, foreign activities, fund-raising or gaming, hospitals, grant-making, certain compensation arrangements, tax-exempt bonds, transactions with interested persons, noncash contributions, major dispositions of assets, and relationships with other organizations. The instructions and glossary should be used to assist in determining how to answer the questions in this part. Some questions require a yes, some a no, and others should be left blank. The checklist should reduce incomplete returns and reduce IRS notices and penalties.

Part V—Statements Regarding Other IRS Filings and Tax Compliance   Part V collects important federal-tax-compliance information in one place and alerts the organization to potential federal-tax-compliance and filing obligations beyond filing the Form 990 annual information return. Questions in this part pertain to employment taxes; information returns; backup withholding; unrelated business income tax; foreign-bank-account reporting; prohibited tax-shelter-transaction reporting; substantiation and reporting of contributions, donor advised funds, and special requirements applicable to organizations described in section 501(c)(7) or (c)(12) and section 4947(a)(1) for nonexempt charitable trusts. The instructions and glossary should be used to assist in determining how to answer the questions in this part. Some questions pertain to other IRS forms, which must be completed if applicable.

Part VI—Governance, Management, and Disclosure   Part VI is new and must be completed by all organizations. It requires information regarding an organization's governing body and management (and their relationships), policies, and disclosure practices. This information includes how and by whom an organization is governed, its governance and management policies and practices, certain relationships between or among its governing and management officials, and how the organization makes certain important information available to its constituents. It defines the governing body as the group of persons authorized under state law to make governance decisions on behalf of the organization and its shareholders or members. The governing body generally is the board of directors (or board of trustees) of a corporation or association or trust.

Part VII—Compensation of DOTKEY, Highly Compensated Employees (HICE) and Independent Contractors   Part VII is a new section and expands the reporting of compensation information on current or former directors, officers, trustees, key employees (DOTKEY), five highest compensated employees (HICE), and five highest paid current independent contractors. Compensation includes amounts received from both the reporting organization and from related organizations (e.g., parents, subsidiaries, brother/sister organizations, supporting organizations). The organization must use a five-year look-back period to determine whether someone was a former DOTKEY or HICE. The new form raises the threshold for reporting from $50,000 to $100,000 for HICE and independent contractors and uses a $150,000 threshold for reporting key-employee information.

Part VIII—Statement of Revenue   Part VIII requires reporting revenue in three categories: contributions, gifts, grants, and other similar amounts; program service revenue; and other revenue. All organizations must complete Part VIII, Column A "Total Revenue," to report gross receipts for all sources of revenue. Organizations, other than section 527 organizations, must complete Columns B through D to report related or exempt function revenue, unrelated business revenue, and revenue excluded from tax under IRS code sections 512 through 514.

Part IX—Statement of Functional Expenses Part IX reports expenses by function (program, management, and general fund-raising) and by natural expense classification (e.g., salaries, office expenses, etc.) Section 501(c)(3) and (c)(4) organizations as well as section 4947(a)(1) (Nonexempt Charitable Trusts) must complete Columns A through D. All other organizations must complete Column A but may complete Columns B, C, and D. If the organization's accounting system does not allocate expenses, the organization may use any reasonable method of allocation. The organization must report amounts accurately and document the method of allocation in its records.

Part X—Balance Sheet This part requires reporting information on the organization's assets, liabilities, and net assets. All organizations are required to complete Part X. For organizations in their first year of operations, zeros should be entered for beginning year amounts. If the return is a final return, zeros should be entered for ending balances.

Part XI—Financial Statements and Reporting Part XI is new and alerts the reader to the level of independence involved in the preparation of the organization's financial statements and how active or involved the board of directors (through a committee) are in the selection and oversight of the CPA/CPA firm and the services they perform. It requires information regarding the organization's accounting method and whether the organization had its financial statements compiled, reviewed, or audited (along with a report) by an independent accountant.

Summary or Purpose of Each Form 990 Schedule

Schedule A—Public Charity Status and Public Support The new Schedule A must be completed by any organization that answered yes to Part IV Checklist—Line 1 (990) or 990-EZ, that states the organization is a section 501(c)(3) or 4947(a)(1) (Nonexempt Charitable Trust), and is not a private foundation that files Form 990-PF. The schedule provides information on an organization's public-charity status and public support that is needed to ensure that an organization's source of revenue is consistent with the reason for receiving exempt status from the IRS. The new Schedule A includes four major and fundamental changes from the prior form: (1) Support and revenue is no longer required to be reported on the cash method of accounting. The organization can now use the same method it uses for its financial reporting (i.e., it can use the accrual method). (2) The IRS has issued new rules eliminating the advance ruling process for section 501(c)(3) organizations and now automatically classifies the organization as a public charity for its first five years of existence. (3) It separates the support schedule into two parts based on the organization exempt classification (Part II and Part III) and tests the level of public support an organization receives. (4) It indicates whether the organization is filing within the first five years of applying for an exemption.

Schedule B—Schedule of Contributors   Every organization must complete and attach Schedule B to their Form 990, 990-EZ, or 990-PF, unless it certifies that it does not meet the filing requirements of this schedule by answering no on Part IV, line 2 of Form 990, or by checking the proper box on line H of Form 990-EZ, or on line 2 of Form 990-PF. Schedule B is required for 501(c)(3) organizations and certain other organizations that receive contributions exceeding certain amounts. It requires the reporting of limited contributor and contribution information, including the name of the contributor, aggregate contributions received, type of contribution, and description of property (for noncash contributions). Organizations must refer to the general rule or the special rules in the instructions to Schedule B to determine whether they must complete Schedule B. Unless the organization is covered by one of the special rules (described later), the general rule requires that every organization that received money or property aggregating $5,000 or more for the year from any one contributor, must complete Schedule B. The special rules apply to 501(c)(3), (c)(7), (c)(8), or (c)(10) organizations and states that organizations that meets the $33\frac{1}{3}$ percent support test of the regulations under sections 509(a)(1)/170(b)(1)(A)(vi), list in Part I only those contributors whose contribution of $5,000 or more is greater than 2 percent of the amount reported on line 1h of Part VIII of Form 990 (or line 1 of Form 990-EZ). The following example illustrates this exception.

A section 501(c)(3) organization, of the type described earlier, reported $700,000 in total contributions, gifts, grants, and similar amounts received on Part VIII, line 1h, of its Form 990. The organization is only required to list in Parts I and II of its Schedule B each person who contributed more than the greater of $5,000 or 2 percent of $700,000, or $14,000. If a contributor gives a total of $11,000, this amount would not have to be reported in Parts I and II because it did not exceed $14,000.

Completion of this Schedule (which also existed in the old version) has always been a very contentious issue, because many organizations and donors do not want their names and addresses disclosed on this form. This is understandable because people or companies that donate money are always asked to give more money (i.e., go to the well where the water is). So many times donor information is omitted or listed as anonymous. The IRS understands this and that is why this schedule is *not*, repeat *not*, open to public inspection. Then why ask for this information at all? Because the IRS needs this information to ensure that certain organizations are meeting their *public support* requirements (i.e., not hiding multiple gifts) and to identify possible quid pro quo transactions (i.e., giving money and getting something back in return).

Schedule C—Political Campaign and Lobbying Activities   Schedule C addresses direct or indirect political campaign activities, lobbying activities, and certain notice requirements for 501(c)(4), 501(c)(5) and 501(c)(6) organizations. Tax law prohibits campaign activities by section 501(c)(3) organizations (i.e., support or oppose candidates for elective federal, state, or local public office). The law does allow 501(c)(3) organizations to expend funds for lobbying activities within specified limits. If they exceed the limits, they could be subject to excise tax on the excess amount. And if excessive (greater than 150 percent over four years), the organization could lose its exempt status.

Schedule D—Supplemental Financial Statements   Schedule D is used to report information on donor advised funds, conservation easements, certain art and museum collections, escrow accounts and custodial arrangements, endowment funds, and supplemental financial information relating to the financial statements. This schedule eliminated many unstructured attachments that were required with the previous form.

Form 990—Schedule E—Schools   This schedule must be completed by NFP schools.

Schedule F—Statement of Activities Outside the United States   Schedule F is required by organizations that provide grants and other assistance to individuals, organizations, or entities outside the United States.

Schedule G—Supplemental Information Regarding Fund-Raising or Gaming Activities   This schedule is used to report professional fund-raising services, fund-raising events, and gaming (if an organization engages in these activities).

Schedule H—Schools   Schedule E must be completed by NFP schools.

Schedule I—Grants and Other Assistance to Organizations, Governments, and Individuals in the United States   Schedule I is required by organizations that provide grants and other assistance to individuals, organizations, or entities in the United States. They only have to report information for each recipient who received more than $5,000 aggregated during the year.

Schedule J—Compensation Information   Schedule J is used to report detailed compensation information for those individuals whose compensation from the filing organization and related organizations, exceed certain amounts reported on the core form, and to provide certain information regarding the organization's compensation practices. It also asks for W-2 income and other benefits to DOTKEY and HICE (e.g., base salaries, bonuses, deferred compensation). The threshold for reporting this additional compensation information for current DOTKEY and HICE is $150,000.

Schedule K—Supplemental Information on Tax-Exempt Bonds This schedule provides additional information on tax-exempt bonds issued by NFP organizations.

Schedule L—Transactions with Interested Persons Schedule L is used to provide information on certain financial transactions or arrangements between the organization and disqualified persons or other interested persons. It is also used to determine whether a member of the organization's governing body is an independent member as indicated on Form 990, Part VI, line 1b.

Schedule M—Noncash Contributions This schedule requires reporting detailed information on noncash contributions received by all organizations in excess of $25,000 during the year. Details include the type of noncash donation received, number of donors, value and method of valuation. Noncash contributions exclude donated services or facilities and also books, publications, clothing, and household goods. The valuation method used could be cost or selling price, replacement cost, opinions of experts, and any other objective and supportable method.

Schedule N—Liquidation, Termination, Dissolution or Significant Disposition of Assets This schedule provides information on certain organizational activities such as ceasing operations, selling or merging the organization, or selling a material portion of the organizations assets.

Schedule O—Supplemental Information to Form 990 Schedule O is a catch-all form. It is a convenient place to explain or elaborate on questions asked in any part or other schedules or to supply additional information. It is basically a lined pad. All organizations must complete this schedule. Filers can use as many schedule O pages as it deems necessary. The instructions state that all narrative answers should have a heading and the heading should be in the order of 990 part (e.g., Part III), line, and column for the main form; and schedule letter, line, and column for 990 schedules. As previously mentioned, Schedule O is also used to provide details on any changes made on amended returns.

Schedule P and Q—Reserved These schedules are not currently used and are reserved for possible future use.

Schedule R—Related Organizations and Unrelated Partnerships   Schedule R is used by all organizations to provide information on transactions with related organizations and with certain unrelated partnerships through which the organization conducts significant activities. This schedule will significantly improve transparency.

Summary

Reporting has come a long way from the first two-page information returns filed in 1942. Most organizations will now have to institute mechanisms and procedures for obtaining and maintaining all necessary information needed to complete a properly prepared Form 990 with all required attachments. The new Form 990 will force organizations to be much more cognizant of certain practices such as related party transactions, which were not required to be reported in the past. It should also improve board oversight because of the increased disclosures. Some organizations will find the new reporting requirements very burdensome, especially smaller NFPs, whereas others will not.

Private Foundation Returns (IRS Form 990-PF)

Introduction

What is a Private Foundation (PF)? Every organization that qualifies for tax-exempt status under IRS Code section 501(c)(3) is further classified as either a public charity or a private foundation. Under IRS Code section 508, every organization is automatically classified as a private foundation unless it meets one of the exceptions listed in IRS Code section 509(a), which allows the entity to be classified as a public charity if its activities are for charitable, religious, educational, or scientific purposes.

As discussed in Chapter 1, PFs typically have a single or only a few major sources of funding (i.e., gifts from one family or corporation rather than from many sources). PFs must have as their primary activity the making of grants (or gifts) to other charitable organizations and/or individuals, rather than the direct operation of charitable programs.

There are three types of PF: private operating, nonoperating (grant or gift making), and exempt operating (very rare). Some tax-law provisions apply to all types of private foundations whereas others only to particular types. An organization's IRS exemption letter will indicate the type of PF the organization is.

A private operating foundation is a PF that devotes most of its resources to the active conduct of its exempt activities as distinguished from the more common grant-making foundations. A museum that is supported by a limited number of individuals would be an example of a private operating foundation. The major difference between a private operating foundation and a public charity is that public charities receive support from a larger pool of donors than the private operating foundation. To qualify as a private operating foundation, the organization must meet an assets test, a support/endowment test, and demonstrate that it distributes substantially all (i.e., equal or greater than 85 percent) of the lesser of its adjusted net income or the minimum investment returns related to the active conduct of its exempt purpose activities. The major advantage to being a private operating foundation is they can receive more donations from individual donors because those donors are allowed to donate up to 50 percent of their adjusted gross income to the private operating foundation as opposed to only 30 percent to a private nonoperating foundation.

A private nonoperating foundation is a PF that make grants (i.e., gifts) to public charities or individuals in order to carry out its exempt purpose. An exempt operating foundation is a PF that is exempt from the excise tax on net income that applies to other PFs, but it must meet certain tests to qualify (e.g., it must have been publically supported for at least 10 years and have a broadly representative board of directors). This type of PF is very rare.

Certain activities can jeopardize the exempt status of private foundations, such as individuals related to the organization receiving more than insubstantial benefits, payment of unreasonable compensation to DOTKEY, participating directly or indirectly in any political campaign, and substantial activities that attempt to influence legislation (i.e., lobbying).

Filing Requirements

All PFs must file Form 990-PF annually if they have taxable income or activity during their operation year. Form 990-PF is a 13-page, 17-part return that can become complicated, technical, and can require detailed calculations. PFs might have to file other forms or schedules such as Form 990, Schedule B (Schedule of Contributors), Form 990-T (Exempt Organization Business Income Tax Return) and Form 4720 (Return of Certain Excise Taxes Under Chapters 41 and 42 of IRC), which is used to determine the excise taxes on acts of self-dealing, failure to distribute income, excess business holdings, and political expenditures,

Most domestic PFs pay an excise tax of 2 percent on their net investment income. Some private operating foundations can qualify for a reduced excise-tax rate of 1 percent.

CHAPTER

15

Contribution/Grant Applications and Reporting

Asignificant number of NFPs derive most of their revenue and support from government grants and contracts and from contributions from individuals, corporations, foundations, and trusts. Many organizations survive by getting small donations from many individuals or companies, whereas others live or die by receiving funds from only a few entities or individuals. The approach to obtaining funds varies widely from pleas made through personal contacts to completion and submission of multipage applications, with the specific method used varying significantly from organization to organization. This chapter will talk about some of the issues involved with soliciting funds, along with related reporting requirements.

Obtaining Support from Individuals, Foundations, Government, and Others

From Individuals and Corporations

Some public charities receive money in the form of small donations from a large number of disinterested individuals. Examples include churches, the Salvation Army, and the Muscular Dystrophy Association (MDA) by way of the Jerry Lewis telethon. A significant number of other public charities obtain funds through the efforts of a small, select group of individuals such as board members, their contacts, and other affluent people. Receipts from these people usually involve some degree of personal relationship or involvement with the organization's programs or activities. The reason individuals give money covers the spectrum from personal experiences to some affinity with the organization's activities or mission. Reasons include obligations as a board member or officer of an NFP to raise money for the organization; family member with disease, infirmity, condition, experience, or other connection; theater, museum, or library patron who appreciates the programs; or a former college/university student or faculty who feels connected to his/her alma mater. The reason for corporate giving usually involves a desire to present the company as a good corporate citizen or the involvement by one or more corporate members with an NFP's Board, management, or activities.

The format for obtaining funds from a large segment of the general public involves mass-appeal advertising on television or in publications, telethons, major events such as marathons or other races, or personal solicitations by a large number of volunteers. Appeals made by a small or select group of individuals are typically more informal, ad hoc, or impulsive, and they do not normally involve a lot of paper work (i.e., no applications). The method is usually through outreach in the form of personal telephone calls, letters, and meetings.

From Government, Foundations, Trusts, and Others

The process of obtaining funds from a government agency or subdivision, foundation, trust or other NFP is normally more involved and usually requires the submission of a written request or completion of an application before being awarded or receiving any funds. The application process varies significantly from entity to entity and even from year to year. Applications typically are time sensitive and must be submitted by a specific date or within a specified time period to be approved (e.g., foundation has available funds only in their current year's budget for research). Many times there is a specific format or procedure that must be followed to obtain funds. Formats and procedures vary significantly from grantor/donor to grantor/donor. For example, some foundations require only a written letter or e-mail, whereas others require a lengthy form to be completed online. Some government agency applications are only a few pages whereas others require a volume of submitted material. Lastly, the level of detail required also varies significantly (e.g., some require current-year information whereas others require three years' audited financial statements, budgets, promotional materials, and letters of recommendation from others).

Most federal, state, and local governmental agencies or subdivisions have a more formal process for requesting grants that include completion of some type of grant request application along with submission of supporting documentation.

Reporting to Donors and Government Agencies

General

Reporting requirements can be broken down into three major areas: (1) donor-imposed reporting, (2) state and local government granting agency/subdivision-imposed reporting, and (3) IRS and state-regulatory-agency imposed reporting. A fourth area, federal reporting requirements (OMB A-133), will be covered later in the next section.

Reporting requirements vary among donors and grantors from no requirements to detailed monthly, quarterly, or end-of-period reports. As a precondition to making a contribution or grant, a donor or grantor can make any reasonable request for how its funds are to be used or what types of reports it requires as long as those requests do not violate any federal or state laws or regulations. The recipient organization has the right to not agree to the donor's demands for use of funds or reporting by not accepting the gift. However, if an organization does accept the gift, it has an obligation to comply with the donor's mandates. It also has to comply with regulatory reporting requirements imposed by the IRS and various states.

Donor-Imposed Reporting Requirements

Individuals and corporations who make large dollar donations typically require very little in the way of reporting. Many don't require anything other than expecting a thank-you acknowledgment. Some request and receive a copy of the organization's annual report, audited financial statement, or Form 990.

Foundations, Trusts, and other NFP reporting requirements are typically more extensive and vary depending on a particular entity's contribution/ grant-giving procedures and can range from a one-sheet report to a reporting package with numerous pages. Depending on the size of the contribution/ grant, the recipient NFP might be required to report how the donation was spent and might have to detail expenditures made by type of expense and compare actual expenditures to an approved budget, if a budget was required. Sometimes the report requires an explanation or description of how the expenditure accomplished the stated purpose of the donation request. Reporting due dates vary and can be on a monthly, quarterly, or annual basis or on an activity, project, program, or restricted basis.

State and Local Government Granting Agency/Subdivision Imposed Reporting

Each government agency or subdivision has its own requirements for requesting funds or reporting their use. The penalty for noncompliance is usually nonreceipt of approved funds, requests to return or reimburse the government for funds spent, or exclusion from applying for future grants.

Most government-grant agreements require the recipient NFP to report how the grant funds were spent. Reports typically include some level of expenditure breakdown compared to a previously submitted and approved budget. Sometimes the report requires an explanation or description of how the expenditures accomplished the purpose stated on the grant request application. Reporting due dates vary and can be on a monthly, quarterly, or annual basis. Many government-grant agreements are expense-reimbursement types. These grants require that the organization first expend funds for preapproved expenditures and then submit a request for reimbursement. Some grant agreements call for the submission of supporting documentation such as copies of vendor bills or organization checks written to pay for expenses.

IRS (Federal) and State-Regulatory-Imposed Reporting (Excluding OMB A-133)

To protect the public and ensure proper tax treatment of donations made and received, the IRS has mandated over the years a number of reporting requirements with which organizations must comply. These include providing donors with a written acknowledgement if receiving donations of cash or property in excess of $250. The acknowledgment should include the donor's, name, date donation was received, and amount of money received. If the organization receives noncash contributions, the written acknowledgment should also include a description of the item/items donated, and if an objective basis is used, the fair value of the noncash donation. The IRS doesn't expect NFPs to be appraisers or evaluators, so NFPs should refrain from valuating goods received unless an objective basis is available and used (e.g., expected sale price at thrift store or listed price of stocks or bonds). If the organization receives more than $75 in cash or noncash contributions and the donor receives back either goods or services (i.e., quid pro quo), then the acknowledgment should state the fair value of the goods and services the donor received in the exchange.

Many organizations will state on the written acknowledgment the value of noncash contributions received based on the amount given to them by a donor. It is no secret that the donor wants to receive the highest value possible in order to receive the greatest tax deduction possible. Sometimes the organization is ignorant of the IRS rules requiring that valuations be made on an objective basis and other times the organization just doesn't want to upset a generous donor. The organization can avoid liability in this situation by simply stating the source of the noncash valuation, that is the donor. The author suggests the following acknowledgment:

Sample Acknowledgment with No Exchange Elements

Dear Mr. Doo Gooder—Thank you very much for your donation of clothes and household items, which you valued at $400. We are a 501(c)(3) designated public charity and as such your gift is eligible for a tax deduction from federal, state, and local income taxes.

Sample Acknowledgment with Exchange Elements

Dear Mr. Doo Gooder —Thank you very much for your purchase of a table at our annual fund-raiser event in the amount of $1,000. Be advised that the exchange value for goods you received equaled $325. Consult your tax advisor for the amount of your payment that might be eligible as a contribution or business-expense tax deduction.

Other Related Information It is not unusual for NFPs to receive donated services. According to IRS regulations, donated services are not tax deductible. However, nonreimbursed, out-of-pocket expenses (e.g., supplies, use of auto) are deductible as contributions. Based on the incorrect belief that donated services are deductible, some contributors will request a statement acknowledging the time they donated with an associated value. If the organization wants to comply with their wishes, the acknowledgment should state that the donation is donated services and again state who is valuing the donation. A sample acknowledgment for donated services is as follows:

Dear Dr. Fre Med—Thank you very much for donating your valuable time at our clinic this summer, which you estimated to equal approximately $10,000 in contributed time.

State-Imposed Reporting Requirements Many states also have regulatory responsibilities and require different types of reporting. For example the attorney general in New York state is responsible for monitoring New York state charities. According to the New York State Charities Bureau web site (a department of the Attorney General)

The Attorney General's Charities Bureau is responsible for supervising charitable organizations to insure that donors and beneficiaries of those charities are protected from unscrupulous practices in the solicitation and management of charitable assets. The Bureau also supervises the activity of foundations and other charities to ensure that their funds and other property devoted to charitable purposes are properly used, and protects the public interest in charitable gifts and bequests contained in wills and trust agreements. The Bureau also maintains a registry of charities and fundraising professionals.

In performing its oversight duties, the Charities Bureau requires that all NFPs operating in New York state submit an annual information return (CHAR500) among other forms if applicable, and will investigate those organizations that are discovered to be noncompliant with New York state laws and regulations.

Federal Grants and Reporting

Federal Awards—Introduction

The federal government is a major source of funds to NFP organizations. They provide funds in a variety of ways from outright grants (similar to contributions) to contracts (similar to exchange transactions or fee for service). Funds can be disbursed as advances or in installments, as expense reimbursements or at the end of a completed activity, project, or program. Funds can come from a federal department (e.g., U.S. Department of Defense) or from thousands upon thousands of subdepartments, divisions, subdivisions, agencies, or subagencies. Funds can even be received as pass-through funds from block grants given to state agencies, subagencies, and local government departments.

The application process can at times be overbearing, and the government has been trying for years to streamline the process. Recently they have improved their web site, which is used to accept grant applications (Grants.gov). This web site is much more user friendly than its predecessors and provides a lot of helpful information for applying for grants.

Over the last quarter century the amount of government awards given to NFP organizations has increased from millions to billions of dollars. As previously mentioned, with increased funding comes increased scrutiny. In 1984, Congress passed the Single Audit Act of 1984 (SAA) (Public Law 98-502) to improve auditing and management for federal funds provided to state and local governments. Funds may include grants, contracts, loans, loan guarantees, property, cooperative agreements, interest subsidies, insurance, and direct appropriations from a number of federal agencies. Before the Act, each federal agency had the authority to require an audit of each federally funded program or activity, and there was no coordination among them. This caused audit overlaps and organizational inefficiencies. Instead of multiple audits, the Act changed the requirements to a single audit: In 1990 the OMB administratively extended the single audit process to nonprofit organizations by issuing OMB Circular A-133, *Audits of Institutions of Higher Education and Other Nonprofit Organizations.* Thus thousands of additional organizations including museums, colleges and universities, school districts, hospitals, and voluntary welfare and health organizations were required to have an audit performed in accordance with the SAA. Congress amended the SAA by passing Public Law 104-156, the Single Audit Act Amendments of 1996. The new law extended the statutory audit requirement to all nonprofit organizations and substantially revised various provisions of the 1984 act (sections reproduced from *Single Audit Act of 1984 with Amendments, Encyclopedia of Business,* 2nd ed., (1999) by Mary Fischer).

Office of Management and Budget (OMB) Circular A-133   The OMB A-133 established standards and consistency for auditing state, local governments, and NFP organizations that receive funds from federal agencies. The SAA of 1984 required that an audit be performed if an NFP received $25,000 or more in federal funds. This was quite onerous, to say the least, for smaller organizations that received even a small sum of money. The SAA amendments of 1996 made a number of significant changes that were enthusiastically welcomed. One of the biggest changes was increasing the audit threshold from $25,000 to $300,000. Another significant change was changing the method of determining the audit threshold from funds received to funds expended.

Current OMB Circular A-133 Requirements

The OMB continued to make amendments to its rules, and effective for years ended after December 31, 2003, the threshold was raised from $300,000 to $500,000. They also modified their regulations to allow an exception to the single, organization-wide audit requirement. The exception was called a program-specific audit, and it basically said that, if an NFP received funds from only one federal grant and the amount was over the reporting threshold, it could have an audit performed that was smaller in scope than the one required for a single audit.

Recipients of federal awards are required to do the following:

- Maintain a system of internal control over all federal programs in order to demonstrate compliance with pertinent laws and regulations.
- Identify all grant programs by Catalog of Federal Domestic Assistance (CFDA) number and title, awarding agency, year of award, and any pass-through entities (if applicable).
- Ensure that audits mandated under OMB A-133 are performed and filed with appropriate federal entities as required.
- Follow up on any audit findings, questioned costs, or compliance issues. This involves specific responses and, when necessary, taking corrective action that will resolve the current and/or previous findings.
- Sign the official data-collection and single-audit submission forms that are prepared in conjunction with the independent auditors' compliance report. The recipient organization is legally responsible for the accuracy and timely submission of these forms even if the auditor prepares the forms.

Auditors of recipients of federal awards are required to do the following:

- Plan and conduct the audit in accordance with GAAS (generally accepted auditing standards) and GAGAS (*Generally Accepted Government Auditing Standards*, if applicable).
- Determine if the organization-wide and federal awards financial statements or schedules are presented fairly in accordance with GAAP.

- Determine if the Schedule of Expenditures of Federal Awards is presented fairly in relation to the organization's financial statements as a whole.
- Perform tests that demonstrate an understanding of the recipient's internal controls in order to support a "low assessed risk" for major programs.
- Determine that the recipient has complied with laws, regulations, and grant agreements through review and testing procedures.
- Follow up on the status of previous audit findings.

Awarding agencies have the following responsibilities in the audit process:

- Ensure that audits are completed and filed on time.
- Provide technical assistance to auditors and recipients who may have audit questions.
- Issue a management decision on financial and compliance audit findings within six months after an audit report has been submitted.
- Ensure that recipients follow up on audit findings and develop and implement a corrective action plan if necessary.

Federal Awards Reporting—Data-Collection Form

The federal government requires the filing of an annual report to the OMB (and, if applicable, to awarding agencies) detailing the total federal expenditures by major program and government agency. The report must be accompanied by the independent *auditor's compliance report.* In the past, the data-collection form and auditor's compliance report were submitted by mail. Then, a few years ago, both of these documents were submitted electronically and by mail. Beginning in 2009, all data-collection forms and auditor's compliance reports are required to be completed only electronically via the Web.

16

Audits—Preparation and Response

What is an *audit?* If you surveyed a random group of people, the most popular answer would most likely be a tax audit performed by the IRS. However, the term *audit* is much broader and encompasses many different types of activities, performed by different individuals for a variety of different purposes or reasons. For example, there are independent financial audits performed for the purpose of providing assurance about whether an organization's financial statements are free of material misstatement. There are also federal compliance audits performed to determine whether an organization is complying with OMB A-133 rules and regulations applicable to each major federal award received. Then there are a number of other types of audits. These include internal control audits (performed to express an opinion on the effectiveness of organization's internal controls); forensic audits (performed to investigate identified or suspected fraud or misrepresentations and are typically used by law enforcement agencies or for legal claims); state or local government granting agency audits (performed to determine whether granted funds were used in accordance with grant provisions); donor audits (requested by foundations, other charities, or individuals to ensure that funds donated were used in accordance with donors stipulated requirements); other regulatory agency audits (performed by the Department of Labor and other regulatory agencies to ensure that the organization is in compliance with all applicable laws; and finally, the IRS audit, which has the responsibility of ensuring that exempt-organization activities are in compliance with their reason for exemption and that taxes are paid on all nonexempt income received.

This chapter will discuss three types of audits that affect a significant number of NFPs. The three are financial records and statements audits performed by independent CPAs, audits performed by government agencies, and audits performed by the IRS. It is important to mention that the following information is based on the author's 30-plus years of accounting and auditing experience and as such is subjective to a degree. Other individuals involved in the audit process might have different experiences or opinions on the topics discussed.

Certified Financial Audits

Many NFPs are required to have their financial records and financial statements audited by an independent CPA or CPA firm. Independence means that the auditor can't be related to the organization (e.g., board member, staff, or related to board member or staff) or connected to the organization in any way that would impinge their independence. Certified financial audits are required for a number of reasons, such as by regulatory bodies (e.g., New York state attorney general if gross income exceeds $250,000 or OMB requirements are met), donors or grantors, board of directors, banks, and sometimes even by management.

Instead of having an audit performed, some organizations might choose or be required to have their financial records and financial statements "reviewed" or "compiled" by a CPA or CPA firm (e.g., New York state attorney general requires a review if gross income is between $100,000 and $250,000). There are important differences between an audit, a review, and a compilation. An audit is an examination of an entity's financial records to ensure that the financial statements are materially (not 100 percent) correct and not misleading. The auditor examines corroborating evidence to support disclosures (e.g., bank statements, invoices). A review is less in scope than an audit. No examination of corroborating evidence is required. Instead, mathematical tests and analytic procedures (comparing last year to current year revenue and expenses) are performed to provide a degree of comfort that the financial statements are materially correct. A compilation is simply the act of *compiling* or putting together information in the form of financial statements. No tests are performed, and the preparer does not make any assertions about the validity of the reported figures. Regardless of the type of service performed, the financial statements should be prepared in conformity to GAAP.

The next few sections will provide the reader with an inside look of how audits are performed, the reasons for performing them, and the views of both the auditor and the recipient of the audit, the auditee.

Audit Requirements

Despite the perception, the goal of the auditor is not to ask endless questions, request unlimited documents, and to be a general pain, although it might seem that way most of the time. The goal of the auditor is to perform all necessary tasks needed to accomplish the goal of issuing an opinion that the accompanied report is materially accurate. The tasks or procedures that are required to be performed are guided by rules known as *Generally Accepted Auditing Standards (GAAS)*, which are rules approved by the Auditing

Standards Board, a rule-making body of the American Institute of Certified Public Accountants (AICPA). With federal grants (i.e., federal compliance audits) the auditor must comply with audit rules issued by OMB, as well as GAAS. GAAS requires that the auditor ask certain questions, obtain and examine various documents, and resolve all questions that might undermine the veracity of the financial statements or other presented reports. Because the goal is to ensure or prove the validity of reported information, the auditor must apply a degree of what is called professional skepticism to the work he or she performs. That is, the auditor cannot simply accept everything they see or hear at face value but must be assured, through examination and testing, that what they are commenting on is materially correct.

Audit Procedures

Before any audit is performed an agreement stating the terms of the audit must be signed by the auditor and auditee. This agreement is called an Engagement Letter. Once an Engagement Letter is signed, the auditor will create a set of workpapers that will support the work performed by the auditor and justify the conclusions reached. A typical sequence of events performed by the auditor is as follows:

- Obtain a copy of the organization's detailed general ledger, trial balance, and, if available, financial statements.
- Ask the organization to send out signed requests, known as confirmations, to banks, insurance companies, and other external parties asking them to corroborate reported amounts.
- Provide the organization with a list of checks and other documents to be retrieved, compiled, and submitted back to the auditor for examination.
- Interview appropriate staff and perform all necessary observations (e.g., counting inventory).
- Examine and compare information on all received documents to information reported in the organization's general ledger and other reports.
- Perform mathematical and analytic tests to determine numerical accuracy.
- Investigate and resolve inconsistencies, questionable amounts, and omitted information.
- Prepare a draft of the auditors report and a report with any problems discovered during the audit and give these reports to the auditee for review and comment.
- Request that the auditee's management submit a letter to them, called a management representation letter, stating their responsibility for the accuracy of all financial statements and reports.
- Prepare and submit the final report to the auditee.

Auditor versus Auditee Perspective

Based on their different roles and responsibilities, the auditor and auditee will usually view the audit process differently. The independent auditor, by circumstance, is on the offense to question and prove the veracity of what they examine. Conversely, the auditee is constantly on the defensive to prove and support their contentions. Therefore, it is natural that friction is sometimes created. It is important that both parties (auditor and auditee) realize that they are not enemies, just people with different goals trying to do their job. Understanding the other party's role and goals goes a long way to reducing animosity. Let's look at some of the problems that sometimes arise.

Auditors' Perspective   Many auditors, especially those starting out or those whose only experience is in auditing, do not understand the internal dynamics of an organization or the competing responsibilities and duties that the accounting department staff has, or they only see their function as an auditor as important or having priority. They don't understand why their requests for documents and information are not being immediately addressed, and they can falsely believe that something underhanded is going on rather than the fact that NFP accounting staff might be over-whelmed with other tasks. Conversely, many organizations place unrealistic demands on the auditors by expecting them to complete their examination in an unreasonably short period of time but do not provide the auditor with requested documents or information to complete their job in a timely manner. They also don't understand that it is difficult to audit a set of financial reports that are inaccurate or incomplete. Just as it is unrealistic to expect a doctor to arrive at an accurate diagnosis without knowing all the medical issues and facts, it is unrealistic to expect an auditor to render an opinion on an organization's financial records that are incomplete or in disarray.

It is also not generally known, except in the public accountancy industry, that auditors (i.e., CPAs) are required by professional organizations (e.g., AICPA) or by law (e.g., New York state) to undergo what is called a peer review or quality review. This is a requirement that CPAs, who perform audits and reviews, have their audit workpapers periodically audited by another CPA or CPA firm. The purpose for this is to verify and ensure that the work they perform is in compliance with all required accounting (GAAP) and auditing (GAAS) rules and regulations. So, when auditors say they are doing something because they have to follow the rules, they are doing what they say because they actually *have* to follow the rules.

Auditees' Perspective   From the auditee perspective (especially the accounting department staff) audits are a necessary inconvenience at best and a thing to fear and loathe at worst. The goal of the auditee is to get through the audit process as quickly as possible so the more normal, daily activities can be resumed. Most organizations are honest and have very little to hide with the exception of some operational, managerial, or procedural practices that could use some improvement. However, there are some organizations where significant problems exist and where they want to hide their fallacies. Staff at these organizations tend to give inconsistent answers, double-talk, provide inaccurate details or schedules, are argumentative and reactive, and continually stall, stall, stall. It is the auditor's job to get at the truth, and in these cases a more assertive or aggressive approach by the auditor is justifiable.

The ideal approach to having an audit completed expeditiously is for the auditor to clearly communicate to the auditee what is needed to perform the audit and for the auditee to collect, organize, and present to the auditor all requested information in a timely manner and answer all questions as quickly, succinctly, and clearly as possible.

Exit Conference and Presentations

As mentioned in Chapter 3, NFP board members have certain legal and ethical responsibilities and duties related to the organization they oversee. One of those duties is *care*. Care requires that directors act in good faith using the degree of diligence, care, and skill, which prudent people would use in similar positions and under similar circumstances. Reviewing the work of the independent auditor and their audit report would fall under this oversight responsibility. It is a common practice for the auditor to present their audit report and any findings to one or more board committees (e.g., audit/budget/finance, executive), if not the full board. If management is present at the presentation meeting, it is not uncommon for the board to ask management to excuse themselves and then ask the auditor if they encountered any problems or issues with management while performing their audit. This allows an opportunity to discuss any issues where written disclosure was not necessary.

Local- and State-Agency Audits

Many state and local government departments or agencies that provide funds to NFPs require that the recipient organization undergo a financial or compliance audit by a representative of the granting department or agency. There are no uniform rules that all government agencies must follow. Audit rules vary among different jurisdictions and different agencies. Some follow mandated rules required by superior departments whereas others have specific guidelines applicable only to their disbursements.

Typically, grant examinations are more detailed and focused than a general, independent financial audit. With these audits, the auditor's goal is to determine whether the grant funds are being used in accordance with the grant agreement (or contract). If the auditors' conclusions are not favorable, the organization has less options or avenues for resolving disputes. Although all audits allow (and many times require) a response from the auditee, the auditee organization is more beholden to the grantor and, therefore, more fearful of disagreeing with the audit findings. There is a justifiable fear that, if they disagree, they might not receive any future grants or might even be asked to return grant money previously received.

Being audited by a state or local government-granting agency is one more necessary evil that NFPs must endure. The more internal controls and *appropriate* accounting policies and procedures an organization has, the more likely that these audits will be no more than a mild annoyance.

IRS Audits

Introduction

The IRS performs a number of audits of exempt organizations each year. The exact number is a heavily guarded secret (for obvious reasons). However, the common belief among NFP auditors is that the percentage of actual field audits performed on filed (or not filed) Forms 990, 990-T, and 990-PF is very small and varies from less than one percent to under five percent a year. A much higher percent receive notices requesting that additional (omitted) information be submitted.

The reason for field audits can be divided into two major categories: (1) required because of reporting errors, reported amounts exceed acceptable thresholds, or inconsistencies in the information reported on the returns; or (2) selected randomly from the general population of returns submitted. Another heavily guarded secret is which thresholds, activities, or disclosures trigger an audit. It is believed that the IRS computers are programmed with algorithms to make these selections.

There are many reasons the IRS performs audits of NFP organizations. The main one is to protect the public and to provide assurance that public donations are going to organizations that are, in fact, performing their publicly stated (and IRS approved) exempt mission. Another one is to gather data on how well laws and regulations are being followed. A third one is to ensure that taxes are paid on all activities that are commercial in nature (unrelated business activities) and not exempt from income taxes. And the last (and least advertised for fear of appearing cold and draconian) is to raise funds through penalties and interest.

Audit Process

In many cases, the process that the IRS follows to perform an audit will be somewhat similar to the following scenario.

The IRS will send a letter (notice of examination) informing an organization that they will be conducting an audit of the organization's financial records. The letter will usually provide certain information, such as: What year or years the audit will cover; Where the audit will be held (e.g., at the NFP's main office); IRS auditor's name and I.D. number; and Reason for audit (can be specific or general). The letter will then list a number of documents required from the organization (the list is usually very general and includes almost everything). Typically the list includes the Trial Balance, General Ledger and books of original entry (cash receipts, cash disbursements, etc.), current and prior years, 990s (sometimes easier to get from the organization than from their own files), publications, brochures, other promotional material, and all other documents deemed related to the audit. The CFO, Controller, or another representative of the organization will then, at some point, contact the IRS agent to set up a mutually convenient time to start the audit. Many times the organization will request that their independent auditor assist with the audit.

Several weeks or months after receipt of the audit notice, the IRS agent or agents will visit the organization, or go to another agreed upon location, to start their audit. The first thing the auditor will do is try to obtain a general understanding of what the NFP does and how it operates and then spend one or more days reviewing documents. The auditor will periodically ask questions and seek to resolve open issues. After completing their field audit, the auditor might discuss his or her overall findings with the auditee. If there is a disagreement as to the findings, the auditor will try to resolve it and may be willing to adjust their findings. If that doesn't resolve the disagreement, the auditor will explain the auditees' rights of appeal. If there is no disagreement as to the findings, the auditor will leave and send a determination letter to the organization within a number of weeks. Findings might include assessments for Excise Tax or UBIT. If the organization is found to be in compliance, there might be no findings or only some suggestions for correcting minor problems or improving internal controls.

Audit Tips

IRS auditors who audit exempt organizations tend to be more sympathetic to the NFP's mission and, therefore, less aggressive in their audit approach than they are with other entities, *unless* they suspect a problem and suspicion can be created simply by dealing inappropriately with the IRS agent. Here are some don'ts that will assist in avoiding problems. *Don't* wait until the last minute when the agent comes in to first gather requested information. *Don't* try to double-talk the agent to cover up a minor infraction. If minor, be upfront. Even if this problem is not minor it might be better to inform the agent of the issue then wait for the agent to discover it., especially if the problem is easily discoverable. The more forthcoming the organization is with the agent in the beginning, the more trusting the agent will be and might even be more lenient. *Don't* have the field audit performed in the organization's accounting office. Have it at an off-site location, such as the CPA's office. This will allow for time to resolve outstanding issues and develop appropriate responses. It is difficult to tell an agent that you can't find supporting documentation without appearing disorganized or inefficient.

Conclusion

NFP organizations have come a long way from the church-run religious groups that existed in colonial times. Today NFPs perform every type of function imaginable and are an integral part of the fabric of our society. Without the multitude of services they perform, the United States and the world would be a much different and colder place.

As the world and the economy have become more complicated, automated, and integrated, so have the operations of all the different types of NFP organizations. As any business entity knows (even one without a profit motive), in order to function properly and be efficient and productive, financial activities must be tracked, recorded, and reported in a timely and accurate manner. Without accurate financial information, appropriate actions can't be taken, important decisions cannot be made, and resources cannot be allocated efficiently. Without clear and accurate reporting, external parties cannot make informed decisions about an organization, which might affect the amount of revenue and support the organization receives. And without accurate financial reporting, regulatory bodies will not be able to ensure that NFP organizations are complying with all the rules, regulations, and laws that justify their reason for existence.

In order to properly maintain financial records and accurately report financial activity, every organization needs competent, knowledgeable accounting/financial staff, consultants, or advisors to assist them. The specific number needed and expertise level required will obviously be based on the size, complexity, and specific needs of each organization. But regardless of the size, competent support is needed. Although most colleges or universities in every part of the country have some type of accounting program and the number of accounting graduates remains high each year, the number of financial programs geared specifically toward the NFP world remains pitifully tiny. With all the changes over the last quarter of the century in the many types of activities that NFPs engage in, and with all the recent changes in accounting and tax rules and laws, it is more important than ever that accountants be trained properly to provide the necessary support needed by NFP organizations. It is one of the goals of the author to see that appropriate training is available to all who seek it.

APPENDIX

Tax-Exempt Organization Reference Chart

This appendix includes the following selection of IRS forms*:

- Form 990: Return of Organization Exempt from Income Tax [Instructions]
- Form 990EZ: Short Form Return of Organization Exempt from Income Tax [Instructions]
- Form 990 Schedule A: Organization Exempt Under Section 501(c)(3) [Instructions]
- Form 990BL: Information and Initial Excise Tax Return for Black Lung Benefit Trusts and Certain Related Persons [Instructions]
- Form 990C: Farmers' Cooperative Association Income Tax Return [Instructions]
- Form 990 PF: Return of Private Foundation or Section 4947(a)(1) Non-exempt Charitable Trust Treated as a Private Foundation [Instructions]
- Form 1065: U.S. Partnership Return of Income [Instructions]
- Form 1023: Application for Recognition of Exemption Under Section 501(c)(3) of the Internal Revenue Code
- Form 1024: Application for Recognition of Exemption Under Section 501(a) for Determination Under Section 120 of the Internal Revenue Code
- Form 1028: Application for Recognition of Exemption Under Section 521 of the Internal Revenue Code [Instructions]
- Form 8718: User Fee for Exempt Organization Determination Letter Request
- Publication 557: Tax-Exempt Status for Your Organization [also in Web/HTML format]

---

*Note: Table A.1 may not include every type of organization that qualifies for some form of federal tax exemption. It should not be considered legal advice and should not be otherwise used to determine matters of law; it is provided for educational purposes only. Please use official IRS materials to ensure your information is completely up to date and accurate.

Table A.1 Derived from IRS Publication 557: Tax-Exempt Status for Your Organization

Section of 1986 Tax Code	Description of organization	General nature of activities	Application Form	Annual return required to be filed	Contributions allowable
501(c)(1)	Corporations Organized Under Act of Congress (Including Federal Credit Unions)	Instrumentalities of the United States	No Form	None	Yes, if made for exclusively public purposes
501(c)(2)	Title Holding Corporation for Exempt Organization	Holding title to property of an exempt organization	1024	990[1] or 990EZ[8]	No[2]
501(c)(3)	Religious, Educational, Charitable, Scientific, Literary, Testing for Public Safety, to Foster National or International Amateur Sports Competition, or Prevention of Cruelty to Children or Animals Organizations	Activities of nature implied by description of class of organization	1023	990,[1] 990EZ,[8] or 990-PF	Yes, generally

All 501(c)(3) organizations are further categorized as one of five types under IRC 509(a):

	Subclass	Section	Description
	Private foundations		All 501(c)(3) organizations that don't qualify as public charities. Some private foundations are additionally subclassified as private operating foundations or private nonoperating foundations, which receive some of the advantages of public charities.
	Public charities	509(a)(1)	Publicly supported charities.
		509(a)(2)	Exempt purpose activity-supported charities.
		509(a)(3)	Supporting organizations for 509(a)(1) or 509(a)(2) charities.
		509(a)(4)	Public safety charities.

501(c)(4)	Civic Leagues, Social Welfare Organizations, and Local Associations of Employees	Promotion of community welfare; charitable, educational or recreational	1024	990[1] or 990EZ[8]	No, generally[2,3]
501(c)(5)	Labor, Agricultural, and Horticultural Organizations	Educational or instructive, the purpose being to improve conditions of work, and to improve products and efficiency	1024	990[1] or 990EZ[8]	No[2]
501(c)(6)	Business Leagues, Chambers of Commerce, Real Estate Boards, etc.	Improvement of business conditions of one or more lines of business	1024	990[1] or 990EZ[8]	No[2]
501(c)(7)	Social and Recreation Clubs	Pleasure, recreation, social activities	1024	990[1] or 990EZ[8]	No[2]
501(c)(8)	Fraternal Beneficiary Societies and Associations	Lodge providing for payment of life, sickness, accident, or other benefits to members	1024	990[1] or 990EZ[8]	Yes, if for certain Sec. 501 (c)(3) purposes
501(c)(9)	Voluntary Employees' Beneficiary Associations	Providing for payment of life, sickness, accident or other benefits to members	1024	990[1] or 990EZ[8]	No[2]

(continued)

Table A.1 (Continued)

Section of 1986 Tax Code	Description of organization	General nature of activities	Application Form	Annual return required to be filed	Contributions allowable
501(c)(10) (also here)	Domestic Fraternal Societies and Associations	Lodge devoting its net earnings to charitable, fraternal, and other specified purposes. No life, sickness, or accident benefits to members	1024	990[1] or 990EZ[8]	Yes, if for certain Sec. 501 (c)(3) purposes
501(c)(11)	Teachers' Retirement Fund Associations	Teachers' association for payment of retirement benefits	No Form[6]	990[1] or 990EZ[8]	No[2]
501(c)(12)	Benevolent Life Insurance Associations, Mutual Ditch or Irrigation Companies, Mutual or Cooperative Telephone Companies, etc.	Activities of a mutually beneficial nature similar to those implied by the description of class of organization	1024	990[1] or 990EZ[8]	No[2]
501(c)(13)	Cemetery Companies	Burials and incidental activities	1024	990[1] or 990EZ[8]	Yes, generally
501(c)(14)	State Chartered Credit Unions, Mutual Reserve Funds	Loans to members	No Form[6]	990[1] or 990EZ[8]	No[2]

501(c)(15)	Mutual Insurance Companies or Associations	Providing insurance to members substantially at cost	1024	990[1] or 990EZ[8]	No[2]
501(c)(16)	Cooperative Organizations to Finance Crop Operations	Financing crop operations in conjunction with activities of a marketing or purchasing association	No Form[6]	990[1] or 990EZ[8]	No[2]
501(c)(17)	Supplemental Unemployment Benefit Trusts	Provides for payment of supplemental unemployment compensation benefits	1024	990[1] or 990EZ[8]	No[2]
501(c)(18)	Employee Funded Pension Trust (created before June 25, 1959)	Payment of benefits under a pension plan funded by employees	No Form[6]	990[1] or 990EZ[8]	No[2]
501(c)(19)	Post or Organization of Past or Present Members of the Armed Forces	Activities implied by nature of organization	1024	990[1] or 990EZ[8]	No, generally[7]
501(c)(20)	Group Legal Services Plan Organizations	n/a	n/a	n/a	n/a
501(c)(21)	Black Lung Benefit Trusts	Funded by coal mine operators to satisfy their liability for disability or death due to black lung diseases	No Form[6]	990-BL	No[4]

(continued)

Table A.1 (Continued)

Section of 1986 Tax Code	Description of organization	General nature of activities	Application Form	Annual return required to be filed	Contributions allowable
501(c)(22)	Withdrawal Liability Payment Fund	To provide funds to meet the liability of employers withdrawing from a multi-employer pension fund	No Form[6]	990 or 990EZ[8]	No[5]
501(c)(23)	Veterans Organization (created before 1880)	To provide insurance and other benefits to veterans	No Form[6]	990 or 990EZ[8]	No, generally[7]
501(c)(25)	Title Holding Corporations or Trusts with Multiple Parents	Holding title and paying over income from property to 35 or fewer parents or beneficiaries	1024	990 or 990EZ	No
501(c)(26)	State-Sponsored Organization Providing Health Coverage for High-Risk Individuals	Provides health care coverage to high-risk individuals	No Form[6]	990[1] or 990EZ[8]	No
501(c)(27)	State-Sponsored Workers' Compensation Reinsurance Organization	Reimburses members for losses under workers' compensation acts	No Form[6]	990[1] or 990EZ[8]	No

Section	Organization	Description	Application Form	Annual Return	Deductible Contributions
501(d)	Religious and Apostolic Associations	Regular business activities. Communal religious community	No Form	1065[9]	No[2]
501(e)	Cooperative Hospital Service Organizations	Performs cooperative services for hospitals	1023	990[1] or 990EZ[8]	Yes
501(f)	Cooperative Service Organizations of Operating Educational Organizations	Performs collective investment services for educational organizations	1023	990[1] or 990EZ[8]	Yes
501(k)	Child Care Organization	Provides care for children	1023	990 or 990EZ[8]	Yes
501(n)	Charitable Risk Pools	Pools certain insurance risks of 501(c)(3)	1023	990[1] or 990EZ[8]	Yes
521(a)	Farmers' Cooperative Associations	Cooperative marketing and purchasing for agricultural producers	1028	990-C	No

[1] For exceptions to the filing requirement, see Chapter 2 and the Form instructions.

[2] An organization exempt under a Subsection of Code section 501 other than (c)(3), may establish a charitable fund, contributions to which are deductible. Such a fund must itself meet the requirements of section 501(c)(3) and the related notice requirements of section 508(a).

[3] Contributions to volunteer fire companies and similar organizations are deductible, but only if made for exclusively public purposes.

[4] Deductible as a business expense to the extent allowed by Code section 192.

[5] Deductible as a business expense to the extent allowed by Code section 194A.

[6] Application is by letter to the address shown on Form 8718. A copy of the organizing document should be attached and the letter should be signed by an officer.

[7] Contributions to these organizations are deductible only if 90% or more of the organization's members are war veterans.

[8] For limits on the use of Form 990EZ, see Chapter 2 and the general instructions for Form 990EZ (or Form 990).

APPENDIX B

Sample NFP Chart of Accounts

Table B.1   Sample NFP Chart of Accounts

SAMPLE NFP ORGANIZATION Chart of Accounts			
Account	**Type**	**Account Description**	**Tax Code**
1901000	Asset	ASSETS (1901000 to 1901999)	
1901001	Asset	CURRENT ASSETS (1901002 to 1901298)	
1901005	Asset	Cash	
1901005.02	Asset	Petty cash	
1901005.04	Asset	Cash - Bank 1	
1901005.06	Asset	Cash - Bank 2	
1901005.10	Asset	Cash - money market	
1901005.80	Asset	Cash - short term investments	
1901010	Asset	Certificates of deposit	
1901050	Asset	Accounts receivable	
1901050.02	Asset	Contracts receivable	
1901050.08	Asset	Clients receivable	
1901100	Asset	Contributions receivable	
1901150	Asset	Grants receivable	
1901170	Asset	Inventory	
1901200	Asset	Prepaid expenses	
1901200.02	Asset	Prepaid insurance	
1901250	Asset	Investments	
1901270	Asset	Allowance for unrealized gains/(losses)	
1901299	Asset	NONCURRENT ASSETS (1901300 to 1901998)	
1901300	Asset	Office equipment	
1901350	Asset	Furniture and Fixtures	
1901360	Asset	Leasehold improvements	

(Continued)

Table B.1   (Continued)

SAMPLE NFP ORGANIZATION			
Chart of Accounts			
Account	**Type**	**Account Description**	**Tax Code**
1901380	Asset	Buildings	
1901390	Asset	Vehicles	
1901400	Asset	Organization costs	
1901420	Asset	Startup costs	
1901450	Asset	Accumulated depreciation	
1901450.02	Asset	Accumulated depreciation - furniture and fixtures	
1901450.04	Asset	Accumulated depreciation - office equipment	
1901450.06	Asset	Accumumulated depreciation - leasehold improvement	
1901450.08	Asset	Accumulated depreciation - building	
1901450.10	Asset	Accumulated depreciation - vehicles	
1901470	Asset	Accumulated amortization	
1901500	Asset	Loans and exchanges	
1901550	Asset	Due from related parties	
1901550.10	Asset	Due from officers	
1901550.15	Asset	Due from employees	
1901550.20	Asset	Payroll receivable	
1901600	Asset	Loans receivable	
1901800	Asset	Security deposits receivable	
1901950	Asset	Other assets	
1902000	Liability	LIABILITIES (1902000 to 1902999)	
1902001	Liability	CURRENT LIABILITIES (1902002 to 19022998)	
1902005	Liability	Cash overdraft	
1902010	Liability	Account payable	
1902030	Liability	Accrued expenses	
1902050	Liability	Payroll payable	
1902060	Liability	Payroll taxes payable	
1902070	Liability	Net payroll clearance	
1902100	Liability	Pension payable	
1902200	Liability	Loans and exchanges	
1902220	Liability	Due to related parties	
1902220.10	Liability	Due to officers	
1902220.15	Liability	Due to employees	
1902250	Liability	Loans payable - short term	
1902300	Liability	Notes payable - short term	
1902399	Liability	LONG-TERM LIABILITIES (1902400 to 1902999)	
1902400	Liability	Deferred income	
1902450	Liability	Loans payable - long term	
1902470	Liability	Notes payable - long term	

Table B.1   (Continued)

SAMPLE NFP ORGANIZATION Chart of Accounts			
Account	**Type**	**Account Description**	**Tax Code**
1902900	Liability	Other liabilities	
1903000	Liability	NET ASSETS (3000 to 3999)	
1903100	Liability	Unrestricted net assets	
1903200	Liability	Temporarily restricted net assets	
1903300	Liability	Permanently restricted net assets	
1904000	Revenue	REVENUE (4000 to 4999)	
1904005	Revenue	Program service revenue	
1904100	Revenue	Membership dues	
1904150	Revenue	Contributions	
1904150.02	Revenue	Contributions - individuals	
1904150.04	Revenue	Contributions - corporations	
1904170	Revenue	Contributions in-kind	
1904190	Revenue	Government grants	
1904200	Revenue	Sponsor income	
1904220	Revenue	Ticket income	
1904250	Revenue	Directory support	
1904300	Revenue	Special events income	
1904320	Revenue	Cost of events	
1904350	Revenue	Auction income	
1904370	Revenue	Cost of auction items	
1904500	Revenue	Investment income	
1904520	Revenue	Interest	
1904540	Revenue	Dividends	
1904560	Revenue	Gains/(losses) on sale of investments	
1904580	Revenue	Unrealized gains/(losses) on investments	
1904650	Revenue	Mailing lists	
1904800	Revenue	Other income	
1904995	Revenue	Release of restricted assets	
1904996	Revenue	Release of temporarily restricted assets	
1904997	Revenue	Release of permanently restricted assets	
1905000	Expense	EXPENSES (5000-6000)	
1905010	Expense	Salaries	
1905010.02	Expense	Officers' salaries	
1905010.05	Expense	Staff salaries	
1905020	Expense	Payroll taxes	
1905050	Expense	Employee benefits	
1905100	Expense	Advertising and promotion	
1905150	Expense	Amortization	

(Continued)

Table B.1 **(Continued)**

SAMPLE NFP ORGANIZATION Chart of Accounts			
Account	**Type**	**Account Description**	**Tax Code**
1905200	Expense	Bank charges and payroll processing fees	
1905310	Expense	Contributed rent and other expenses	
1905350	Expense	Depreciation	
1905400	Expense	Dues, books, and subscriptions	
1905450	Expense	Equipment leases and rentals	
1905500	Expense	Equipment purchases	
1905550	Expense	Event costs - other	
1905600	Expense	Insurance	
1905650	Expense	Interns	
1905700	Expense	Interest	
1905750	Expense	Local transportation	
1905800	Expense	Miscellaneous	
1905850	Expense	Office expenses and supplies	
1905950	Expense	Outside contractors	
1906050	Expense	Political expenditures	
1906100	Expense	Postage and delivery	
1906150	Expense	Printing	
1906200	Expense	Production	
1906250	Expense	Professional fees	
1906300	Expense	Program expenses - other	
1906350	Expense	Recruitment	
1906400	Expense	Relocation	
1906450	Expense	Rent	
1906500	Expense	Repairs and maintenance	
1906550	Expense	Telephone and communications	
1906600	Expense	Trade shows	
1906650	Expense	Travel, conferences, and meetings	
1906750	Expense	Utilities	
1906800	Expense	Vehicles	
1909000	Expense	Undistributed expenses	

APPENDIX C

Abbreviations

AICPA	American Institute of Certified Public Accountants
A/R	Accounts receivable
A/P	Accounts payable
BIDs	Business Improvement Districts
CFO	Chief Financial Officer
CORP.	Corporation
CPAs	Certified Public Accountants
CR.	Credit
DOTKEY	Directors, Officers, Trustees, and Key Employees
DR.	Debit
EIN	Employer identification number
FASB	Financial Accounting Standards Board
FICA	Federal insurance contribution act (Social Security)
FMV	Fair market value
FUTA	Federal unemployment tax act
FV	Fair value
G/L	General ledger
HICE	Highest compensated employees
INC.	Incorporated

IRC	Internal Revenue Code
IRS	Internal Revenue Service
LDC	Local Development Corporations
NFP	Not-for-Profit Organization
OMB	Office of Management and Budget
PFs	Private Foundations
POA	Power of Attorney
PR	Permanently restricted
PV	Present value
SFAS	Statement of Financial Accounting Standards
SIA	Split-interest agreement
SL	Straight line
SOP	Statement of Position
SUI	State unemployment insurance
TIN	Taxpayer identification number
TR	Temporarily restricted
UR	Unrestricted

Glossary

Accounts payable   Obligations to pay for goods and services that have been acquired on open account.

Accounts receivable (trade)   Amounts due the organization from sales of products or services.

Accounting tenets   Principles or theories of accounting that dictate in the most general terms how financial activity should be treated and are the underpinnings of GAAP.

Accrual basis   Basis of accounting that records the financial effects of transactions and other events and circumstances that have cash consequences for the entity in the periods in which those transactions, events, and circumstances occur, rather than only in the periods in which cash is received or paid by the entity.

Accrued expenses   Estimated obligations (usually expenses) that have been incurred but aren't supported by a vendor bill or other documentation.

Accumulated depreciation   Sum of depreciation charges taken from date of asset purchase to current date.

Advisory board   Group of people who provide some level of advice to an NFP board or management, who are not usually board members and do not have the same legal and fiduciary responsibilities of board members.

Amortization expense   Portion of intangible assets and deferred charges allocated to current period expense (similar to depreciation expense).

Amortization of discount   Periodic adjustments made to account for differences between initial recorded discount value (PV) and current value.

Annuity   Series of payments or receipts over a period of time.

Assets   Probable future economic benefits obtained or controlled by a particular entity as a result of past transactions or events.

Audit report (independent)   Report prepared by a CPA or CPA firm that states whether the financial statements included in the report present fairly the audited organization's financial position, results of operations, and cash flows in conformity with GAAP.

Bank reconciliation   Comparison of transactions listed on a bank statement with the transactions listed on an organization's books (i.e., G/L).

Beneficiaries   Individual or entity that will receive benefits from a trust or other financial arrangement.

Board of directors   Individuals entrusted with the responsibility of ensuring that an organization accomplishes its purpose for being in existence (its mission).

Board of trustee   Similar to board of directors.

Bookkeeper   Individual whose primary responsibility is recording all financial activity in one or more books of record. Although still used, this term is becoming antiquated since financial transactions are typically maintained using computers and software and not physical books.

Budget   A monetary plan, guide, and tool to assist an organization's management in allocating existing and future resources and to assist in evaluating deficiencies and accomplishments in operations based on financial results.

Budget variance   Difference between actual financial results and budgeted amounts.

Bylaws   Document that specifies in broad terms how the organization will operate and be governed.

Capital lease   Lease (or rental agreement) where the purchaser is actually purchasing the asset rather than renting it because, by the end of the lease period, most of the asset is used up.

Cash   Currency (bill and coins) on hand and demand deposits held at banks and other financial institutions (checking and savings accounts).

Cash equivalents   Investments that are highly liquid and will be converted to cash in such a short period of time that a change in their value is highly unlikely.

Certified public accountant   Individual who satisfied all educational, examination, and experience requirements within a proscribed state jurisdiction.

Charitable gift annuities   Similar to charitable remainder trust but no actual trust is set up.

Charitable lead trust   Donor establishes a trust naming an NFP as beneficiary until the agreement terminates (e.g., donor or spouse dies), at which time the plans assets revert either to the donor or to another beneficiary.

Charitable remainder trust   Donor establishes a trust in which assets are contributed to an NFP in exchange for receiving distributions for a specific period of time and upon termination (e.g., death of donor or other beneficiary) the NFP gets to keep assets.

Chart of accounts   List of all account names and numbers in an organization's general ledger.

Check request form   Form used by purchaser or other employee requesting that payment be made for the purchase of goods or services and approved by authorized personnel.

Collections   Works of art, historical treasures, or similar assets that are (1) held for exhibition to the public, for educational purposes, or for research in furtherance of public service and not financial gain; (2) protected, cared for, and preserved; and (3) subject to a policy requiring any proceeds from the sale of collection items to be reinvested in other collection items.

Combined financial statements Presenting together the financial statements of two or more interrelated, commonly controlled organizations after eliminating all interorganizational transactions.

Commercial enterprise An organization whose purpose is to maximize its profits by providing products or services.

Common stock Securities that represent ownership interest in a corporation that typically provides the owner with rights to sharing profits, losses, dividends, appreciation, and depreciation.

Compensated absence Payment to employees for time not worked (e.g., vacation and personal time off).

Consolidated financial statements Presenting together the financial statements of two or more entities in which one has a controlling economic or financial interest over the others after eliminating all interorganizational transactions.

Contingencies Uncertain, existing conditions that may create a possible benefit (i.e., gain) or a legal obligation in the future that are based on past transactions or events.

Contributions Voluntary, unconditional transfer of assets to an entity or assumption of their liability by another entity.

Contributions in kind Voluntary, unconditional donations of noncash, goods, facilities, or services.

Contra asset account Accounts used for tracking the reduction in the gross cost of an asset such as accumulated depreciation and allowance for bad debt.

Control environment Encompasses the organization's general philosophy, the organizational structure and methods of authority, personnel procedures, external influences, and the ability to monitor its activities.

Credit Right side of a transaction that represents a decrease to certain types of accounts and an increase to other types of accounts.

Debit Left side of a transaction that represents an increase to certain types of accounts and a decrease to other types of accounts.

Deferred income/revenue Receiving money in advance for providing goods or services in the future (i.e., received before it is earned).

Defined benefit plan Retirement plan where specific benefit amounts are calculated to be received in the future, based on employees' age, years of service to the organization, or salary earned.

Defined contribution plan Retirement plan in which individual accounts are set up for each participant and benefits are based on a combination of contributions made, earning on contributions invested, and any other participants' forfeitures allocated to individual accounts.

Deposits in transit Cash deposited in an organization's bank account but not included on the bank statement due to timing.

Depreciation   Allocation of a portion of the total cost of a tangible asset over its estimated useful life.

Discount rate   Interest rate (i.e., percent) used to calculate PV.

Donations (*see* **Contributions**)

Donor advised funds   Charitable giving vehicle wherein an individual, family, or corporation makes an irrevocable, tax-deductible contribution of personal assets to a charity and at any time thereafter can exercise a right to make a recommendation on either uses of the account, such as providing advice about how to invest or make distributions from the account.

Donors   Individuals, corporations, or other entities that make contributions to an NFP organization.

Double-entry system   System that promulgates that every entry made to a business' financial records (also know as books) has two sides—a debit and a credit—and is balanced.

Employee   Generally anyone who performs services for an organization that is controlled by the organization about what will be done and how those services will be performed.

Endowment funds   A fund created by a donor contribution with the stipulation that the fund must be held in perpetuity and permanently restricted; the income earned must be used for unrestricted or restricted purposes in accordance with the donor's wishes.

Equity method of accounting   Requires that the NFP record the purchase of the shares of the commercial entity at its fair value and recognizes investment income each year based on the percentage interest the NFP has in the invested company if the NFP has the ability to exercise significant influence over operating and financial policies of the commercial entity. Significant influence is assumed when stock ownership is between 20 and 50 percent.

Exchange transactions   Purchase of goods or services for money or another asset.

Executive director   Senior manager at an NFP organization who oversees operations and personnel and implements board of directors decisions.

Excise tax   Tax incurred by NFP organizations for various allowed (e.g., private-foundation investment income) and disallowed (e.g., supporting political campaign) activities.

Exempt organization   Organization exempt from paying income or other taxes by the Internal Revenue Service or other governmental regulatory body.

Expenditures   Outflows of cash or other resources.

Expense   Using up of an asset or incurring some type of liability (or obligation) to create or generate revenue.

Expense reimbursement grants   Grant provision that requires the organization to first incur approved, budgeted expenses before receiving any grant proceeds.

Fair value   The price that would be received to sell an asset or paid to transfer a liability in an orderly, arms-length transaction between market participants at the measurement date.

Federal unemployment tax   Required payments to the federal government for future unemployment benefits of terminated employees based on a percentage of all current employees' salary up to maximum amount.

Fee for service   Payment of money or other asset in an arms-length transaction in exchange for services performed.

FICA   Federal Insurance Contribution Act (a/k/a Social Security). Federal law that requires that both employers and employees contribute to a program that provides future monetary and medical benefits to retirees, the disabled, and children of deceased employees.

Financial Accounting Standards Board   The designated private-sector organization for establishing standards of financial accounting that govern the preparation of financial statements.

Fiscal year   Discrete period of time (usually 12 months) used by an organization to account for its operations that can end in any month (e.g., June or December).

Fund accounting   Method of accounting that required an organization to separate its major activities into separate categories or funds (e.g., operating fund, special-use fund). Each fund maintains its own assets and liabilities, sources of revenue, and support and expenses. Each fund also is self-balancing and has its own general ledger accounts. No longer an acceptable method of accounting under GAAP.

General journal   Separate book or file used to record miscellaneous transactions where all debit and credit entries balance to zero as opposed to specific journals that are used to enter specific activity such as cash disbursement journal or cash receipts journal.

General ledger   A book or computer file that stores all detail or summary financial transactions of an organization.

Generally Accepted Accounting Principles   Composite of various standards, conventions, and rules for recording, categorizing, and summarizing transactions and preparing financial statements or reports that accurately reflect an organization's operations at a particular point in time and with the least subjectivity or variability.

Generally Accepted Auditing Standards   Rules for properly performing a certified financial audit approved by the Auditing Standards Board, a rule-making body of the American Institute of Certified Public Accountants (AICPA), that requires that the auditor ask certain questions, obtain and examine various documents, and resolve all questions that might undermine the veracity of the financial statements or other presented reports.

Highly compensated employees   Defined by the IRS as one of the five highest compensated employees of an organization (including employees of a disregarded entity of the organization) other than officers or key employees. The five highest compensated employees are determined by the amounts of reportable compensation for the calendar year ending with or within the organization's tax year.

Historic cost   Money paid or other resource given up or foregone, to acquire, produce, consume, or exchange another asset.

Independent contractor   A person who provides services to an organization but who is not treated as an employee.

Intangible assets   Assets with no physical substance such as patents, copyrights, trademarks, and goodwill.

Internal controls   The system of policies and procedures that an organization uses to: ensure the reliability of financial reporting, comply with all required laws and regulations, protect its assets, and ensure that its resources are used properly to achieve its organizational mission efficiently and effectively.

Internal Revenue Code   Domestic statutory tax law of the United States covering income tax, payroll taxes, gift taxes, estate taxes, and statutory excise taxes.

Internal Revenue Service   The federal agency responsible for enforcing the U.S. Treasury Department's revenue laws.

Inure   Accrue or flow to the benefit of someone.

Investment portfolio   A pool of different investments owned by an organization that can include marketable securities (stocks and bonds), real estate, investment in partnerships, and any other income-producing asset.

Joint costs (fund-raising)   Expenditures (or costs) that have functional elements of fund-raising, and one or all of the following: programs, management, and general.

Key employee   Defined by the IRS as someone who earns a significant salary (e.g., >$150,000) and has authority to make major organizational decisions or significant control over the organization activities.

Liabilities   Probable future sacrifices of economic benefits arising from present obligations of a particular entity to transfer assets or provide services to other entities in the future as a result of past transactions or events.

Loans payable   Legal obligation to pay a specific sum of money at a specific period of time.

Marketable securities   Equity and debt securities that are listed on a public exchange that can be readily bought or sold.

Net assets   Difference between what an organization owns and what it owes, broken down into three categories: unrestricted net assets, temporarily restricted net assets, and permanently restricted net assets.

Notes payable   Written promise to pay a specific sum of money at a specific period of time in the future.

Notes to financial statements   Material disclosures required by generally accepted accounting principles that are not presented on the face of financial statements but accompany those statements as a supplementary document.

NFP mission   The purpose an NFP organization is created, reason for existence, and perpetual goal.

NFP organization   A legal entity or group formed for some purpose other than to make a profit and not owned by any one or more individuals or entities.

Office of Management and Budget   Cabinet-level office of the president of the United States whose predominant mission is to assist the president in overseeing the preparation of the federal budget and to supervise its administration of executive-branch agencies. The OMB also evaluates the effectiveness of agency programs, policies, and procedures; assesses competing funding demands among agencies; sets funding priorities; and ensures that agency reports, rules, testimony, and proposed legislation are consistent with the president's budget and with administration policies.

Operating leases   Agreement for the rental of property between a user of the property (lessee) and the renter of the property (lessor) for a specific sum of money.

Operating year   Discrete period of time (usually 12 months).

Payroll service company   Commercial company that handles payroll-related functions, such as calculating payroll taxes, processing payroll checks, remitting payroll taxes, submitting required reports to regulatory agencies, and preparing payroll reports for management.

Payroll taxes   All federal, state and local income taxes, Social Security, and Medicare taxes (FICA) withheld from wages paid to employees along with the employers' portion of FICA. Sometimes included in this category are employer payments for federal and state unemployment tax, state disability, and workers' compensation, which are technically insurance and not payroll taxes.

Permanently restricted net assets   Assets that are restricted from use by one or more donors. Typically the principal amount (i.e., the amount of the original gift) must be held in perpetuity (i.e., forever) by the organization and the income earned on invested assets can be used for either unrestricted or restricted purposes in accordance with donors' stipulations.

Petty cash   Bills and coins kept on hand in a box, envelope, or drawer to pay for small, incidental expenses, such as local transportation (subways, taxis), meals for staff meetings, and postage.

Pledges   Promise to make a donation at a future point in time. Pledges can be unconditional or conditional (based on some nonguaranteed occurrence).

Pooled investments   Combining of investments into one single portfolio fund to earn a larger return or reduce investment management fees or other investment costs.

Power of attorney   A legal document that enables an individual to designate another person, called the attorney in fact (as opposed to an attorney-at-law), to act on his/her behalf (as agent) until some point in the future as specified in the document or required by law.

Prepaid expense   Expenses paid for before benefits are received and recorded as an asset in the organization's general ledger in accordance with accrual-based GAAP rules. The asset is subsequently reclassified to an appropriate expense account in the year the benefit is received.

Present value   Current worth (value) of future sums of money, calculated by discounting future amounts at an appropriate interest rate (opposite of compounded interest).

Program expense   Direct and indirect (allocated) expense related to the performance of a major organization's program.

Program service revenue   Revenue generated from program activities that includes any products or services provided by an NFP organization.

Public charity   Organization classified by the Internal Revenue Service as a qualifying, Internal Revenue Code section 501(c)(3) tax-exempt organization that derives a significant portion of its revenue and support from the general public.

Private foundation   Organization that receives most of its funds from a small number of individuals or entities, such as from one family or corporation, and has as its primary activity the making of grants to other charitable organizations and individuals, rather than operating charitable programs.

Private operating foundation   Private foundation that devotes most of its resources to the active conduct of its exempt activities but doesn't receive enough funding from the general public to be classified as a public charity.

Realization   The converting of an asset or right to an asset into cash (e.g., actually receiving a pledged donation).

Recognition   Including a transaction in the organization's general ledger (e.g., recognizing or recording a promise to make a contribution or pledge receivable).

Refundable advance   Money that is received from a governmental agency or other entity, which might not be earned and might need to be returned.

Release of restricted funds   The recognition of restricted contributions or grants as unrestricted assets after the time or purpose restriction has been met.

Review (accountant's report)   Analytical, numeric tests and other procedures performed by a CPA or CPA firm to ascertain whether the organization's financial statements are materially correct and free of misstatement. It differs from a financial audit in that no corroborating documentation is examined.

Separation of duties   The partitioning of various accounting and authorization duties and responsibilities to different individuals to remove the degree of control a single individual has over a particular process, thereby reducing the opportunity of someone doing something improper or illegal, such as misappropriating assets.

Single Audit Act   Legislation passed by Congress in 1984 (and amended in later years) to improve auditing and management for federal funds provided to state and local governments and NFP organizations, by, among other things, reducing overlaps caused by the simultaneous performance of audits by different federal agencies.

Split-interest agreement   Created when a donor contributes assets directly to an NFP or places assets in a trust for the benefit of the NFP organization, but the NFP is not the sole beneficiary of the assets or the income generated from the assets.

Straight-line method   Simplest method for determining what portion of an asset's cost to allocate as a current year's expense. Method requires that the asset's cost be divided by its estimated useful life in years and the result recognized as a current-period depreciation or amortization expense.

Statement of activities   One of the three financial statements required to be presented in order to be in compliance with GAAP. It shows the major categories of income and support and expenses categorized by major program and supporting services (management and general and fund-raising) and covers a specified period of time (usually one year). This statement is similar to the income statement (or statement of profit and loss) that is presented by commercial entities.

Statement of cash flows   One of the three financial statements required to be presented in order to be in compliance with GAAP that shows the cash receipts and cash disbursements during a specified period (e.g., one year), classified by three principal sources of use: operations, investing, and financing.

Statement of Financial Accounting Standards   Accounting standards promulgated by the Financial Accounting Standards Board that is an integral part of generally accepted accounting standards.

Statement of Financial Position   One of the three financial statements required to be presented in order to be in compliance with GAAP that shows the totals of major categories of assets, liabilities, and net assets at a particular point in times. This statement is called the balance sheet for commercial entities.

Statement of Functional Expenses   One of the four financial statements required to be presented by voluntary health and welfare organizations (VHWO) in order to be in compliance with GAAP. This statement is optional for all other organizations. This statement is a two-dimensional report that shows expenses by function (e.g., program and supporting services) and by natural classification (e.g., salaries, office supplies).

Statement of position   Publications produced by the Auditing Standards Board of the American Institute of Certified Public Accountants that provide technical guidance to auditors on a wide range of subject matter.

Statutory employee   Rules embodied by federal statute that classify workers as employees.

Statutory nonemployee   Rules embodied by federal statute that classify workers as not employees.

Support   Income that is not generated through an exchange transaction (i.e., by providing a product or services) and includes contributions, grants, contributed facilities, and services.

Temporarily restricted net assets   Assets (cash, receivables, etc.) received over one or more years that are restricted by the donor until some future time or for a specific purpose. Once the restriction is met, the assets become unrestricted and can be used for any legitimate purpose.

Trial balance   List of the totals or balances of each account in the general ledger at a particular point in time.

Trust   Agreement with an individual or entity to take title to property owned by a grantor (donor) and to protect or conserve it for either the grantor or the trust's beneficiary or beneficiaries.

Trustee   Empowered to manage the trust and ensure in most cases that the trust investments earn an appropriate return.

Useful life (estimated)   Estimated period of time an asset (e.g., property and equipment) is expected to be useful or productive and may not correspond to its actual physical or economic life.

Uniform Management of Institutional Funds Act   Document (Act) prepared in 1972 by members of the National Conference of Commissioners on Uniform State Laws that provided guidance and authority to charitable organizations about the management and investment of funds held by those organizations.

Uniform Prudent Management of Institutional Funds Act   Updated the Uniform Management of Institutional Funds Act in 1994 and has been enacted by 43 jurisdictions (as of 2009). The act updates rules on investment decision making for trusts, including charitable trusts, and imposes additional duties on trustees for the protection of beneficiaries.

Unrelated business income   Income from a trade or business that is regularly carried on by an exempt organization and that is not substantially related to the performance by the organization of its exempt purpose or function, except that the organization uses the profits derived from this activity.

Unrelated business income tax   Taxes on income derived from activities not related to the organization's exempt purpose (see **unrelated business income**).

Unrestricted net assets   Similar to the capital account of a commercial company. It is the excess of NFP's assets over their liabilities and it can be used for any legitimate purpose.

Voluntary Health and Welfare Organization   Organizations formed for the purpose of performing voluntary services for various segments of society and are tax exempt, supported by the public, and operated on an NFP basis.

About the Author

Laurence Scot was born and raised in New York City, graduated with a BA in Political Science from Queens College and an MBA in accounting from Pace University Lubin School of Business. After college he held responsible accounting positions in such prominent organizations as the law firm of Shearman and Sterling, the American Institute of Certified Public Accountants (AICPA), and Coopers and Lybrand, and is certified to practice in both New York and New Jersey.

Mr. Scot is the co-founder and co-managing partner of Skody Scot & Company, a midtown CPA firm formed in 1990 that specializes in servicing the NFP community. Like many other professionals, he believes strongly that giving back to the community and being involved in civic and philanthropic endeavors is important to a balanced and rewarding career. To that end, over the years he has volunteered his time to a number of worthwhile organizations, activities, and causes including: board chair: NYC Industries for the Blind, Mayor's Small Business Advisory Board, NYS Society of CPAs—Data Processing Committee, and Murry Bergtram High School for Business—Business Advisory Council; board treasurer: NJ Center for Tourette Syndrome Association of NJ, American Lung Association of Brooklyn; and board member: NYC Department of Finance Tax Reform Committee, and Con Edison Small Business Committee.

In recognition for his involvement and contributions of time, resources, and expertise, Mr. Scot has received a number of awards and citations over the years including: *SBA's 2000 Community Service Award* (U.S. Small Business Admin.), *2000 Citation for Community Service* (Manhattan Borough President), *1999 Accounting Advocate of the Year Award* (U.S. Small Business Admin.), *1998 School-to-Work Award* (NYS Educ. Dept./NYC Bd. of Educ./ NYS Dept. of Labor), *1996 Entrepreneur of the Year Award* (Crain's New York Business), and recognition letters from several NYC Commissioners. He has also been profiled in *New York Newsday* and quoted in a number of prominent publications such as *New York Times, Crain's NY Business,* and *Technology Today.*

Mr. Scot has a passion for teaching and has taught undergraduate and graduate classes at several colleges and has been lecturing and giving seminars to CPAs, bankers, NFP directors and officers, management, and entrepreneurs for over 20 years on a variety of subjects. Some of these include: *Best Practices and Good Financial Mgmt* (Merrill Lynch Philanthropic Congress), *Understanding Not-For-Profit Accounting and Financial Statements* (JP Morgan Chase), *Converting to an Inexpensive Accounting Program* (NYS Society of CPAs), *Financial Accounting for Not-For-Profit Organizations* (Support Center of New York), *Tax Tips to Residents, Doctors and Other Healthcare Professionals* (LI College Hospital, Beth Israel Hospital, and SUNY Health Science Center at Brooklyn), and *Employee or Independent Consultant/Contractor?* (New York Software Industry Association).

Recently, Mr. Scot created a first-of-its-kind, in-class, NFP accounting certificate program being offered at New York University SCPS, where he currently teaches. The material for this book is a culmination of Laurence Scot's 30-plus years of accounting and business experience and his many years servicing NFP organizations and the material covered in the certificate program.

For more information about Mr. Scot please visit Laurencescotcpa.com.

Index